D1376816

LOUISIANA The Pelican State

LOUISIANA

NEW EDITION

The Pelican State

EDWIN ADAMS DAVIS

LOUISIANA STATE UNIVERSITY PRESS
BATON ROUGE   1975

For DEBORAH CLAIRE (*Debbie*)
and DEIRDRE ANNE (*Dede*),

my granddaughters

ISBN 0–8071–0162–1 (text edition)
ISBN 0–8071–0163–X (trade edition)
Library of Congress Catalog Card
    Number 75–8468
Copyright © 1959, 1961, 1969, 1972, 1975 by
Louisiana State University Press

First edition, 1959
Second edition, 1961
Third edition, 1969
Fourth edition, 1975

Frontispiece: The Mississippi River south of
Baton Rouge. Photograph by David King Gleason

CONTENTS

CONTENTS

MAPS

ACKNOWLEDGMENTS

Factual material for this book was gathered during my more than forty years of studying, researching, and teaching Louisiana history at Louisiana State University. I have gleaned information from historical books and journals, newspapers, family letters, diaries and other manuscripts, business records, parish and state governmental archives, and from the accounts of numerous travelers who visited Louisiana in years past. My affection for and understanding of the complex civilization of Louisiana was developed gradually over these many years through acquaintanceship with countless citizens in all walks of life and in all sections of the state. It is my hope that this book will inspire Louisianians to a greater love for their state and country and will increase their knowledge and appreciation of our history.

For professional advice and criticism, I am indebted to Academic Vice-President Raleigh A. Suarez, McNeese State University; Dr. Joseph G. Tregle, Jr., Department of History, University of New Orleans; and A. Otis Hebert, Jr., former director, State Archives and Records Service, and presently director, Acadian Folklore Museum, University of Southwestern Louisiana.

At the Louisiana State University Library in Baton Rouge, I was assisted by Virginia M. Ott, now retired, Department of Archives; Evangeline Lynch, Louisiana Room; Michael Sotille, Circulation Department; Frances Tigott, Newspaper-Microfilm Room; Edith M. Sims, Social Science Department; Helen Palmer, Humanities Division, and Jimmie H. Hoover, Government Documents Department.

I also received assistance from former Governor Sam H. Jones, Lake Charles; Vernon L. Strickland, State Department of Commerce and Industry; Emogene Pliner, Public Affairs Research Council of Louisiana; Leon Sanders, formerly of KTBS Television Three, Shreveport; Louis J. Nicolosi, state supervisor of social studies, State Department of Education; Secretary of State Wade O. Martin, Jr.; Assistant Secretary of State J. R. Nelson; Rex Laney, Research and Statistics Division, Office of the Secretary of

State; A. Leon Hebert, attorney, Baton Rouge; and Dr. R. C. Kemp and Dr. Martin J. Broussard, also of Baton Rouge.

I am indebted to Edith Atkinson, former librarian, and Harriet Callahan, present librarian, Louisiana Department, Louisiana State Library, for bibliographical assistance, and to Willie M. Prophit, former secretary of the publication office and editorial assistant, *Louisiana History*, Louisiana State University, for counseling on vocabulary levels.

Several public school educators working in the field of Louisiana history read the original manuscript and made valuable suggestions, among them Margaret M. Bradbury of Shreveport, Opal M. Shea of Lake Charles, Elva G. Marks of New Orleans, Helen Bankston of Hammond, and Watt Black of Baton Rouge. Through the years numerous public and private schoolteachers have noted factual errors or have made suggestions for improvement of the text. To each of them I offer my thanks and appreciation.

Patrick Kennedy has given me special advice on educational techniques and specific problems concerning the teaching of Louisiana history. For his assistance I am most grateful.

To Sandra Gunner, State Supervisor of Ethnic Studies, State Department of Education; to the Acadian Minority Task Force; and to the Task Force on Ethnic Minorities Studies, I want to express my appreciation.

I also thank Mary McMinn, of Charleston, West Virginia, former Louisiana State University Press editor, for advisory and editorial services. Charles East, director, Leslie E. Phillabaum, associate director, and Martha Lacy Hall, editor, Louisiana State University Press, gave of their talents to make this a better book.

My granddaughters—Deborah Davis, who gave stenographic aid, and Dierdre Davis, who made recommendations on word identification—were most helpful.

My wife, La Verna Rowe Davis, has been an active researcher, editor, critic, and collaborator at all stages of researching and writing the book.

To each of the above and to numerous other persons in Louisiana I owe a great debt of gratitude.

EDWIN ADAMS DAVIS

INTRODUCTION:
THE HERITAGE OF A LOUISIANIAN

Louisiana is one of the most interesting states of the Union. Between Opelousas and Morgan City lies the heart of the romantic "Cajun" country. In the Felicianas, along the rivers and bayous in the southern sections of the state, and in several areas of North Louisiana are numerous antebellum plantation homes. Grand Isle is a picturesque Gulf Coast fishing and resort village. Amid the orange groves in the deep delta country of the Lower Mississippi are the villages of fishermen and trappers of varied nationalities who retain many of their native customs.

New Orleans is one of the most "different" cities in the United States, its modern business district on Canal Street just a stone's throw from the aged and graceful buildings of the Vieux Carré, the old quarter. Elsewhere in the state are cane fields, huge industrial complexes, offshore oil rigs, pine forests, salt mines.

All of these are a part of our Louisiana heritage. One of the most important is the land. Another is the people. And there is of course the rich heritage of our history.

The Land

Importance of the Land. Geography has affected all phases of Louisiana life from the days of early settlement to our own times. The most important geographical features of the Pelican State include its location, boundaries, and shape; its climate, rivers, and lakes; and the surface of the land. Together with the location of underground resources, these geographic features are determining factors in the agricultural, industrial, and general economic life of modern Louisiana.

Location and Size of Louisiana. Louisiana lies at the lower end of the Mississippi River Valley and is bounded by Arkansas, Mississippi, Texas, and the Gulf of Mexico.

Louisiana is not a large state, for it has only approximately 48,500 square miles of land and water area.

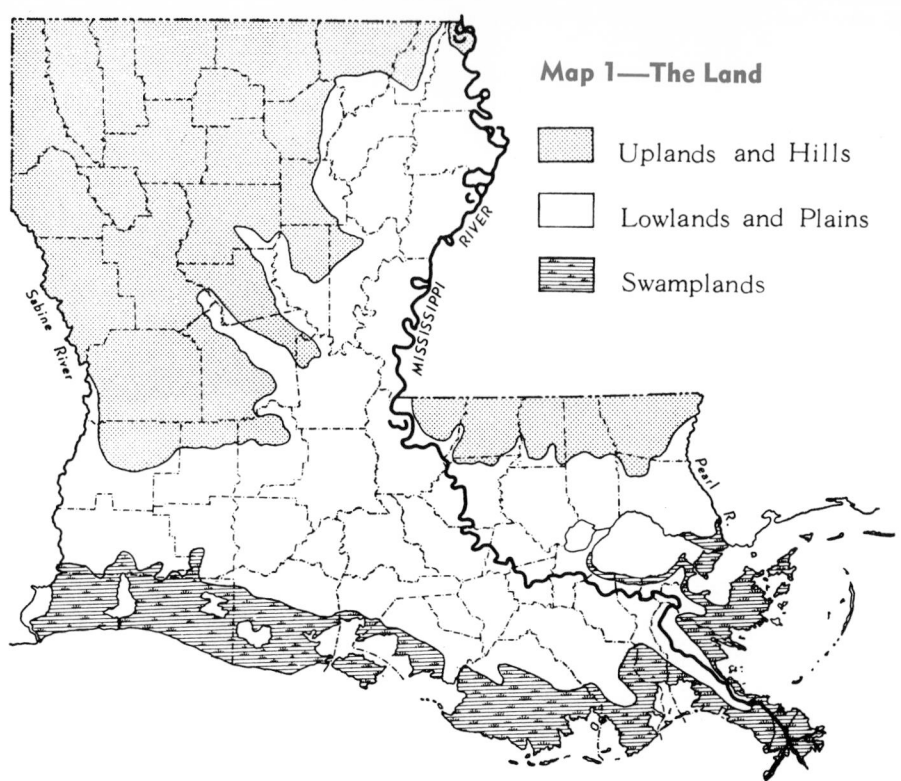

Map 1—The Land

	Uplands and Hills
	Lowlands and Plains
	Swamplands

It ranks thirty-first in size among the fifty states. About 3,500 square miles of this total area is in lakes and some 650 square miles in rivers. Louisiana's ragged coastline measures a little over 750 miles and is exceeded only by those of Alaska, Florida, Hawaii, California, and Maine. The state measures nearly 300 miles from east to west and some 375 miles from north to south.

If one looks carefully at a map, Louisiana appears to be a short, wide boot with a very ragged and well-worn sole, heel, and toe.

Climate. Most of Louisiana has a humid, semitropical climate which is much the same over most of the state. Snow rarely falls in the southern sections, and in the northern parishes a

heavy snowfall measures only a few inches. The average rainfall in the northern areas is about forty inches a year, but in South Louisiana sixty-five inches a year or more is not unusual. Tropical storms originating in the Gulf of Mexico sometimes pass through the southern coastal areas.

The Surface of the Land. All of Louisiana lies within a large southern region known as the Gulf Coast Plain. This plain is divided into two parts, however—the upland and the lowland districts.

The Louisiana uplands are divided into three sections. The Florida Parish Uplands lie in the northern part of what are known as the Florida Parishes, in the southeastern portion

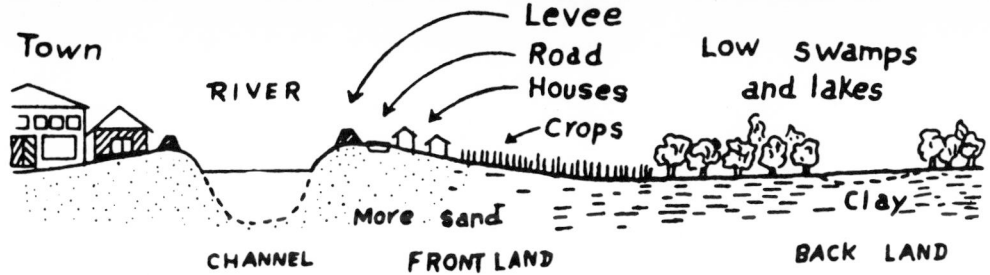

of the state. The North Louisiana Uplands are in North and Northwest Louisiana between the Red and Ouachita rivers. The West Louisiana Uplands are southwest of the Red River and north of the southwestern Louisiana prairies. The highest areas in the state are the Kisatchie Hills in Natchitoches and Vernon parishes, the Tunica Hills in West Feliciana Parish, and the so-called Driskill Mountains in Bienville and Claiborne parishes.

The Louisiana lowlands may be divided into two sections. The Mississippi River Plain is narrow in the northeast and widens in triangular fashion south of Baton Rouge. The higher portions of this plain are called "front lands" because they front the Mississippi and other rivers and bayous, whose flooding slowly built up leveelike ridges. Behind the "front lands" are the "back lands" and behind them the swamps. The Gulf Coastal Plain lies west of Southwest Louisiana. The Coastal Marshes along the Gulf of Mexico are sometimes protected by barrier beaches of sand and shells.

Soils of Louisiana. The state's fertile soil is its basic resource. It is porous and warm and is very deep in most sections. It may be divided into two general divisions; the upland soils and the lowland soils. Alluvial soils are those which were deposited by the overflowing of rivers and bayous. Few regions in the world have as much alluvial soil as Louisiana, about one-third of the state being covered with it.

Rivers and Lakes. Rivers have been the great architects of Louisiana, for much of the land was slowly built up by their deposits during floods. In recent years levees have been constructed to protect the land from floodwaters. But the rivers and bayous determined the paths of settlement, for until the coming of the railroads and the hard-surfaced highways, they dictated the routes of Louisiana commerce and travel.

The Mississippi is Louisiana's most important river. It has been called by many names. Some Indians named it *Michi Sepe*. The Choctaws called it the "old-big-strong" river, and the Spanish gave it the romantic name of Rio de Flores (river of flowers). The "front lands" and the levees have caused the streams to flow away from

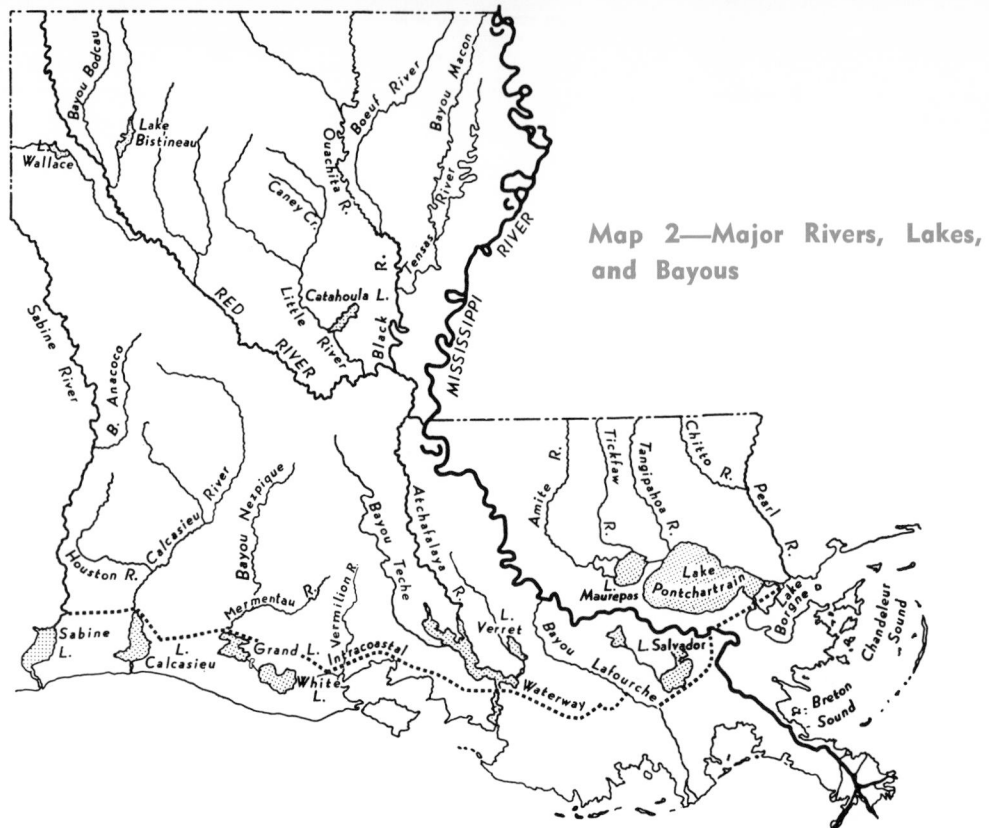

Map 2—Major Rivers, Lakes, and Bayous

the Mississippi, so that only the Red River flows into it from the west and none from the east, south of Baton Rouge.

The Red River is the second largest Louisiana waterway. The Ouachita–Black River system is so called because the Ouachita and other streams join to form the Black River. The Sabine River separates the southwestern part of Louisiana from Texas, and the Mississippi and Pearl rivers serve as part of the boundary between Louisiana and the state of Mississippi.

The words *river* and *bayou* are sometimes misunderstood in Louisiana. *Bayou* really means a sluggish inlet or outlet of a lake or bay, or one of several mouths of a river. According to that definition, Bayou Teche is

really a river, and the Atchafalaya River is a bayou, for the Atchafalaya carries a large amount of the water of the Mississippi to the Gulf of Mexico. From 1904 until recently, Bayou Lafourche was cut off from the Mississippi by the levee and so was technically a river. But it is now a bayou again, due to the construction of a large pumping station at Donaldsonville which pumps in water from the Mississippi.

One of the most frequently misunderstood physical features of Louisiana is the Isle of Orleans, or Island of Orleans as it is sometimes called, which is not an island at all. The land that makes up the Isle of Orleans is bounded by the Mississippi River on the south and southwest and the Gulf

xiv

Mouths of the Mississippi

of Mexico on the east. Going from west to east, its northern boundary is Bayou Manchac (once called Iberville River), the Amite River, Lake Maurepas, Lake Pontchartrain, Lake Borgne, and Mississippi Sound. But this area was called the Isle of Orleans long before Louisiana was purchased from France in 1803.

Vegetation. The plant and forest areas achieve striking contrasts in Louisiana. It is these contrasts, together with the luxuriant growth of all types of vegetation, that give the state much of its beauty. More than 150 species of trees are native to Louisiana. Shrubs, vines, and smaller plants grow in profusion.

Louisiana has three very spectacular and beautiful trees. The live oak, clad in Spanish moss, is a sight not easily forgotten. The cypress, which grows best in swamp and lowland areas, is distinguished by feathery green foliage

and a wide cone-shaped base. Its roots, called knees, frequently grow above the surface of the water or swampland in order to get air. The magnolia, another native tree that grows best in South Louisiana, produces large, fragrant flowers and has been transplanted into all parts of the state.

Many varieties of pine grow in the uplands. Other families of trees grow naturally in all sections of the state. Numerous ornamental trees are native or have been imported—pride of China (chinaberry), bitter orange, sweet olive, mimosa, palm, and banana, to name a few.

Shrubs and flowers include the honeysuckle, clematis, camellia, azalea, crape myrtle, jasmine, and spirea. Lilies and irises are found in many varieties. When Alexander Campbell, a noted Protestant minister, visited Louisiana in 1839, he described one of the planter's homes: "He literally resides in the midst of gardens...

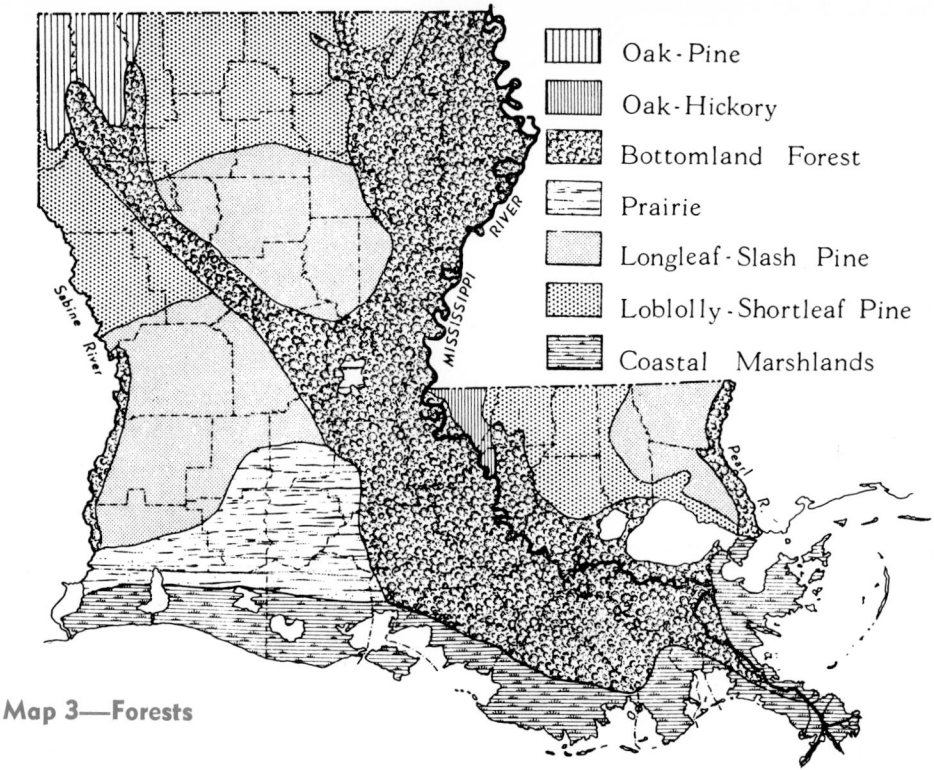

Legend:
- Oak-Pine
- Oak-Hickory
- Bottomland Forest
- Prairie
- Longleaf-Slash Pine
- Loblolly-Shortleaf Pine
- Coastal Marshlands

Map 3—Forests

with flowers that bloom in January."

Animal Life. Louisiana offers an attractive home for many forms of animal life. The rivers, lakes, and Gulf waters teem with both freshwater and saltwater fishes. The southern coastal region is probably the most important winter home in North America for wild geese and ducks, as well as being a year-round home for sea and freshwater birds.

Only a small number of the larger quadrupeds survive in the state. The buffalo, for example, which used to live in the northwestern and western regions, were all killed years ago. Deer are plentiful in many of the lowland and upland wooded sections. Black bears, cougars, and panthers (also called the catamounts) are sometimes sighted along the Atchafalaya or Tensas rivers or in other wooded lowlands. Mink, raccoon, skunk, and opossum are found over the entire state. Timber wolves are now almost extinct, but foxes, dam-building beavers, and the ferretlike otter are plentiful. Wild hogs are occasionally seen in more remote swamp and timber areas. Coyotes have come into the state from Texas and have been seen east of Baton Rouge.

Louisiana is the home of many different kinds of birds. The state bird, the Brown Pelican, nests in salt-marsh areas along the Gulf Coast and at the mouth of the Mississippi River. These sections are also the homes of ducks and geese and many smaller birds, including gulls, terns, sandpipers, herons, bald eagles, and egrets. The wooded uplands and the less swampy lowlands also have their share of bird life. Here the bird watcher sees and hears woodpeckers, quail, cardinals, mockingbirds, orioles, and numerous other species. Wild turkeys are occasionally discovered along the rivers and in the swamps, and in the pinewood uplands.

Gulf game fishes include tarpon, king mackerel, sharks, giant rays, and jewfish. Flounder, Spanish mackerel, redfish, and trout are the most important marketable varieties. Turtles, shrimp, crabs, and oysters are also of great commercial value. Commercial fishing provides a living for many citizens of the state.

The most important freshwater game fishes are bass, trout, crappie (*perch* to many Louisianians), and sunfish. Catfish is the most important freshwater commercial variety. Louisiana bullfrogs live in such numbers and are of such size as to make the state a leader in the production of froglegs as a table delicacy. Crawfish are found along the bayous and streams, and Breaux Bridge calls itself the "Crawfish Capital of the World."

Louisiana's reptiles are numerous but few are harmful. Most spectacular is the alligator, found in swamps and along a few bayous in the southern part of the state. Poisonous snakes include the rattlesnake and the water moccasin, or cottonmouth. A cousin of the cottonmouth, the copperhead is sometimes called the highland moccasin. The coral snake is even more poisonous and is found in timber or canebrake areas.

Natural Resources. No state has been so blessed with such a variety and quantity of natural resources as Louisiana. The list of land surface resources is almost endless—rich agricultural and grazing lands, forests with numerous varieties of timber, streams and lakes for fishing, natural waterways for the transportation of products and consumer goods. The surface water of rivers, bayous, ponds, lakes, and other streams is a fabulous asset to Louisiana's economic and recreational facilities. There is, for example, an average daily flow of more than 400 billion gallons of surface water along the state's six major rivers—the Mississippi, the Atchafalaya, the Red, the Ouachita, the Sabine, and the Pearl.

Louisiana forests fall into several groups. Pine timber is most important in the upland portions of the state. The hardwood forests of ash, elm, oak, and red gum grow in the basins of the Red and Mississippi rivers, and cypress and tupelo trees grow in the swamp areas. However, most of Louisiana's timber areas have been cutover and are now in the process of regrowth.

Underground resources include vast quantities of petroleum, natural gas, sulphur, salt, gypsum, sand and gravel, stone for quarrying, and fresh water for manufacturing purposes or for human and animal use. It has been estimated that Louisiana has enough ground water to furnish every citizen of the United States with several thousand gallons every day. And Louisianians are just beginning to tap the resources in the ground underneath the coastal waters of the Gulf of Mexico.

Except for iron, coal, and a few other basic minerals, Louisianians could live very well on what they produce within their own state.

The People

Louisianians, like Americans in general, are descended from immigrants who came from many nations. Some of these immigrants came directly to Louisiana during the 1700's, others during the 1800's, and still others have arrived during this century, even during the last few years. Mexicans and Cubans are good examples of those who have only recently arrived in the Pelican State.

The French Period, 1699–1762. During the French era of Louisiana history, the largest group of immigrants came from France, generally from the vicinity of Paris or from the western coastal regions. But other nationalities also came—people from Germany, Holland, and in smaller numbers from several other countries. The Germans and the Dutch most frequently were from the lower Rhine River Valley.

The first black slaves were brought from the West Indies during the first decade of settlement of the Louisiana colony. By 1720, however, slaves were being brought in larger numbers from the French West Indies and directly from Africa, usually from the region north of the Gulf of Guinea in West Africa.

During the entire period, numerous French Canadians made the long trip southwestward from the St. Lawrence River Valley and from Acadia and other settled areas north and east of the present state of Maine.

The Spanish Period, 1762–1803. The Spanish opened the doors of Louisiana to many more Europeans than the French had done. They also permitted Central and South Americans and English settlers in the colonies along the Atlantic seaboard to migrate to Louisiana. The Spanish gave land, tools, and supplies to these settlers and made them welcome in their colony.

Soon new settlers began to arrive from the West Indies, the English colonies, and from Spain and other European nations. Acadians who had been scattered after they had been sent away from their homes in Nova Scotia, located along the streams and bayous of South Louisiana. Large

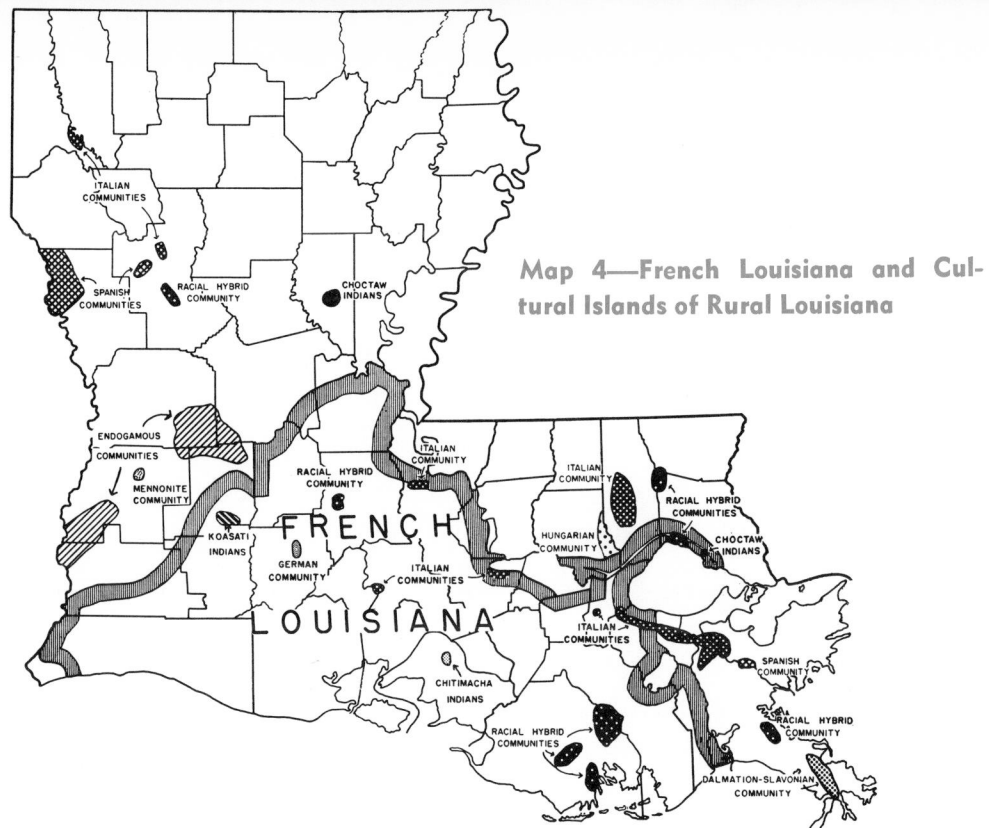

Map 4—French Louisiana and Cultural Islands of Rural Louisiana

numbers of slaves were brought from the West Indies and from Africa, and some West Indian free Negro planters brought their slaves with them to Louisiana and established plantations or businesses in the settled areas.

Great Britain had acquired East and West Florida in 1763, and large numbers of Scottish and English settlers established themselves in what are now the Florida Parishes, east of the Mississippi River and north of Lakes Pontchartrain and Maurepas.

At the end of the Spanish period, Louisiana was about ten times larger in population than it had been when the Spanish acquired the colony.

American Years from 1803 to 1860. Louisiana grew fantastically after its purchase in 1803. New settlers poured in from all the American states. They came down the Mississippi River on rafts, in flatboats, and in crude, home-made scows. After 1812 many came downriver in steamboats and during the 1850's many more rode "the cars" (trains) into New Orleans. Thousands reached the city from Latin American lands or from the Atlantic seaboard or from Europe in sailing ships, and during the last years of the period in steamships, particularly from Ireland and Germany.

Thousands of slaves were brought westward from the older southern states. Many slaves were smuggled into Louisiana from Africa or from the West Indies long after the importation of slaves became illegal in 1808. The last slaves were apparently smuggled into Southwest Louisiana in February, 1865, according to a slave ship's records checked by this writer during the middle 1930's.

The years from 1803 to 1860 were years of rapid population growth in Louisiana.

Population Growth During the Last One Hundred Years. After the Civil War ended in 1865, Americans from the northern states flocked to Louisiana in large numbers. Many brought wealth with them, but others acquired property because of the unsettled conditions which followed the war.

European immigration to the state continued, although many of the newcomers moved on up the Mississippi River to settle midwestern lands or to establish themselves in such cities as St. Louis, Cincinnati, Milwaukee, and Chicago. The Irish continued to arrive, as did Germans, in large numbers. The Irish and Germans were joined by Italians and by smaller numbers of immigrants from other countries. And at some period—it is not known just when—a small number of Chinese settled along the southeastern coast where they became commercial fishermen. The latest to arrive have been the Mexicans and the Cubans.

During recent years, owing to the rapid industrialization of the state, large numbers of Americans from other states are moving to Louisiana.

The People of Modern Louisiana. The people of present-day Louisiana are descended from many nationalities and races—British, French, Spanish, Canary Islanders, European West Indians, Germans, Italians, Indians whose ancestors lived here when the first explorers came, free Negroes from Santo Domingo and Cuba, black slaves from Africa, Chinese, Irish, Acadians from the Atlantic Seaboard or from Canada or other places who finally found their way to Louisiana, Hungarians, Russians, and others.

But the members of these groups have done comparatively little to preserve their cultural heritage.

It was not until 1911 that Rodolphe Lucien Desdunes, a Creole of color, published his *Nos Hommes et Notre Histoire (Our People and Our History)* and in 1937 that Charles Barthelemy Rousseve brought out *The Negro in Louisiana: Aspects of His History and His Literature*. During the last decade, however, other black students of the Negro's role in the history of Louisiana have begun to do serious research in this neglected field. The modern historian has a broader opportunity for contributions to Louisiana and American Negro history than those of any other state.

French Louisianians have only begun to take real pride in their nationalistic heritage during the last two or three decades. It was not until 1933 that Louise Olivier of Louisiana State University began her crusade for the

Louise V. Olivier

preservation of the French language and culture in Louisiana. The final drive was led by Jimmie Domengeaux of Lafayette, the late Roy Theriot of Abbeville, and others. The Organization for the Development of French in Louisiana (CODOFIL) was officially created by legislative act in 1968, and since that time has been enthusiastically directed by Chairman Domengeaux.

The first issue of *Acadiana Profile*, "A Magazine for Bi-Lingual Louisiana," edited and published by Bob Angers of Lafayette, appeared early in 1969. It has received strong approval in the French-speaking area of Louisiana and is extending its circulation beyond the borders of the state.

Other groups should follow the example of the Acadians, for all citizens of the state should take a greater pride in their nationalistic or racial heritage—and in their historical heritage as Louisianians.

The Historical Heritage

A State with a Fabulous History. The romantic and historic past, the bustling present, and the boundless future are happily combined in modern Louisiana. Here is found a rich blending of Old World and New World cultures.

The old civilization of Louisiana is fast disappearing. But there are still many reminders of the past in modern Louisiana: lovely antebellum homes like The Shadows at New Iberia and Rosedown in West Feliciana, old parish courthouses, peaceful cemeteries like those at Grand Coteau or in Grace churchyard at St. Francisville, the Vieux Carré in New Orleans, the Old State Capitol at Baton Rouge, statues like the one of Evangeline at St. Martinville, Old Fort Macomb near New Orleans—now in ruins because a small group of Louisianians made no effort to save it from destruction.

And there are the names that we use every day without thinking that they too are a part of our historical heritage.

The Shadows on the Teche, New Iberia

Place-Names of Louisiana. Place-names are the names given to towns, parishes, rivers, lakes, bayous, swamps, and other geographic locations. The names of Louisiana parishes, for example, indicate their own romantic story. Some, like Avoyelles, Natchitoches, Ouachita, and Caddo, were named for Indian tribes; others were given Indian names, like Calcasieu (crying eagle), Catahoula (beloved lake), and Tangipahoa (ear of corn). Others recall the French period: Baton Rouge (red stick), Terrebonne (good earth), Plaquemines (persimmons). La Salle, De Soto, Iberville, and Bienville were named for explorers or colonial leaders, and Iberia,

Concordia, East Feliciana, and West Feliciana reflect the Spanish period. St. James, St. Martin, and St. John the Baptist have a religious origin. Some were named for American statesmen like Washington, Franklin, or Jefferson. Others were named for such Confederate leaders as Jefferson Davis or General P. G. T. Beauregard.

Flags Over Louisiana. Nearly a dozen different national flags have flown over Louisiana or sections of the present state—more than over any other state in the Union.

The flags of colonial Louisiana during the French and Spanish periods include the golden lilies of Bourbon

A New Orleans patio

France, the golden castles and red lions of imperial Spain, the crosses of St. George and St. Andrew of Great Britain, another flag of Spain which carried the bars of Aragon, and then the new flag of Revolutionary France, the same tricolor that France has today.

In December, 1803, Louisianians saw another emblem unfurled to the breeze at New Orleans, the stars and stripes of the United States. In 1810 the people of Spanish West Florida (the present Florida Parishes) revolted against Spain, captured Baton Rouge, and hoisted their Bonnie Blue Flag. The Free State of West Florida be-

came a part of Louisiana two and a half months later.

Louisiana seceded from the Union in January, 1861, and for about a month the old state flag served as the emblem of an independent Louisiana. Then the representatives of the "Free, Sovereign, and Independent" State of Louisiana adopted a flag similar to that of the United States except that it had a single yellow star in a red field. After Louisiana joined the Confederate States of America in March, 1861, the Stars and Bars of the Confederacy became the national flag. After the Civil War the people of Louisiana welcomed the stars and stripes of Old Glory again.

And it is more than possible that the "snake-on-the-cactus" tricolor flag of Mexico flew over a part of the southwest corner of the state. During the years 1821–1826, before the Sabine River boundary had been definitely settled, several small Mexican cavalry patrols crossed the river. They moved into the so-called Neutral Ground or Sabine Strip along the Old Natchitoches Trace and then perhaps moved southward to the land of the Crying Eagle along the lower waters of the Calcasieu River, then back into Texas.

A Land of Tales and Legends. Louisiana is a state about which many legends have been woven and tall stories told. Some of these tales and legends have elements of historical fact, but some have been deliberately made up by Louisianians themselves for the entertainment of friends or tourists.

One story is told that the Customhouse at New Orleans has a foundation made of cotton bales, though cotton bales would hardly serve this purpose. The real foundation of the building consists of cypress pilings, topped by heavy cypress logs, the whole covered with a thick layer of concrete.

There is a story that when French Prince Louis Philippe visited Valcour Aime, a wealthy Louisiana planter, in 1798, the dishes of gold that were used at a banquet were afterwards tossed into the Mississippi. There are two things wrong with this fine story: first, Valcour Aime was a very sound businessman and would never have thrown away golden dishes; second, he was not born until 1798 and therefore would not have been old enough to have entertained the prince in the first place.

There are many mosquito stories, some of which were invented by travelers and others by Louisianians themselves. For instance, there is one set of mosquitoes that stings you all day and another set that stings you all night. In Northeast Louisiana two mosquitoes can whip a dog, and four can hold a man down and hogtie him. Along the Lower Mississippi River one never kills a mosquito, he butchers him. In some places mosqui-

toes torment alligators to death, and sting mules right through their hoofs.

And fog yarns were commonplace. Fogs were particularly bad during early February, 1838. The New Orleans *Picayune* described how "some fifty laborers were busy with spades, axes, crowbars, &c. endeavoring to open a pathway through the fog." Blasting with gunpowder "did loosen it a little." A postscript to the story read: "The butchers at Slaughter House Point being unable to force their pirogues through the fog, climbed up about 40 feet, and finding the air sufficiently thin at that height, they hauled their beef up after them, and trundled it across the city on top of the fog, by means of wheelbarrows."

Preservation of a Great Heritage. Louisianians of the past and those of the present have done too little to preserve their interesting and unusual historical heritage. There are signs, however, that they are finally beginning to awaken to the fact that they live in the midst of historical relics of many kinds and that at least some of these legacies from the past must be preserved.

Will future citizens of Louisiana be able to preserve their great historical heritages, the good things from their old civilization, while continuing to keep in step with modern technical and material progress?

The answer is up to each new generation.

LOUISIANA The Pelican State

Southern Indians
and a method
of killing alligators.
From an engraving
by Theodore De Bry

PART ONE
Louisiana's
Earliest
Inhabitants

1. THE LOUISIANA INDIANS AND THEIR CIVILIZATION

Before the Explorers Came. It is believed that the first Indians to come to the area of present-day Louisiana came several thousand years ago and settled along the Gulf Coast and along the shores of the inland rivers and streams. Numerous prehistoric Indian village sites have been found in various sections of Louisiana.

These Indians used harpoons and spears and constructed crude habitations by covering a tepeelike wooden framework with grass, leaves, and skins. They burned out logs for boats. They cooked food by the stone-boiling method, which was the dropping of stones into bucketlike leather containers supported by stakes driven into the ground.

These people finally invented bows and arrows or acquired them from other tribes. They learned to make a crude pottery, and they domesticated dogs for protection and hunting and for food. Still later they began making a few everyday tools and utensils, to

3

Hard work with shovel and wheelbarrow was needed during the excavation of this Louisiana Indian mound.

do some farming, and to build burial mounds for their dead.

During the last thousand years before the arrival of European explorers they began to build more-or-less permanent houses grouped together in sizable villages, some of which were surrounded with earthen walls and ditches for protection. The Indians produced a greater variety of food grains and vegetables.

They fashioned larger and larger boats and began to travel more. They traded for horses with the nearby Texas Indians and began to raise their own. Those of northern Louisiana developed a sizable trade with their neighbors in Arkansas.

The Indian Groups and Where They Lived. The Louisiana Indians may be divided into six general families or language groups, each of which can be subdivided into tribes. Each group lived in a definite area and each spoke its own language. A variety of the *Muskhogean* tongue was understood by some persons in nearly all of the villages, and thus it served as a common language for the members of different language groups.

Those people who belonged to the *Muskhogean* group occupied almost all of southeast Louisiana east and north of the Mississippi River, part of present-day Pointe Coupee Parish, and a strip of land a few miles wide

4

Much of the work of excavation of a mound must be done carefully with brushes and small tools.

south of the Mississippi. The Tangipahoas, who had villages on the shores of Lake Pontchartrain, and the Acolapissas, who lived just west of Pearl River, were the most important tribes. The Houmas lived in the Feliciana parishes, and the Bayougoulas lived near the present village of Bayou Goula in Iberville Parish.

Those who spoke the *Caddoan* language occupied the northwestern quarter of the state, with most of their important villages along the Red and Saline rivers, Bayou D'Arbonne, and the upper part of Little River. Unlike the other Louisiana Indians, the Caddos moved around a great deal, for they used horses as domesticated ani-

mals. There were, of course, no state boundaries as we know them today. The Caddo Indians also ranged into parts of present-day Texas and Arkansas. Two tribes of this group were the Kadohadacho and the Washita.

The Indians who spoke the *Tunican* language lived in northeastern Louisiana, east of the Ouachita River and north of the present-day town of Harrisonburg. These Indians we call the Tunicas.

The civilization of the people who spoke *Atakapan* and who lived in southwest Louisiana along the Calcasieu, Mermentau, and Vermilion rivers was generally lower than that of the other linguistic groups.

5

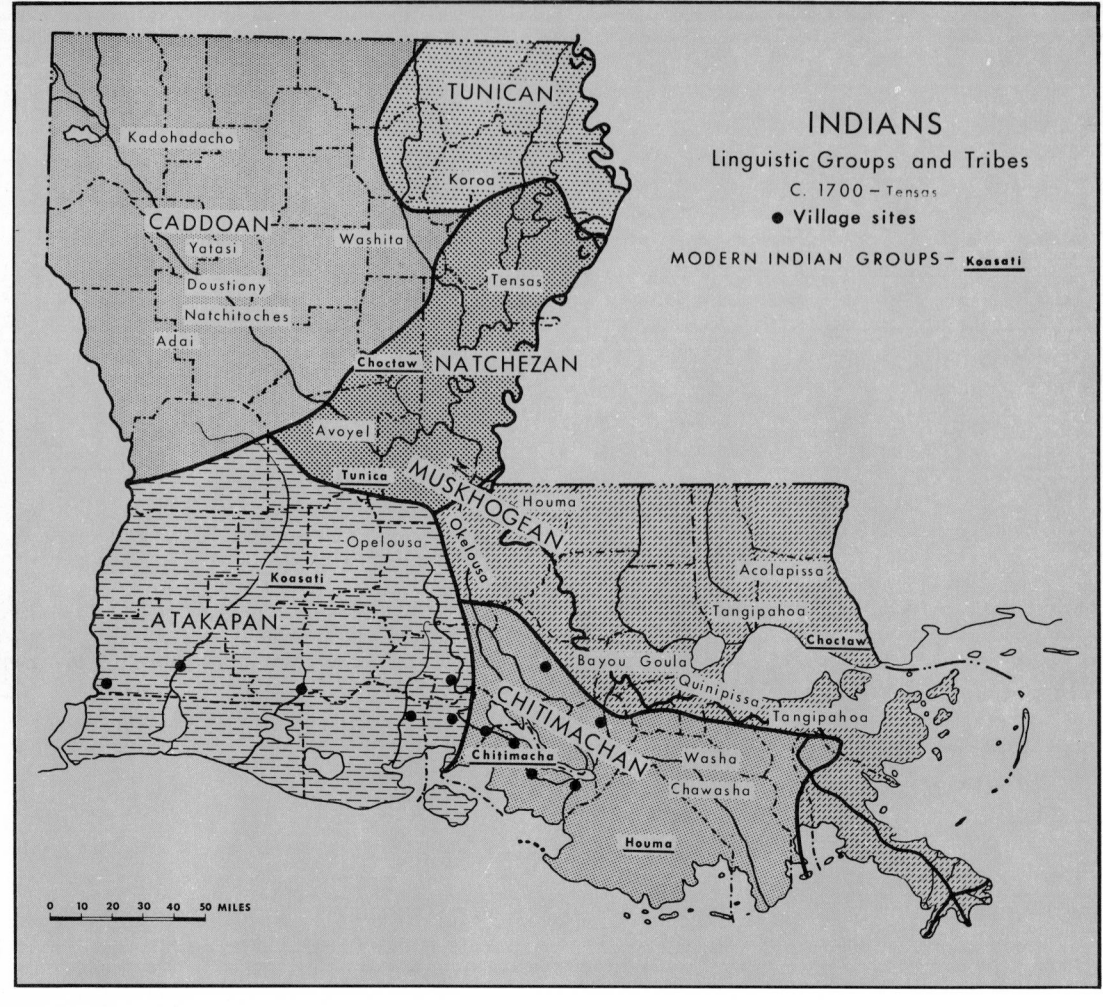

Map 5—Louisiana Indians, 1700

The country east and northeast of Alexandria was the home of the *Natchezan* group, who possessed a high degree of culture. The most important of their villages were near present-day Natchez, Mississippi, and in Concordia Parish. In addition to this Natchez tribe, other leading tribes were the Tensas, who lived near Marksville, and the Avoyel, for whom Avoyelles Parish was named.

The *Chitimachan* group lived east of Bayou Teche and south of the Mississippi River. Along with the *Muskhogeans,* they were great fishermen, and their most important villages were located on the shores of the numerous lakes of this region and along Bayou Lafourche.

The *Atakapan* group was the largest of the six and had about 4,200 members when the French first settled

Louisiana warriors on the trail of an enemy. From an old French engraving.

Louisiana. The *Muskhogean* family was second with 3,500 and the *Chitimachan* third with 3,000. Those who spoke *Caddoan* numbered about 2,500. The two smallest groups were the *Natchezan* with 1,200 and the *Tunican* with only about 500 members.

The land occupied by these six language groups had no specific boundaries, though it was understood that one group should not settle or hunt or fish in the area where another group lived. The rivers of Louisiana, therefore, did not mark the boundaries of the lands of the tribes or groups.

Tribal Warfare. In general the Louisiana tribes were peaceful. The Tuni-

can family was the most warlike, and the Koroa tribe, which belonged to this family, the most cruel. The Assinais, who were of the *Atakapan* group, were probably the most warlike individual tribe.

Shortly after the arrival of the French in Louisiana, there were two important Indian wars. In 1700 the Quinipissas went to live with the Bayougoulas, but after a short time the latter suddenly killed most of the Quinipissa men and adopted the women and children into their tribe. In 1706 there was a war between the Tunicas and the Houmas.

Most of the Louisiana Indians tortured and killed their prisoners. The Assinais were probably the only Loui-

7

siana Indians who practiced cannibalism as a part of their religion. One of the early settlers who visited the tribe later wrote: "Neither my comrades nor I could eat until after we had quit those cruel cannibals."

Houses, Tools, and Weapons. The Indian villages were most often built in a large circle around an open space, which was used for dances, games, meetings, and religious ceremonies, but some of the smaller villages were only a row or two of huts set along a river or bayou. There were no palisades or walls around the towns.

The Indians of South Louisiana built their houses of wood, canes, or reeds, and roofed them with grass, palmetto leaves, or cornhusks. They were usually round, about fifteen feet high, with small doors but no windows. There was a large hole in the top of the roof to let out the smoke from the cooking or heating fire and to let in light.

In North Louisiana the houses were better made, for the climate is somewhat colder there. Heavy posts were set in the ground and around the posts was woven a kind of framework, which was then plastered with clay or mud. House decorations were uncommon, though the Koroas sometimes adorned their cabins with pieces of shining copper.

The Indians had little furniture. Beds were made by planting four short posts in the ground and weaving on top of them a cane or reed frame, which was then covered with moss, grass, or the skins of animals. There were a few pottery cooking pots, water bottles, and storage jars; some red, black, or yellow baskets made of split cane; and woven mats on the ground. It was the custom to keep a small fire burning in the cabin, for warmth in winter or to drive out the mosquitoes in summer. If the weather was mild only a small torch made of dried canes was needed for these purposes.

The Indians had very few tools and weapons, all of which were crude. Bows were made of wood. The cane arrows had hardened points or were tipped with bone splinters, deer horn tines, garfish scales, or flints. Blowguns with cane splinter darts feathered with thistledown were used for hunting birds and small animals. They had stone knives, hatchets, and stone-pointed spears. Crude hoes were used for cultivation of their fields. Bone fishhooks, barbed fish arrows, nets made of cedar wood strips and funnel-shaped fish traps were used to catch fish.

Although there were a few bark canoes, most of the boats were made by hollowing out large cypress logs. André Pénicaut, one of the early French settlers, describing how this was done, said that the Indians built a large fire at the foot of a tree and "kept it up until the tree fell to the ground. Then they burned it off at the desired length. When they had burned the tree sufficiently for their

Indians fashioning a dugout canoe.
The men in the background are felling
a tree with fire.

"Caddo Indians Gathering Wild
Grapes." Artist, George Catlin.

purpose, they extinguished the fire with moist earth, and scraped out the tree with large thick shells. They then washed the canoes with water so as to give them a fine polish." Some of these large pirogues were thirty and even forty feet long. Cane rafts were used for crossing streams or bayous.

Food. An abundant supply of animals, fish, fowl, grain, fruits, berries, nuts, and vegetables made food plentiful. Bear, deer, small animals, and alligators lived in the forests, prairies, and swamps. Buffalo roamed the northwestern and western sections of the state. Three varieties of corn, numerous kinds of roots, plant shoots, grain from native grasses, many varieties of beans, sweet potatoes, cabbage, pumpkins, melons, and other vegetables were grown. Peaches, plums, mulberries, persimmons, grapes, and numerous kinds of berries and nuts grew wild or were planted. Bees furnished wild honey. Salt was extracted from either sea water or water from saline springs or dug from near-surface deposits.

The Indians generally boiled or roasted their meats. They had separate cooking pots for meats and fish, for they did not like to mix the flavors. Most of their bread was made of corn meal which had been ground with a large wooden mortar and pestle. They made a kind of porridge of ground corn called *sagamite* and to this were sometimes added beans, meat, and even fruits. Bear fat and deer tallow

were used for seasoning. The Indians dried their fruits and vegetables and also smoked and dried their meats for preservation during the winter or summer months.

André Pénicaut described how they lighted their fires: "They take a small piece of cedar wood, the size of one's finger, and another small piece of mulberry wood, which is very hard. They put them side by side between their hands and by spinning them together, like making chocolate froth, they make a little piece of fuzz come out of the cedar wood and catch fire. This can be done instantly."

Clothing. Animal skins were used for clothing by the Indians, as well as cloth woven from grass and mulberry-wood fibers, or from various kinds of feathers. Some Indian men were fully clothed with shirt and pants, some with only pants, and still others with only a breechcloth. The women wore long fringed skirts and loosely fitting tunics tied at the waist with a belt or cord. Moccasins were worn by some tribes only in winter but by others during the entire year. Children were dressed like their parents, though frequently the smaller youngsters wore no clothing at all.

It was customary for the men's hair to be cut short, but the women left theirs long and it was either coiled around the top of the head or hung in long braids down the back. The men did not wear beards. Pénicaut wrote that they removed the hair from their

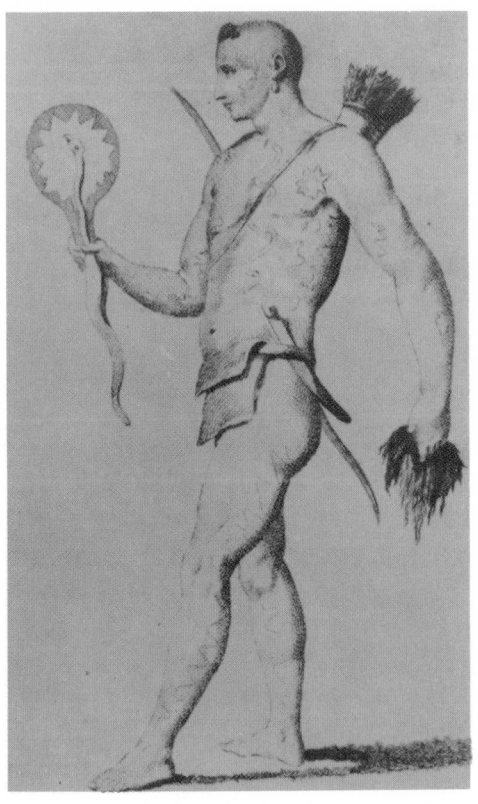

This elaborately tattooed northwest Louisiana brave carries a scalp and holds a tribal or religious emblem. From an old French engraving.

girls were given much training in physical fitness; their diet included raw eggs and a special kind of tea. The boys practiced running, and many wonderful stories are told of their swiftness. It is said that one of the Louisiana Indians could outrun a horse for short distances and that he made his living by running. The children were taught courtesy and respect for the adults of the village.

Most Louisiana Indians were very polite. When the Bayougoulas, for example, met a friend they placed their hands over their own faces and breasts, then over the hands of their friends. After this they raised their hands upward with the palms outward in a form of salute. When an Indian met a Frenchman during the early colonial years he said, "Is it you, my friend?" before stopping to talk.

faces with "shell ash and hot water as one would remove the hair from a suckling pig." Most of the Louisiana Indians painted or tattooed their legs, arms, and faces, and some of them painted their teeth black. They used many kinds of ornaments—necklaces, rings, bracelets, nose rings, earrings, and breastplates.

Education. Indian life was simple and centered around the family; the girls were trained in the household arts; the boys were taught how to fish and hunt and how to fight in case of war with another tribe. Both boys and

Social Life. Many persons believe that Indians were serious people who had very little social life, but this is not true. The Indians had regular rules and customs of behavior, and enjoyed different amusements such as sports, games, and dances.

The Louisiana Indians had many different kinds of races, running games, and ball games. One of their ball games was called the *tole* game. It was played on a large field about

11

The Red River Valley five thousand years ago

two hundred feet long with a pole set in the ground at each end. The players divided into two sides, and a goal was scored by touching the ball to the pole at the opposite end of the field; thus, it was somewhat similar to our modern game of soccer football. During the summer a favorite sport for boys was the blindfold swimming race. Sometimes boys and girls, wrapped and tied in blankets or skins, were rolled down small hills, and younger children played "tag" and marbles just as they do today.

There were many kinds of musical instruments, for the Louisiana Indians loved to dance, but they were generally used for keeping time rather than for producing music. Horns were made from canes or reeds, and rattles were fashioned out of gourds filled with pebbles. Skins were tightly stretched over wood or earthenware to form drums, and whistles were either carved from wood or molded from clay. A favorite instrument was made from alligator skins. The skin was prepared by ex-

posing the body of the alligator to ants until they had eaten all the flesh and the tender parts of the skin, which was then carefully dried. The sound was produced by raking a stick across the rough, irregular top.

Most of the larger villages had a dance house which was used for social as well as religious dances. The Choctaw Indians of Bayou Lacomb, who had moved to Louisiana from Alabama, had seven different dances which they always performed in the same order. One of these, the "Tick Dance," was danced in this fashion. All the dancers locked arms and formed two lines facing each other. They then began to sing and as they sang they moved forward toward each other. They stamped first the right foot, then the left, at each step looking down at the imaginary ticks they were crushing beneath their feet.

Most Louisiana Indians loved to tell stories, tales, and legends, some of which were related in a special sing-song voice.

Medicine. Medicine was considered a part of religion, and many of the medicine men were also the priests or ministers of the villages. With little knowledge of surgery, if they failed to set a man's broken leg, for example, they sometimes entertained him for a few days and then strangled him. No crippled children or adults were permitted to live. Indians had little resistance to infectious diseases such as measles, diphtheria, or smallpox, which were introduced by the explorers from Europe.

Louisiana Indians were, however, not too far behind Europeans in the practice of medicine at the time the French came to Louisiana. They used herbal remedies of many kinds. The Louisiana historian Charles Gayarré says they had discovered and were using over three hundred medicinal herbs. One Frenchman who came to Louisiana reported that the Indians carefully guarded their knowledge of these herbs and refused to share it.

Small huts, like ovens, were used for sweat baths and for boiling a variety of medicinal herbs. For stomach disorders the Indians used sumac seeds, ripe persimmon pulp, rhubarb, snakeroot, and sassafras. They treated toothache with a pulp made of acacia wood, and reduced swellings with a brew of elderberry roots. But their universal remedy was sweet-gum tea, which they said "gladdens the heart."

Religion. The Louisiana Indians worshiped many gods. The Tunicas, for example, had nine gods—the sun, thunder, fire, and the gods of east, south, north, west, heaven, and earth. They were very careful not to tell Father Jacques Gravier anything about their gods when he visited them during the early 1700's. In 1712 Father Gabriel Marest reported that "nothing is more difficult than the conversion of these savages. . . . We must first make men of them and afterwards work to make them Christians."

The Indians of the Natchitoches region worshiped in small round temples, and every morning, after rubbing their bodies with a white mud, they entered them, held up their hands, and prayed. In their many religious ceremonies dancing played an important part. The Chitimachas held regular dances at different seasons of the year; the summer dance ceremony lasted six days and was the longest and most important. All the men were painted red and wore feathered bands around their heads. The music was furnished by gourd rattles and rough alligator skins. Dancing was followed by great feasts in each village.

Marriage ceremonies varied with each tribe, some, especially those for important people, being long and elaborate. In one tribal ceremony the young man collected a group of his male friends and went to the house of his bride-to-be. Before arriving there they would see the girl with some of her friends, and when the young man tried to catch her, she was protected by them. When she was finally caught, everybody went into the house, and the couple were seated in the center of the group and questioned by the older men. When all of the questions were answered, the marriage ceremony was performed and there was a great feast, after which the people danced until daybreak.

Later History of Louisiana Indians. During the eighteenth century, tribal conflicts, wars against the French, and enforced migration north and westward constantly reduced the native population of Louisiana. The French seem to have had no recognizable Indian policy beyond furnishing a limited number of gifts and inferior-quality trading goods. The Spanish, on the other hand, tried to protect the Indians, made regular treaties with the tribes, and gave them large amounts of gift goods at regular intervals. But all of the tribes had been materially reduced in number by the time of the Louisiana Purchase and a few, including the Natchez, had been completely exterminated. The Avoyel tribe, for example, in 1698 was estimated at about 280, but by 1805 only a half-dozen members were left; in 1698 the Tunicas were estimated at nearly 500, but in 1803 only slightly more than 50 were living in the northeastern section of the present state.

The decline in Indian population continued after the purchase of Louisiana. Their lands were gradually sold to white men, whole tribes moved out of the present state limits, white men's diseases carried off large numbers, and some intermarried with whites or blacks and left their tribes. In 1880 only about 850 Indians were scattered through more than ten parishes, and a decade later the number had declined to 628. Chahta-Ima, Father Adrien Rouquette, the noted poet-missionary to the Choctaws, died in 1887, and with his death sympathy for the Louisiana Indian ceased. By 1950 the Indian population had declined to 409, comparatively few being of pure blood.

But in 1970 some 5,350 Indians were recorded as living in the state. This dramatic increase seems to be accounted for by the fact that many persons who could claim being of Indian descent did so in order to receive federal assistance. Probably the largest groups now living in the state are the Houmas, who live in Terrebonne Parish, and the Koasati, in Allen Parish, who moved to Louisiana about a hundred and fifty years ago. Most of the Louisiana Indians today have lost their old ways of life, and are now farmers, trappers, and fishermen.

Indians have contributed much to Louisiana life. They gave the white man many vegetables and fruits; they taught the early settlers how to make a living in the forests and swamps; and they gave to Louisiana many of the names of her parishes, streams, and cities.

14

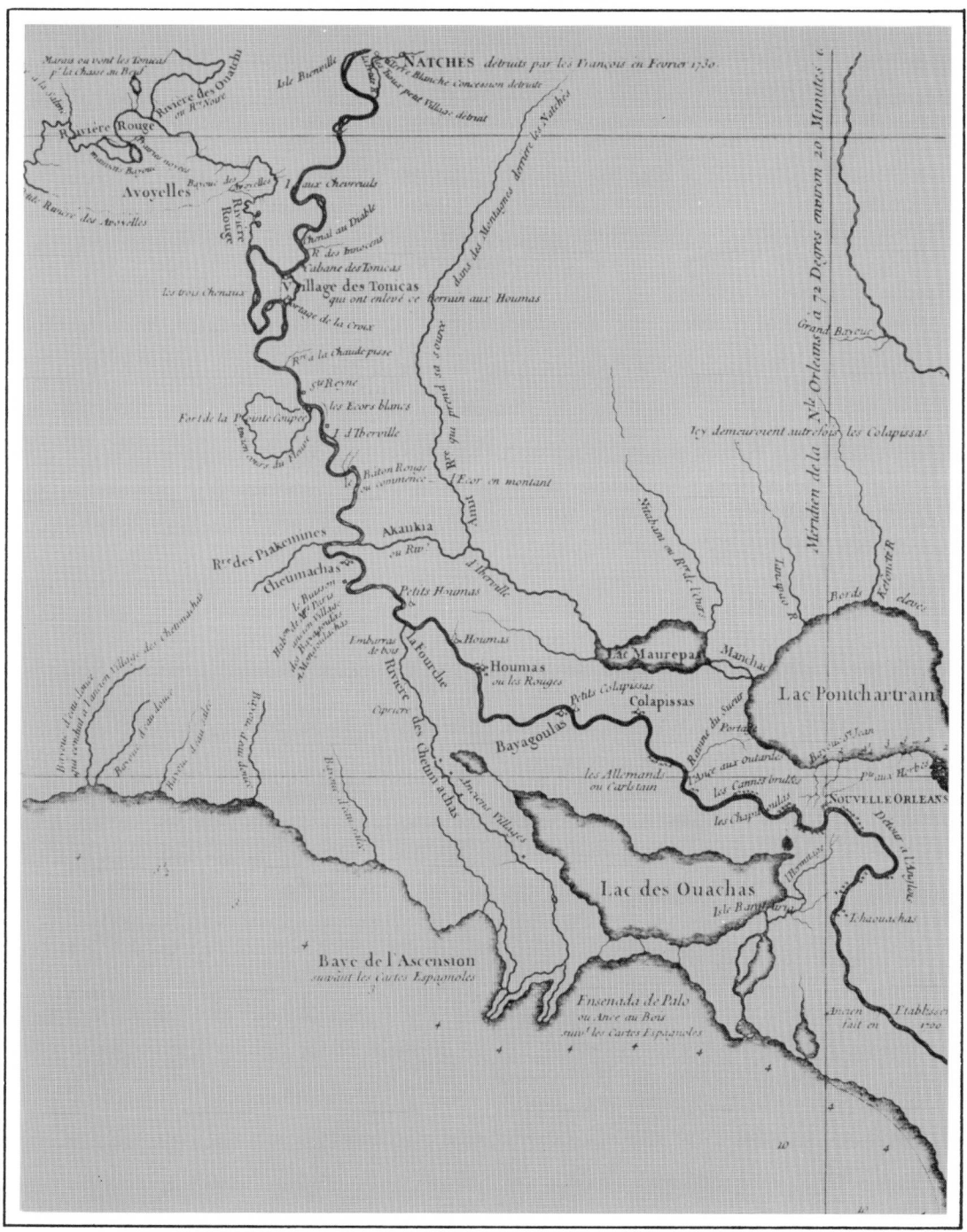

Map 6—Where the French first came into contact with Louisiana Indians

PART TWO
Louisiana
as a French Colony,
1699–1762

2. THE FRENCH ESTABLISH A COLONY

Explorations of the Spanish and the French. Within twenty years after the discovery of America the Spanish explored and settled the islands of the West Indies. During the next thirty years the Spanish explored most of the southeastern part of the United States and discovered the Mississippi River.

In 1513 Ponce de Leon landed in Florida and a few years later tried to plant a colony on its west coast, but was driven off by the Indians. Alonso de Pineda sailed along the Gulf Coast in 1519 and found the mouth of a large river, in all probability the Mobile River. Pánfilo de Narváez, landing in Florida in 1528 to establish a colony, lost most of his men fighting Indians. He built some crude boats and started westward along the coast of the Gulf of Mexico, but near the mouth of the Mississippi River his little fleet was wrecked and only a few men escaped. Alvar Cabeza de Vaca (whose name means "head of a cow") and a few

Moscoso's departure for Mexico.

others traveled across the southern part of what is now Louisiana, and after eight years of wandering finally reached Mexico.

In 1539 Hernando de Soto reached the west coast of Florida with some six hundred men. Hearing of a rich Indian nation, he began to search for it, and for four years he ranged from Florida to Arkansas, but never found the gold and riches he sought. He died, probably in southeastern Arkansas, and was buried in the Mississippi River. The survivors of his army, led by Luis de Moscoso, tried to reach Mexico by marching across northern Louisiana and Texas, but overland travel was too difficult. They returned to the Mississippi, built boats, floated down the river, and then followed the Gulf Coast to Mexico. For nearly one hundred and forty years after this no

other Europeans visited the Lower Mississippi Valley.

The French founded Quebec in Canada in 1608, and their explorers and fur traders pushed quickly westward along the Great Lakes. Nearly fifty years later, Pierre Esprit Radisson reached the western shores of Lake Superior, where he and his men heard of a great river which ran southward toward the Gulf of Mexico. Within the next few years the French had explored the upper portions of the great river.

At this time a French fur trader and explorer named René Robert Cavelier, Sieur de La Salle, lived in Canada. He made plans to explore the Lower Mississippi River country and secured the aid of another explorer named Henri de Tonti. Tonti was an Italian whose right hand had been blown almost off by the explosion of a grenade during a battle against the Spanish. Without waiting for a doctor, he himself cut off the mangled hand, which was later replaced with an iron one, so that he was called *Bras-de-fer* ("Iron Arm,") or "Iron Hand."

La Salle and Tonti started down the Mississippi River early in 1682 with fifty-four French and Indians, including thirteen Indian women and children. They reached the mouth of the river on April 7 and two days later La Salle took possession of the country by planting a large wooden cross in the ground. On it was inscribed: "Louis the Great, King of France and Navarre, reigns, April 9, 1682." He named the land "Louisiane," meaning "the land of Louis." Two years later, La Salle left France with some four hundred people to found a colony in Louisiana,

La Salle takes possession of Louisiana, April 9, 1682

but he missed the mouth of the Mississippi and finally established Fort St. Louis near Matagorda Bay in Texas. The colony failed and La Salle was killed by his own men.

Both Spain and France now claimed the land of Louisiana, which would belong to the first nation settling there successfully.

France Plans to Settle Louisiana. For some years after the death of La Salle in 1687, France seemed to forget about Louisiana, though there were some leaders in France and Canada who continued to urge the settlement of the Lower Mississippi Valley.

Great Britain, France, and Spain, the three greatest powers of western Europe, were engaged in a struggle for the control of the entire continent of North America. The Spanish had founded St. Augustine, Florida, in 1565; the British had settled Virginia at Jamestown in 1607; and the French had established Quebec a year later. France now controlled the St. Lawrence River Valley in Canada, the Great Lakes region, and the Ohio and Upper Mississippi river valleys. She wished to keep the Lower Mississippi Valley from falling into the hands of Spain or Great Britain. This could be accomplished by establishing a colony near the mouth of the river. The French especially feared the British.

After the death of La Salle, the Count de Pontchartrain, an important government official in France, became ambitious to expand French posses-

sions. In 1694 Henri de Tonti, the friend and companion of La Salle, offered his services in establishing a Louisiana colony. Three years later, a Canadian, the Sieur de Remonville, proposed the organization of a company to send out an expedition of settlement. The same year Tonti published a book called *La Salle's Last Discoveries in America,* which described the geography, the Indians, and the resources of the Mississippi Valley. It became very popular in France and caused many of her people to begin thinking about Louisiana.

But the British had not been idle. About this time Father Louis Hennepin, who also had been a member of some of La Salle's exploring expeditions, became a subject of the King of Great Britain. In 1697 and 1698 he published two books urging William III to take possession of the entire Mississippi Valley.

The secret agents of Louis XIV of France soon discovered that the British were planning to found a colony in Louisiana. The Count de Pontchartrain realized that he had to take immediate action. He held conferences with French and Canadian leaders. It was decided that there were two possible methods for the settlement of Louisiana. Colonists could either be sent along the Great Lakes and down the Mississippi River under the leadership of a man like Tonti, who knew the country, or they could be sent by ship directly from France. The latter plan was chosen. In their search for

Pierre le Moyne, Sieur d'Iberville

an experienced naval commander and a good leader to head the expedition, they considered many Frenchmen and Canadians and finally chose a Canadian, Pierre le Moyne, the Sieur d'Iberville.

Iberville. The Sieur d'Iberville was born in Canada in 1661, the third son of Charles le Moyne, a native of Dieppe, France, who had emigrated to Canada when a young man. Charles le Moyne had married a French girl named Catherine Primot. They had fourteen children. Their sons Iber-

ville, Bienville, Chateauguay, and Serigny were to distinguish themselves in Louisiana.

Reared in Canada, Iberville was an active youth, who joined the French navy while still in his teens. He became commander of a warship and later a whole fleet, winning victories against the British in Hudson Bay and off the coast of Newfoundland. He was a great hero to the Canadians. The Governor of Canada once remarked of him that he was "as military as his sword and as used to water as his canoe." His experience and success against the British made it obvious that the Count de Pontchartrain and his advisers would select him to make the settlement in Louisiana.

The Voyage of Settlement. Iberville began immediately to organize his expedition at La Rochelle. He collected food, clothing, weapons, tools, and other supplies, and secured two frigates called the *Badine* and the *Marin* and two small storeships. Crews of Canadians and other experienced sailors were assembled, a total of about three hundred men.

On October 24, 1698, the expedition put out from the harbor of Brest, France, with Iberville in command of the *Badine*. The little fleet sailed directly to Santo Domingo, where it was joined by a French warship, the *François,* for it was feared that the British might attack. Here, at Santo Domingo, Iberville secured the services of Laurent de Graaf, a celebrated ex-pirate, as a pilot. The ships then sailed past Cuba and up the west coast of Florida. Turning westward, they anchored off Santa Rosa Island, near the entrance to Pensacola Bay.

The Spanish had settled Pensacola in 1696 and would not permit the French to enter their harbor, so Iberville's fleet moved on westward to Mobile Bay. In the area, the explorers found an island on which was a heap of bones. They first called it Massacre Island, but later changed the name to Dauphin Island after the eldest son of the King of France. As they had seen

no British ships, the *François* returned to Santo Domingo.

Iberville next sailed southwest to the Chandeleur Islands, then northward to Cat and Ship islands. The latter was so named because it had a good anchorage on the land side. Cat Island was given this name because it swarmed with animals somewhat like foxes or cats, probably either opossums or raccoons. Here the little fleet anchored. The next day, February 13, 1699, Iberville and his brother Bienville rowed to the mainland and visited the Biloxi Indians.

Several days later Iberville, accompanied by Bienville and about fifty Canadians and sailors, set off in two large boats and two canoes to find the mouth of the Mississippi River. Iberville planned to go up the river and choose a place for the new settlement. The fleet was to remain in the harbor at Ship Island, and if supplies should run short or Iberville did not return within six weeks, the *Marin* was to return to France for additional supplies.

Exploration of the Lower Mississippi. Iberville pushed slowly southward, threading his way around and between the many islands. The wind was usually against him, so the pulling was hard, and fog slowed up his progress. The islands were low and marshy, offering little protection from the winter winds; wood was scarce and sometimes his men had no fires. Water could be had only by digging into the

22

"The Harbor of La Rochelle" by Jean-Baptiste Camille Corot

sands of the low beaches. One night after a stormy day the men had to build a platform on which to sleep, for the water covered the low island on which they were camped.

The storm continued the following day but the party pushed on, and late that afternoon they rounded a sort of cape. The wind drove them toward a series of jutting crags with calmer water between them. Iberville wrote in his journal: "As I neared the rocks, I perceived that there was a river. I passed between two of the rocks in twelve feet of water, the sea very heavy. . . . I found the water sweet and with a very great current." The "rocks" were not rocks at all, but drift logs covered with mud. The river was the Mississippi. It was March 2, 1699.

The next morning the party started up the river, and on the fourth day reached a settlement of Bayougoula Indians, several of whom offered to guide them up the river. The Indians showed them a letter which Tonti had written to La Salle in 1685. At that time Tonti had come down the Mississippi to assist La Salle in establishing his colony, but La Salle had missed the mouth of the river.

Iberville continued up the Mississippi past the village of the Mongoulacha Indians. He passed the site of the

23

present-day capital of Louisiana, where he saw a red pole with the heads of fish and bear stuck upon it, and so he named the place Baton Rouge, which means "red pole" or "red stick" in French. He passed Pointe Coupee, where the Mississippi was just beginning to cut through its loop and isolate what is now False River, and on March 20 reached the villages of the Houma Indians.

After being entertained by the Indians, Iberville started on his return trip. At Bayou Manchac, below Baton Rouge, he turned eastward with a few men, returning to Cat Island by way of Bayou Manchac, the Amite River, and Lakes Maurepas, Pontchartrain, and Borgne. Bienville continued on down the Mississippi to its mouth, then turned northward to Cat Island. The two brothers arrived at Cat Island within a few hours of each other.

Fort Maurepas, the First Settlement. Iberville now determined to establish a settlement on the Gulf Coast instead of at some point on the Mississippi. The riverbanks were low and the land behind them swampy. He feared, too, that large ships would not be able to cross the bars at the mouth of the river. If a fort were built on the coast, France would be able to control the mouth of the Mississippi and in addition might gain possession of the entire northern shores of the Gulf of Mexico.

Iberville explored the shores of the Bay St. Louis and the other bays and inlets eastward as far as Mobile, finally choosing the projection of land on the eastern side of Biloxi Bay as the site for his settlement. The little fleet anchored in the bay and the men began immediately to construct a small fort. By May 1, 1699, it was completed and named Fort Maurepas, in honor of the French prime minister. It was a small square fort armed with twelve cannon. On each side was a deep ravine and at the back a deep trench was dug to provide additional protection. Ensign de Sauvole was put in command, with Iberville's brother Bienville as lieutenant and second in command. The fort was garrisoned by seventy men and six shipboys with provisions for about six months.

On May 4, Iberville sailed for France with the *Badine* and the *Marin* to get new colonists and additional supplies. He had been successful in rediscovering the Mississippi River and in planting the settlement which was to grow into the French colony of Louisiana.

The Early Years. The early years were filled with hardships for the little colony. Many of the Canadian settlers were hunters and trappers, called *coureurs de bois,* who did not like to till the soil. Neither did the colonists who had come from France like to farm, much preferring to explore the region in search of gold and other precious metals. They were also unhappy because they had no wives to help them with household duties and make homes for them. No crops were raised the first year, which caused a heavy drain upon the supplies which had been brought from France.

About four months after the departure of Iberville, Bienville, on another exploring trip up the Mississippi, had an adventure which has become famous in the story of early French Louisiana. On his way down the river, at a short distance below present-day New Orleans, he saw a twelve-gun British ship. The British had decided to establish a colony near the mouth of the Mississippi, and Lewis Banks, captain of the vessel, was looking for a suitable site. Bienville boldly sailed up to the British ship and informed Banks that he was in French territory. He also told him he had a fleet a short distance upriver and that the British must leave immediately. Believing what he had been told, Banks turned around and departed downstream. This place on the Mississippi is still called "English Turn."

Iberville returned from France in early December, 1699, with supplies and new colonists. Having been told of Bienville's encounter with the British, Iberville ordered him to build a fort on the Mississippi at the first solid ground. Bienville selected a site about fifty miles upriver on the east bank, where he and his eight men built a low stockade, a small blockhouse, and a powder magazine. The blockhouse was a two-story, twenty-eight-foot-square fort made of cypress logs and armed with two eighteen-pound and four four-pound cannon. A few months later Father Jacques Gravier wrote that the twelve-foot-wide moat had not yet been finished but that there were "five or six cabins detached one from another and roofed with palm-leaves." The name Fort de la Boulaye was given to the little fortification, though no record remains of just why it was so named.

Tonti arrived from Canada with ten canoes, fifty men, and a cargo of furs while Bienville was still building Fort de la Boulaye. Having heard of Iberville's settlement, he had brought the furs for export to France. During this period Iberville explored the Mississippi River as far north as Natchez and sent Pierre le Sueur up the Mississippi in search of minerals. Le Sueur returned with some blue and green earth which he thought contained copper, but it contained no minerals.

Iberville again voyaged to France for supplies and colonists, and returned in December, 1701, his last voyage to the Louisiana colony. He found only about one hundred and fifty persons remaining in his colony: the rest had died. Supplies had run short and for some months the garrison at Fort Maurepas had had only a little corn to eat. He decided to move most of the colonists to a better location, where the soil was richer and where the harbor was deep enough to float large ships.

Mobile. Early in 1702, Iberville moved most of the settlers to Dauphin Island.

A landing made during Iberville's exploration of the Mississippi

A little later he built another settlement on the west side of Mobile Bay about thirty miles from the Gulf, and left only a small garrison at Fort Maurepas. Sauvole had died the preceding summer, so Bienville, who was now the second in command to his brother, began the construction of the fort which was named Fort St. Louis de la Mobile.

Fort St. Louis was much larger than Fort Maurepas, being about 375 feet square, and having four batteries of six cannon each. Within the fort were a guardhouse, a storehouse, a residence for the commandant, a house for the officers, and a chapel. The soldiers' barracks were constructed outside the palisade. Nearby, homes were built for the settlers.

Iberville left Louisiana for the last time on April 27, 1702. Before leaving he gave some good advice to the French government in one of his dispatches. He wrote that it was "necessary to send here honest tillers of the earth" and not men who came to Louisiana solely with the intention of making a fortune. But he left his colony well supplied and with the first lessons of colonization already learned. He had planned to return, but war broke out between France and Great Britain and his naval duties kept him occupied. He died of yellow fever in Havana, Cuba, in 1706.

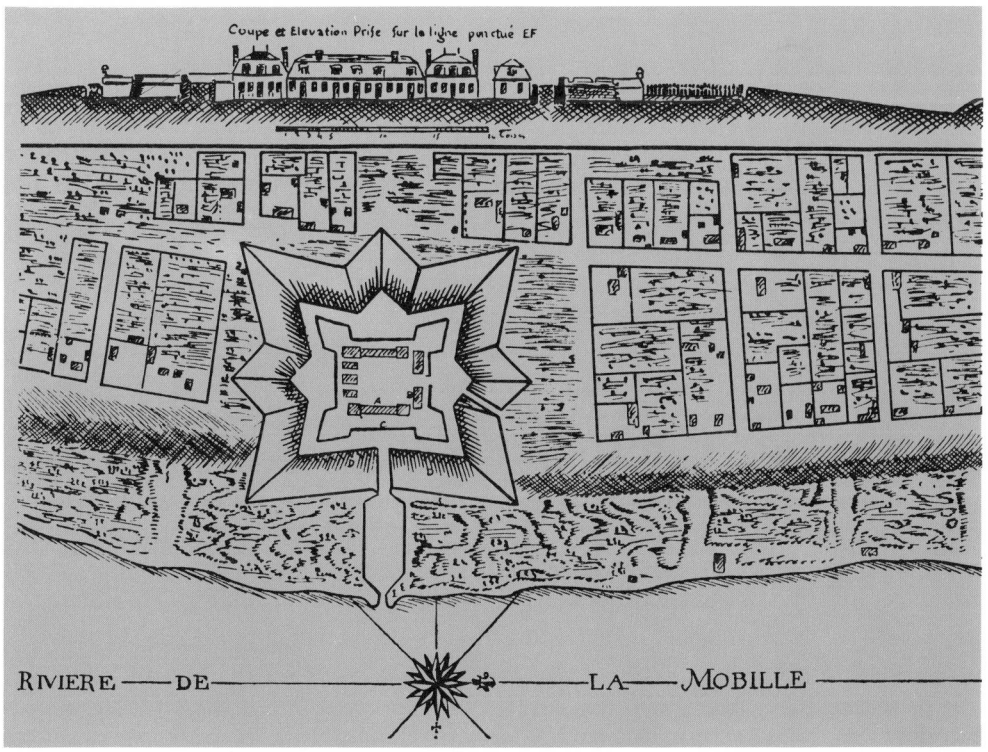

Coupe et Elevation Prise sur la ligne ponctué EF

RIVIERE — DE — LA — MOBILLE

Adrien de Pauger's plan of Fort St. Louis de la Louisiane at Mobile.

Iberville had succeeded where La Salle had failed. He had planted the colony of Louisiana, and though small it was firmly rooted. Not only an inspiring leader, he had also been a practical one. He advocated the extension of agriculture as the colony's chief means of livelihood and urged the emigration of families and of young women to marry and make homes for the young settlers. No French colonizer has a better record of heroism, work, and self-sacrifice. He well deserves to be called "The Founder of Louisiana."

Slow Growth of the Colony. The little settlements at Fort St. Louis de la Mobile, Fort Maurepas, and Fort de la Boulaye grew slowly during the years after 1702. A few farms were established along the Gulf Coast and along the banks of the Lower Mississippi. Voyagers and traders arrived every year from the Great Lakes region or the Upper Mississippi with furs and other trading goods. But disease, famine, and storms harassed the settlements. The colonists quarreled among themselves. The home government kept them so busy searching for mines and pearl fisheries, trying to domesticate the buffalo for their "wool," and raising silkworms, that they had to depend upon vessels from France to supply the major portion of their provisions.

Iberville, the other leaders, and the priests had pleaded for the establishment of homes. "With wives," Iberville said, "I will anchor the roving *coureurs de bois* into sturdy colonists." "Send me wives for my Canadians," wrote Bienville. "Let us sanction with religion, marriage with Indian girls," penned the priests, "or send wives of their own kind to the young men." Accordingly, in the summer of 1704, twenty-three young women arrived, girls who, according to the priest, "were reared in virtue and piety, and knew how to work." The same ship, the *Pelican,* also brought seventy-five soldiers, four families of artisans, a curate, and two Gray Sisters.

The colonists looked over the sides of the vessels toward a land which they believed to be one of fabulous riches, where life would be easy and work not too difficult. They were disappointed, "dumped, like ballast," as Louisiana historian Grace King wrote, "upon the arid, glittering sands of Dauphin Island or Biloxi, ill from the voyage, without shelter, without food, without employment." Many of them, unaccustomed to the climate and the hardships, died within a short time.

In 1704 Mobile had only 195 inhabitants; among them were 8 officers, 72 soldiers, 14 naval officers and sailors, 10 shipboys, 40 Canadians, 16 laborers, and 23 women or girls. In that year Jean François le Camp was born to Jean le Camp and his wife—the first birth to be recorded in the colony.

The colony was in bad condition. The people were in rags, and the soldiers wore skins rather than their worn-out uniforms. The colonists ate acorns, a little corn which they had raised, and wild game and fowl which were obtained by hunting. Their wooden houses, roofed with palmetto or straw thatch, were poorly built. They had made a start, however, in raising chickens and livestock. A report stated that they had "14 cows; 4 bulls, of which 1 belongs to the King; 5 calves, 100 hogs, 3 goats, 400 chickens, which the commissary has preserved carefully for breeding."

In September, 1704, a yellow fever epidemic took the lives of thirty-five persons, including the gallant and experienced Tonti, whose loss was a severe blow to the colonists. Alcée Fortier, one of Louisiana's noted historians, called him "the most chivalric of the explorers of America."

By 1708 the little colony boasted 279 persons, not counting Canadians and Indian slaves, and in addition "50 cows, 40 calves, 4 bulls, 8 oxen, 1400 hogs, and 2000 hens." But two years later, excluding the soldiers, sailors, and Canadians, there were only 178 inhabitants. The others had died.

Beginnings of Trade. The fur trade

28

with the Upper Mississippi and the western Great Lakes region had begun in 1700 when Tonti brought the first shipment of furs down the river. During the years that followed, the governors of Canada opposed the trade in furs, hides, corn, meat, and other products, one of them writing that the goods in many instances belonged to Canadian creditors. But as it was easy to float boats down the great river, the trade continued.

As early as 1701, Iberville had begun to investigate the possibilities of trade with the West Indies—Havana was, after all, only fifteen sailing days from Biloxi. But the Spanish officials were slow to start trade outside their own possessions. In 1704, however, the French were able to do the Spanish a favor; Pensacola needed flour, lard, and munitions of war, and Bienville sent the needed supplies. Two years later he again sent flour to Pensacola.

By 1708 the trade with Cuba and the other West Indies islands was well established, though it was still frowned upon by some of the Spanish officials. It was upon this trade that the Louisianians depended for much of their supplies during Queen Anne's War (the war between France and Great Britain) when foodstuffs could not be received regularly from France.

After 1703 the French government maintained a storekeeper at the Balize, near the mouth of the Mississippi. He handled all the supplies, food, ammunition, and other goods sent over from France and was required to keep a strict "account of merchandise and ammunition received and distributed." The early settlers had very little metallic money. For the most part they traded and bartered, or depended upon "bills of credit" which were issued by the governor of the colony.

Bienville and the Louisiana Colony. Until 1712 there were only two important government officials in Louisiana. The Governor, as the representative of the King, was at the head of civil, military, and naval affairs, while a Commissioner served as the auditor, treasurer, and chief storekeeper of the colony. The Curé guided the religious life of the people. There were no courts of law, for the officials decided disputes and punished criminals.

Only three persons served as Governor: Iberville during 1699, Sauvole from 1699 to 1701, and Bienville from 1701 to 1713. Bienville was an able governor, doing the best that could have been done under the circumstances. During the yellow fever epidemics of 1701 and 1704 he saved his colony from ruin and perhaps from abandonment. Through both sternness and friendly persuasion, he made the colonists begin raising agricultural products. When the great flood of 1709 overflowed the fort and the town at Mobile, he simply moved them down the river the next year to a higher location at the present site of Mobile. The new fort was named Fort St. Louis de la Louisiane.

Though he was to remain in Loui-

St. Denis selects a site for a French trading post near present-day Natchitoches.

siana for many years, Bienville's first years had been the hardest. By 1712 the Louisiana colony was permanently established and could boast a population of about four hundred persons, including twenty slaves. It is with good reason that Bienville has been called "The Father of Louisiana."

3. LOUISIANA UNDER ANTOINE CROZAT

Antoine Crozat, the Merchant. During the early 1700's there lived in Paris a great merchant named Antoine Crozat. Although the son of a peasant, he had become one of the richest men in France and had been made a Marquis by the King.

Crozat had made huge profits from the Guinea Company, which traded in Africa, and from the Asiento Company, which imported African slaves into the New World. Louisiana had been described to Crozat as having splendid opportunities for agriculture, mining, and trade. He believed that given sufficient opportunity he could turn the French colony into a money-making investment.

Crozat's Grant. In September, 1712, Crozat secured a royal charter which granted Louisiana to him for a fifteen-year period. He was granted all the territory called Louisiana south of what is now Illinois. He was to have all the commercial rights formerly held by the King, including the importing and exporting of goods and the privilege of working mines and searching for precious stones, of course yielding to the King the "Royal Fifth." He was given all the land that he might cultivate and all manufactories which he might establish. He was given the use of all property belonging to the King. He was granted the exclusive right to import slaves from Africa.

Crozat in return was obligated to continue the laws of France in Louisiana and to send two ships from France each year with supplies and colonists.

Governor Cadillac. The colonists learned that Louisiana had been granted to Crozat during the early summer of 1713, when Governor Antoine de la Mothe Cadillac arrived, but it made little difference to them. They were extremely poor and were enduring a hand-to-mouth existence. There were only two companies of soldiers, fifty men to a company, in the colony, while some seventy-five Canadians performed various services for the King. The rest of the population totaled about three hundred persons, but these were scattered along the Gulf Coast west of Mobile and up the Mississippi River about as far as Pointe Coupee.

The new Governor had spent over twenty years in the service of the King in Canada. He had founded Detroit and had lived under frontier conditions in Canada. He was a man of courage, had a great deal of energy, and was rigidly moral and pious. He had also been given Royal instructions to govern his colony "with justice and mildness . . . like a good father."

On the other hand, Cadillac was proud and vain. He wore a "ponderous wig, the curls of which spread like a peacock's tail," and was both quarrelsome and bad-tempered. He was interested principally in making money though he had made little in Canada, while his ancestral castle in France was so run-down that the local wags called it "Cadillac's Rookery." His superiors in Canada had accused him of being "more interested in making money for himself than in the good of his establishment." Other Canadians had said that he was "hated by the troops, by the inhabitants, and by the savages."

Cadillac was very critical of the little colony. He wrote back to France that Dauphin Island "consists of a score of fig-trees, three wild pear-trees, and apple-trees of the same nature, a dwarfish plum-tree, three feet high, with seven bad-looking plums, thirty plants of vine, with nine bunches of half-rotten and half-dried-up grapes, forty stands of french melons, and some pumpkins." On another occasion he wrote that "the colony is not worth a straw for the moment; but I shall endeavor to make something of it, if God grants me health."

With characteristic energy, he went to work.

Work of Cadillac. Acting under instructions of the French government and Crozat, Cadillac first reorganized the government of the colony. An attorney general became his legal adviser and the lawyer of the people. He organized a court and advisory body called the Superior Council. He put into operation the so-called "Custom of Paris," which was simply the laws and legal customs of that section of France in the vicinity of the capital. He encouraged agriculture, offered plans for raising tobacco and indigo, and promoted the Indian fur trade. He sent out parties to plant settlements and encouraged trade with the Spanish in Mexico and Florida, with the British colonies, and with the islands of the Caribbean. In fact, he tried any sort of economic venture which would make the colony more self-sustaining and give a profit to Crozat.

Extending the Frontiers. In 1714 Cadillac called upon Louis Juchereau de St. Denis to establish a post on the Red

Fort St. John Baptiste de Natchitoches

River in what is now northwest Louisiana. Spain had been gradually pushing her settlements into Texas and western Louisiana, and the Governor wanted to stop them at the Sabine River.

St. Denis had come to Louisiana with Iberville and was an intelligent and energetic young man to whom the freedom of the Louisiana frontier greatly appealed. He soon became friendly with the Indians and familiar with the entire Lower Mississippi region.

St. Denis, with a sergeant and twenty-five soldiers, took three boats loaded with Indian trading goods, munitions, and supplies, and chose a site at Natchitoches for the new fort. It was well that the French had arrived at this time, for the Spanish had already sent out one expedition to start a settlement near the same place. Some years before, a few Spaniards had settled near present-day Robeline.

As soon as Fort Jean Baptiste de Natchitoches was completed, St. Denis took his trading goods and proceeded southwest to the Spanish post of San Juan Bautista, on the Río Grande. Here the Spanish Commandant made him a prisoner, and during the weeks which passed St. Denis fell in love with the Commandant's granddaughter, Manuela. He was taken to the City of Mexico and later was returned to San Juan Bautista, where he continued his courtship of Manuela. The girl's father at last gave his consent to the marriage, and in 1716 Señorita Manuela de Sanchez y Ramon became the bride of St. Denis.

For several years St. Denis traded with the Indians of western Louisiana and eastern Texas, and in 1722 he was appointed Commandant of the Natchitoches District, which included all of northwest Louisiana. He died in 1744. Louisianians during this period maintained that St. Denis deserved to have been made Governor of Louisiana.

In 1716 Bienville completed a fort on the high bluff overlooking the Mississippi at Natchez which had officers' and soldiers' quarters, a magazine, and storage buildings within the walls. The fort was named Rosalie, after the wife of the Count de Pontchartrain. At about the same time, forts were built on the Alabama River and on the Wabash River, north of the Ohio. These forts, together with those at Mobile and Dauphin Island, gave France several strongholds with which to protect Louisiana from the British and the Spanish.

Agriculture and Commerce. Cadillac, acting under orders from Crozat, did what he could to encourage agriculture but the colonists did not like farming. Money could be made from tobacco and indigo but it involved very hard work, as did the cultivation of corn and vegetable crops. A few settlers, however, did produce food crops and in some years there was a surplus. For the most part the settlers in Louisiana at this time were Canadian hunters, fortune seekers from

The building of Fort Rosalie.

France, or those who had been sent to Louisiana instead of to the jails of the mother country.

In order to secure labor for the fields, Crozat imported Negro slaves from the West Indies. Five hundred were brought over in 1716 and about three thousand the following year. Afterward, most of the slaves were brought from Africa.

Cadillac had hoped to make a personal fortune for Crozat and for himself from gold and silver mines and from pearl fisheries, but despite the fact that he sent out numerous expeditions, none was discovered.

Gradually the French won the battle with the British for the Indian trade in hides and furs. The overland trade with Texas and Mexico, which was carried on from Natchitoches generally, sometimes ran to several thousand livres a year. The trade with Spanish Florida made a little profit. However, the colony did not prosper and brought in no profits to Crozat, the proprietor.

Recall of Cadillac. Cadillac's temper steadily grew worse. He quarreled with the officials. On one occasion some of the soldiers sent a committee to see the Governor and complained that they had nothing to eat but corn. The Commissary-Commissioner defended the soldiers, so Cadillac "gave him a good rapping on the knuckles." When the people framed a petition demanding free trading privileges with all countries, the Governor complained that they "have dared to meet without my permission."

Cadillac's daughter fell in love with Bienville, and when he ignored her infatuation, she enlisted the help of her father, who offered her hand to him. But Bienville did not love the young lady, so he told the Governor that he must forever remain unmarried. The Governor then became his enemy. Bienville later wrote in one of his dispatches that "the cause of Cadillac's enmity to me, is my having refused to marry his daughter."

By the summer of 1716, Cadillac had reached the end of his patience with the colony of Louisiana. His troubles were constant and he had gathered no riches. He had tried to carry out his orders, but many projects had failed. He wrote back to France in disgust: "Decidedly, this colony is a monster without head or tail."

Crozat had also lost patience with Cadillac. He wrote to the Governor and told him bluntly that the evils present in Louisiana were the result of his inefficient administration. The Governor and the Commissary-Commissioner were dismissed. The Minister of Marine in France wrote that their intellects were "not equal to the functions with which his Majesty has entrusted them."

Bienville served as Acting Governor until the new Governor arrived.

End of Crozat's Colony. Bienville held his second governorship for a little less than a year. In March, 1717, Jean Michiele, Seigneur de Lepinay, the new Governor, arrived. He was a naval officer who had served more than twenty years in Canada. Governor Lepinay brought with him a new Commissary-Commissioner, three companies of infantry, and fifty colonists. He brought Bienville the decoration of the Cross of St. Louis, and title to Horn Island, just east of Ship Island off the Gulf Coast.

Lepinay had hardly landed in Louisiana before he and Bienville began to quarrel, and soon the colony was divided, one group supporting Bienville and the other the new Governor.

In France, Crozat's financial affairs had taken a turn for the worse, so he reconsidered his Louisiana venture. He had spent over 1,250,000 livres. What had he gained? There were only about seven hundred people in his colony, including the soldiers of the army. Trade with the Spanish and British colonies had not been successful and several millions of livres worth of goods were still in Louisiana for want of a market. The hoped-for mines had produced no minerals and the pearl fisheries no pearls.

Then Crozat received word that Lepinay was doing no better than had Cadillac. In early August, 1717, he addressed a petition to Louis XV, begging to be released from the agreement, and the ministers of the King accepted his proposal.

New Orleans, 1719

4. JOHN LAW'S LOUISIANA

John Law. The chief character in the Louisiana drama from 1717 to 1731 was a Scottish banker and businessman named John Law. The drama concerns two companies which he organized and which for a time controlled Louisiana. Next to Iberville and Bienville, Law contributed more than anyone else to Louisiana's development during the French period.

Law was the son of a wealthy Edinburgh goldsmith and banker. Early in his youth he showed ability in mathematics, finance, and commerce, but at the age of twenty he had already gambled away his fortune. He killed a man in a duel and fled to France, where he soon gained another fortune at the gambling tables.

Law studied finance, particularly the methods of the Bank of Amsterdam, and developed the idea that

France could greatly increase her wealth by printing huge quantities of paper money. He had little difficulty in selling his scheme to the Duke of Orléans and other governmental leaders. In 1716 he organized the General Bank of France and the following year its paper money was accepted as currency in all France. In 1718 it became the Royal Bank of France, with Law as Director-General.

The Company of the West. The Scotsman conceived the idea of using some of the deposits of his bank for the development of Louisiana. He organized the Company of the West and shares of stock were offered for sale to everyone in France. Law promised that huge profits were to be made in Louisiana and that everyone who purchased shares of stock would become wealthy.

36

John Law

The shares sold at 500 livres each and could be bought on credit with only a 25 per cent down payment. The people became very excited over this prospect of easy wealth, and Law had no difficulty in selling his stock.

In 1717 Louisiana was turned over to the Company of the West on approximately the same terms which had been granted Crozat in 1712. In 1719 all of the French trading and colonizing companies were merged into one large one called the Company of the Indies, and the Company of the West was included in this merger.

The Company of the Indies an-

nounced great plans for the development of Louisiana. Large numbers of settlers were to be sent to the colony, new settlements were to be established, and agriculture was to be promoted. Trade was to be extended with the Spanish in Florida and Mexico, with the British in their southern colonies, and with the Illinois country. Currency would be sent to Louisiana to give the people more money with which to buy goods.

Government Under the Company of the Indies. The governmental officers and Superior Council were left largely

37

as they had been under Crozat. Each of the more important settlements of Biloxi, Dauphin Island, Mobile, Natchez, and Natchitoches had a Commandant, who was both the civil and military official.

The headquarters of the colony was first at Dauphin Island, but by 1719 had been moved to Fort Maurepas. Shortly afterward a part of Fort Maurepas burned and the capital was moved to New Biloxi, on the other side of the bay. The capital of Louisiana remained at New Biloxi until August, 1722, when it was moved to New Orleans.

In 1721 Louisiana, which then included most of the Mississippi Valley, was divided into nine governmental districts, each under the charge of a Commandant and a Judge. The following year three large religious parishes were created, and turned over to the Carmelite, Jesuit, and Capuchin orders. Except for the Florida Parishes, present-day Louisiana was given to the Capuchins.

Bienville became Governor of Louisiana for the third time in 1718. He returned to France in 1725 and left Pierre Dugué de Boisbriant serving as Acting Governor. Étienne Périer became Governor in 1727 and served until 1733, two years after Louisiana became a royal colony again. Under Bienville and Périer, from 1718 to 1733, Louisiana made steady progress.

The Founding of New Orleans. Bienville had always wanted to build the

capital of the Louisiana colony on the Lower Mississippi River, but it was some years before he had the opportunity to found his new city.

In 1717 he wrote the directors of the Company telling them of a crescent bend in the Mississippi which was safe from tidal waves and hurricanes. The new capital should be built here. A colonist named Le Page du Pratz, who arrived in Louisiana about this time, commented that "a better choice could not have been made." He also complimented Bienville by writing: "It is not every man that can see so far as some others."

Early in 1718, Bienville left Mobile with about fifty men, including a few carpenters and twenty-odd convicts, and spent much time that year directing the building work. Progress was slow, but by the end of 1719 a number of huts and storage houses had been built, so Bienville began to move supplies and troops to his new town.

The chief engineer of the colony, Le Blond de la Tour, had opposed Bienville's plans. When an assistant engineer, Adrien de Pauger, arrived in the colony in 1720 he was ordered to draw the plans for the new city. He reached New Orleans in March, 1721, and under his supervision the town soon began to take shape. Drainage ditches and canals were dug, a wharf was built, low levees were thrown up, a cemetery was located, and a church and government buildings were constructed.

The central portion fronting the

Adrien de Pauger surveys the site of
New Orleans.

river was occupied by the church, with
the priest's house on the left and a
guardhouse and prison on the right. In
front was the Place d'Armes, or parade ground, to the left of which was
a market place fronting the river,
while scattered about the river front
were government warehouses. Bienville built his home on the site of the
present-day customhouse and in front
of this building erected a powder
magazine. At the other extreme end of
the town were the quarters of the soldiers. Today we call the eleven-by-
seven-block rectangle, which made up
the French town, the "Vieux Carré" or
Old Square.

Bienville named his new capital
Nouvelle-Orléans, New Orleans, in
honor of Louis Phillipe, Duke of Orléans and Prince Regent of France.

New Colonists for Louisiana. The
Company of the Indies had difficulty
in getting settlers to come to Louisiana, so the French government began
to release people from prisons and
houses of correction, upon their agree-
ing to go to the colony. These men and
women were chained together and
driven along the roads of France toward the port towns like droves of
cattle. At night they were locked up
in barns and when shelter could not

Settlers for the Louisiana colony. A cartload of French criminals and poor people waiting at a French port. An old woodcut.

be found were forced to lie down in ditches, while guards stood over them.

But still not enough people could be found, so orders were given to kidnap the poor and send them to Louisiana. There was no time to choose or select or examine or ask questions. As Grace King has written, "It was a dog-catcher's work; and dog-catchers performed it. Streets were scoured at night . . . the contents of hospitals, refuges, and reformatories were brought out wholesale, servant girls were waylaid, children were kidnapped." Soon the word "Louisiane" became hated for it meant a place of exile, far from France.

Indescribable hardships were suffered by these immigrants on the voyage to Louisiana. The captains of the ships were paid according to the number of people they brought over, and so they packed the greatest possible number into their vessels. Conditions

on board were very bad, the food was moldy and sometimes rotten, and the water was stale and usually impure. Hundreds died. Out of 213 persons who sailed on one ship, only 40 reached Louisiana alive.

Criminals and people of bad character do not make good citizens and soon the Company realized its mistake and adopted a new method of securing settlers. Large grants of land called "concessions" were given to wealthy or noble Frenchmen or other Europeans, in return for which these men agreed to settle families on their lands. Smaller grants of land called "habitations" were given to the less wealthy. But these offers did not attract enough settlers.

The Company then tried another method. The expenses of European families migrating to Louisiana would be paid. Each family would also be

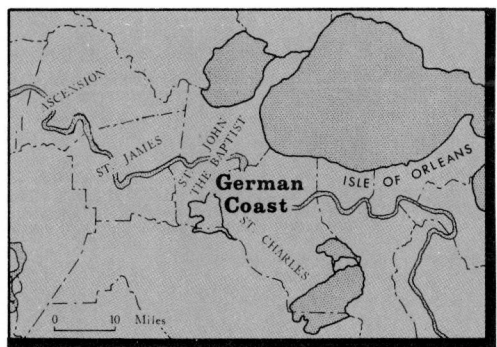

Map 7—The German Coast above New Orleans

given sizable plots of land, horses and oxen for the cultivation of fields, and pigs, sheep, chickens, furniture, kitchen utensils, and food supplies until the first harvest.

Pamphlets and handbills were published, but the descriptions of Louisiana were not correct. They said that four crops could be raised each year; that the Indians were very friendly and did most of the work; that there was plenty of game, including deer and bear. Many Frenchmen and other Europeans believed these descriptions and came to Louisiana.

Several thousand Germans and many Swiss arrived, most of whom changed their names to the French spellings. But they remembered their German origin. Even today their descendants say with pride: "We are the descendants of those Germans who turned the wilderness into a paradise."

During those early years most of the settlers lived very hard lives. The Company did not keep its promises. The ship captains turned the supplies over to the soldiers or sold them for the Company's profit. The settlers were dumped off the ships onto the beaches of Mobile or Biloxi or at the landing at New Orleans without shelter and without food. Some of them were forced "to subsist on what they might be able to catch on the beach, standing for the most part of the day in the salt water up to the waist."

No one knows how many settlers arrived during those years after 1717. Over eight hundred came in 1718 and this number more than doubled the population of the colony. In 1722, nine ships arrived with over four thousand settlers. But it is certainly true that more settlers came during these years than at any other time while the French held Louisiana.

In the fall of 1727 the first group of *filles à la cassette,* or casket girls, arrived. They were called casket girls because each of them had a small trunk filled with personal belongings, a sort of hope chest which had been given her by the Company. They were marriageable young ladies of good character and were housed by the Ursuline nuns in a large building guarded by soldiers until they found husbands.

Negro Slaves Sent to Louisiana. Additional slave labor was needed. During the summer of 1719 the ships *Grand Duc du Maine* and *Aurora* arrived

41

from Africa with about five hundred slaves, so the Company built a slave-trading station across the Mississippi from New Orleans where Algiers is today. It was called the "Plantation of the Company." Here the slaves were distributed or were sold to the colonists.

By 1724 slaves had become so numerous that Bienville felt it necessary to enact special legislation for their management and control, so the *Code Noir,* or "Black Code," was promulgated. While the Black Code dealt mainly with slaves, Article 1 ordered all Jews expelled from Louisiana and Article 3 permitted "the exercises of the Roman Catholic creed only." Many of the articles protected the slaves. They must be properly clothed and fed, cared for in sickness and old age, and must not be shackled or tortured. On the other hand, slaves from different plantations could not assemble, and no slaves were permitted to carry weapons or sell goods without permission of their masters.

Establishment of the Jesuit Plantation and the Coming of the Ursulines. In 1726, Jesuit Father Ignatius de Beaubois secured permission to establish a headquarters at New Orleans for Jesuits on their way to missionary assignments up the Mississippi and to secure the services of the Ursuline nuns for educational and medical work. The first Ursuline nuns arrived in August, 1727, and were temporarily quartered in Bienville's house, which thus became the first convent within the limits of what would become the United States. A permanent convent was completed in 1734. In addition to their teaching duties, the sisters took charge of the military hospital and ministered to soldiers and citizens alike who needed medical attention.

The Natchez Indian War. On December 2, 1729, a ragged, half-starved, half-dead man staggered into New Orleans. He told the excited people that the Natchez Indians had risen against the French and had massacred all of the settlers at Fort Rosalie and in the surrounding country. He had been away from the fort and had thus escaped. A few other fugitives appeared within a few days and confirmed his report.

The Natchez had been at peace with the French for some years, and many settlers had established farms among them. Several of the red men had already visited France, one of whom had said that in Paris he liked best the Street of the Butchers' Shops, because they had so much meat there. He had seen men who "had their hair done up like women [they were wearing wigs]; that he had a strong suspicion they used rouge and that they smelled like a crocodile."

But a Commandant named Chepart had been sent to Fort Rosalie. He was an iron-handed man who treated his soldiers and the Indians harshly and planned to become rich through the establishment of a large plantation. When the Indians did not

This old French print (1726) shows Indians in a large canoe on the Mississippi near New Orleans.

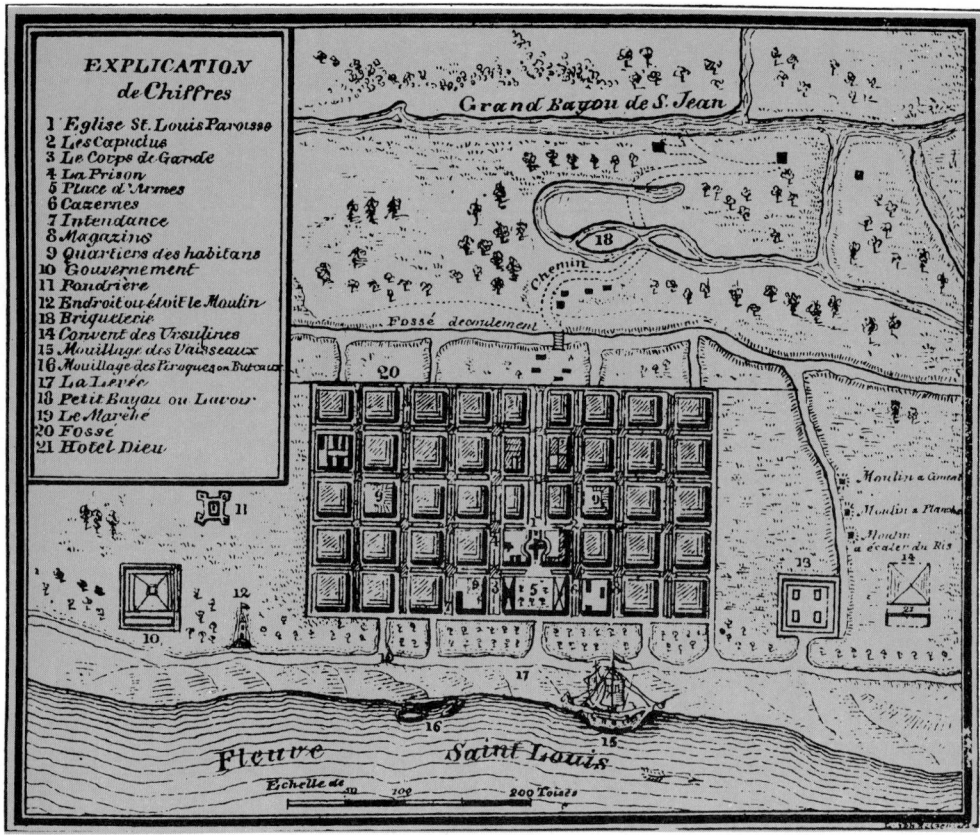

EXPLICATION de Chiffres

1 Eglise St. Louis Paroisse
2 Les Capucins
3 Le Corps de Garde
4 La Prison
5 Place d'Armes
6 Cazernes
7 Intendance
8 Magazins
9 Quartiers des habitans
10 Gouvernement
11 Poudrière
12 Endroit ou était le Moulin
13 Briqueterie
14 Convent des Ursulines
15 Mouillage des Vaisseaux
16 Mouillage des Piroques ou Buteaux
17 La Levée
18 Petit Bayou ou Lavoir
19 Le Marché
20 Fossé
21 Hotel Dieu

Map 8—New Orleans, about 1728

want to give up their village of the White Apple or their land, Chepart became enraged and said that they must leave just as soon as the harvest was over. Chepart was warned that the Indians were planning to revolt, but he did nothing. On November 26, 1729, the Indians began a massacre and killed nearly three hundred persons.

Some of the Louisiana Indians joined in the uprising and many settlers west of the Mississippi were killed. One settler, however, who lived off the coast of present-day Terrebonne Parish, drove away the attacking Indians in a very peculiar manner. Upon seeing them, Sylvain Filiosa grabbed a kettledrum and banged it so loudly that the Indians stopped and gazed in alarm at the unknown and strange weapon. From this time Filiosa and his island were called "Le Timbalier," the kettledrummer.

The French marched against the Natchez. The Indian forts were destroyed and most of the Indians were

44

killed or captured and sent as slaves to Santo Domingo. The few who escaped moved further westward into Louisiana or joined the Chickasaws. The Natchez ceased to exist as an organized Indian nation.

Growth of Towns and Villages. New Orleans grew slowly during those early years. By 1721, however, it was a sizable village, and two years later Father Pierre Charlevoix wrote that there were about a hundred rude houses, a church, several warehouses, and other buildings in the town. He predicted that "this savage and desolate place, which is still almost covered with trees and canebrakes, will one day be an opulent city, and the Metropolis of a great and rich colony."

A storm destroyed the church and many other buildings in 1723, but the latter were reconstructed and a new brick church soon replaced the old wooden one. Four small forts called St. Jean, St. Charles, St. Louis, and Bourgogne, were built at the four corners of the little town and were connected by a low earthen wall.

In 1727, when the Ursuline Sisters arrived, one of them wrote back to France: "Our town is very handsome, well constructed and regularly built." She continued that the streets were large and straight, the houses well built and whitewashed, and that "the colonists are very proud of their capital."

In 1719 a fort had been built on the present site of Baton Rouge, and four years later a trading post named Les Rapides was established at present-day Pineville. By 1720 Natchitoches had nearly a hundred inhabitants, who made a good living from agriculture and trade with the Indians. Other villages were established and new settlers opened up farms along the rivers and bayous of southeast Louisiana.

But the pioneers faced many hardships. The land had to be cleared of trees and brush, and they had to learn how to plant crops in the climate of Louisiana, which was different from that of France. Domestic animals were difficult to secure; good prices were not always received for their farm products; there were droughts and storms. "But the greatest torture," wrote Father Paul du Poisson, "is the mosquitoes, the cruel persecution of the mosquitoes." This little creature had caused more problems for the French in Louisiana than had any of the animals, other insects, or forces of nature, and Father Poisson continued for two more pages to explain how hateful the little insects were.

Despite all these hardships, however, the colony made slow but steady progress.

Company of the Indies Gives Up Louisiana. When the directors of the Company of the Indies received word of the Natchez massacre and the Indian war, they agreed they could not furnish the money which would be necessary to rebuild the colony. They had tried to make Louisiana a profitable

Failure of Law's bank

colony, but now all their efforts seemed lost.

John Law's "Mississippi Bubble" had burst in 1720. The stockholders of his bank, suspecting that all was not well with their Louisiana investments, began to withdraw their deposits. Shortly thereafter France was flooded with paper money, and foreign investors also began to withdraw their investments. The government refused to accept the bank's paper money, and the run on the bank continued. Soon it could not pay its depositors. Law

escaped from France to Belgium, and died in 1729, in poverty and obscurity, in Italy.

While most of the people hated Law for the ruin which he had caused, one of the stockholders wrote the following:

> *Monday bonds I bought;*
> *Tuesday gains unthought;*
> *Wednesday my home to date;*
> *Thursday I rode in state;*
> *Friday I danced with glee;*
> *Saturday—woe unto me!*

Early in 1731 the directors of the Company asked the King to take back their charter and the following November he issued a series of orders which ended the Company's control of Louisiana.

Work of John Law and the Companies. John Law, the Company of the West, and the Company of the Indies had done great things for Louisiana. Law had found Louisiana a colony with fewer than a thousand inhabitants; the Company of the Indies left it with a population of about 7,500, including Negro slaves. Several towns and settlements had been founded; agriculture was well established, although not all of the needs of the settlers could be supplied; and New Orleans had been built into a town of which its people were proud. Despite the shortcomings of John Law and the impracticability of some of his ideas, Louisiana owes him a great debt of gratitude.

5. THE LAST FRENCH GOVERNORS

Bienville's Last Governorship. Étienne Périer was Governor for two years after the Company of the Indies returned Louisiana to the King. The Chickasaw Indians, who had always been enemies of the French, caused trouble. The colonists were discontented because a hurricane had caused a food shortage. Some of the government officials had grown lax in performing their duties, and there were disagreements among the members of the Superior Council.

Périer lost interest in Louisiana. Though a man of integrity, he was somewhat brisk and harsh, which hampered good relations with the Indians and with his subordinates. He finally resigned and Bienville was again appointed Governor.

Bienville had been living in France since his last governorship, but he left there as soon as possible and arrived in Louisiana in 1733.

The Chickasaw Indian War. Bienville was almost wholly occupied with the Chickasaws during his last governorship and had to declare war against them. He ordered Pierre d'Artaguette, a Commandant in Illinois, to gather an army and meet him in the Chickasaw country in May, 1736. He himself

Jean Baptiste le Moyne, Sieur de Bienville, "The Father of Louisiana."

47

would raise an army in Louisiana, move up the Mobile River, and join D'Artaguette. Their combined force would have little difficulty with the Chickasaws.

D'Artaguette and his little army of forty-eight soldiers reached the appointed place, but Bienville, who had been delayed because of almost constant rains and a violent storm, was not there. For ten days D'Artaguette searched the area looking for the Governor, and finally decided to attack the Indian villages without waiting for Bienville. He captured one village, but he and some of his soldiers were taken prisoner during the attack on the second village. Bienville reached this place a few days later and, believing that D'Artaguette and his men had not yet arrived, attacked the strong Indian fort but was defeated. The Indians burned D'Artaguette and fifteen of the soldiers to death.

Mathurin le Petit, who was one of the prisoners not burned, reported that the doomed men chanted a prayer, which the Indians called a "song to go above," while they were being led to the two huge fires. They did not "interrupt their singing amid the fire until they fell, half burned or suffocated by the flames."

The Louisiana colonists were much saddened by the deaths of D'Artaguette and his men, and for many years they told stories about him and how he had fearlessly attacked the Indians. These stories gradually became legends, and anyone wishing to speak of something very old said that it was "as old as the time of D'Artaguette."

Bienville never recovered from this defeat. More than a hundred French soldiers had been killed. What had gone wrong? Whose fault was it? The two armies had simply not coordinated their movements. Together they could have defeated the Indians; separately they had been defeated. He took the blame upon himself.

Bienville continued the war against the Indians but was never able to inflict a decisive defeat. Finally, in 1740, the Chickasaws sued for peace. But the Governor was so disappointed at his failure to win the Indian war that he asked permission to resign his governorship. He was getting old and had lost the energy of his youth. It is certain that he was a brokenhearted man.

Bienville's Last Years in Louisiana. Bienville spent the next three years engaged in routine matters of administration. He continued to encourage trade and agriculture. He aided in the relief of suffering when two hurricanes hit the Gulf Coast in the fall of 1740. He proposed the establishment of a school in New Orleans where the boys could be taught geometry, geography, and other subjects. He wrote that "young men brought up in luxury and idleness are of little use."

The new Governor arrived in New Orleans in May, 1743, and in mid-August, Bienville sailed for France, after nearly forty years in Louisiana. He had traveled Louisiana's bayous and rivers and had threaded its forests. He had attempted to keep the Indians at peace and had worked to build the colony into a proud possession of France. Years later, he tried in vain to prevent the transfer of Louisiana to Spain. The Father of Louisiana died in Paris in 1767 at the age of eighty-seven.

The Grand Marquis. Pierre Rigaud, Marquis de Vaudreuil, the new Governor, was the son of a Governor of Canada and belonged to a family which was very influential at the French court. He had a genial and kindly nature; he had soldierly courtliness and great dignity and his manners were elegant; and he enjoyed giving magnificent entertainments, formal ceremonies, and military displays. Throughout his governorship, he maintained in New Orleans a fashionable little court which closely resembled the magnificent court of the indolent, pleasure-loving King Louis XV at the palace at Versailles in France.

Vaudreuil's Indian Problems. The Chickasaws had continued to cause trouble, for their peace with Bienville had been only a truce. Most of them preferred to trade with the French rather than the British, but it was difficult for Vaudreuil to get trading goods from France. So the Indians traded with the country which had the most goods at the cheapest prices.

In 1747 the Indians made a raid down the east bank of the Mississippi for some distance south of Baton Rouge, and the settlers fled to New Orleans. The next year they again moved down the left bank of the Mississippi, killing and plundering as they went. Some of the settlers escaped by crossing the river, where the militia defended them. In 1752 the Chickasaws once more went on the warpath and Vaudreuil led a force of over seven hundred men against them. Their villages were burned and their cornfields destroyed, and without means of subsistence, they sued for peace.

Development of the Colony Under Vaudreuil. Vaudreuil encouraged agriculture, and it was not long before larger quantities of cotton, tobacco, rice, and other crops were being grown. In good years, some of these products were exported. Myrtle wax was produced for the making of candles and for other purposes. Salt, rough-sawed lumber, and bricks were manufactured for home use and for shipment to France or to the West Indies.

A census was taken in 1744, and it was found that the colony had slightly over three thousand white inhabitants, about eight hundred soldiers, and over two thousand slaves. This census revealed that the total population had declined since the Company of the Indies had turned the colony back to the King in 1731. On the other hand there was considerably greater prosperity than there had been before.

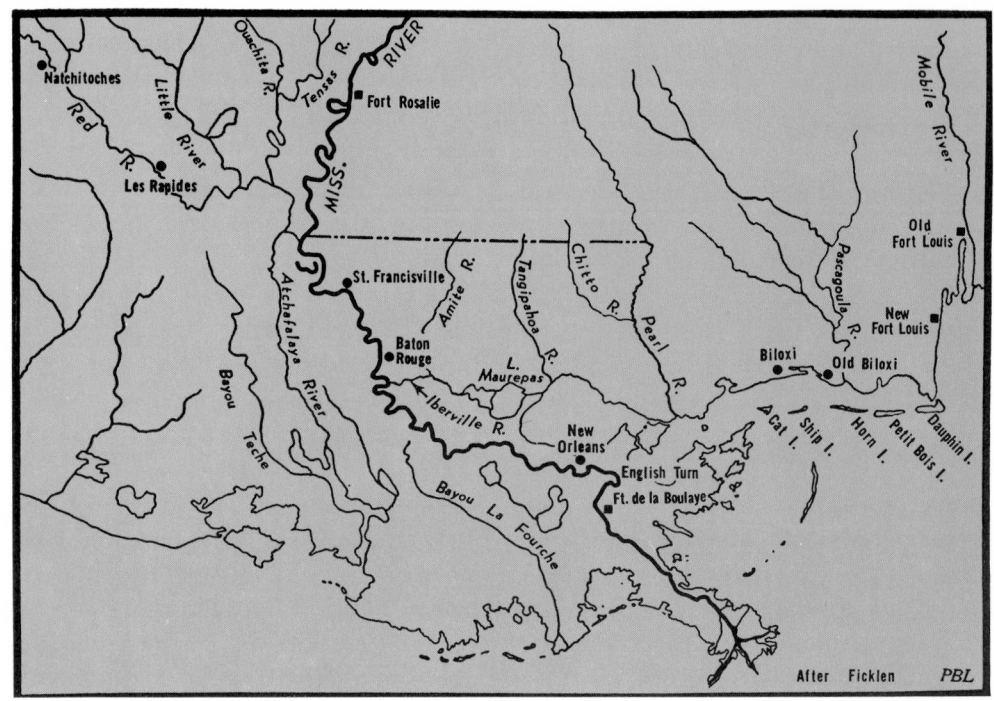

Map 9—Early French settlements in Louisiana

End of Vaudreuil's Governorship. The Governor was very popular in New Orleans because of his numerous balls and dinners; for the first time the wealthy citizens of the colony had a fashionable social life. The common people, however, were not so happy with their Governor. They accused him of favoring the soldiers, who bullied and insulted the citizens, and said that he surrounded himself with a small group of favorites who flattered him and who received many economic privileges. They said that the government officials were merely his tools, that his expenses were too high, and

that his wife was making large profits from illegal business transactions.

One of the reports sent back to France charged that Madam Vaudreuil "keeps in her own house every sort of drugs, which are sold by her steward. . . . The husband is not ignorant of this. He draws from it a handsome revenue."

However, Governor Vaudreuil remained in favor with the officials in France and he was promoted to a similar post in Canada in 1753. His governorship was long remembered in Louisiana for its luxury and military display, for its grand balls, and for the refined manners of the upper-class society. During later years, when hard times came, many people enjoyed recalling the good old days of the *Grand Marquis.*

Governor Kerlerec. Louis Billouart, Chevalier de Kerlerec, was a bluff, hearty, honest naval officer with twenty-five years of service to his credit. He was accustomed to discipline, which he insisted should be rigidly enforced. He was not a man of great ability, however, and simply could not handle adequately the many problems which faced the colony during his term of office. The French and Indian War was being fought between France and Great Britain during most of his governorship, and as a result he faced many difficulties. But he did the best that could have been done under the circumstances, and one of the colonists admitted that he had "qualities of heart very different from those of his predecessor."

Kerlerec's Problems. The Indian trade caused Kerlerec much trouble, for the British had plenty of trading goods and their prices were lower than those of the French. All Kerlerec could do was to play the tribes against each other and to try trading the goods which he had. He begged France to send over well-trained, well-disciplined troops and argued that Swiss troops were better than French troops. He strengthened New Orleans by erecting a palisade around the city and by rebuilding the battery at English Turn. In the channel at the entrance of the Mississippi he anchored an old ship which could be sunk to keep out British ships. But during the French and Indian War, Louisiana seemed to have been forgotten, for France could not assist the colony.

Conditions in Louisiana grew worse, and as they grew worse, Kerlerec's discipline tightened. The Commandant at Cat Island forced his soldiers to cultivate his garden and to do other personal work. He stole their supplies, trading them to the Indians or to the settlers. Finally a few of the soldiers revolted and killed the Commandant. Kerlerec held the trial of the soldiers in New Orleans and several of them were executed.

The morale of the colony declined. The Jesuits and the Capuchins were engaged in what some of the people called a religious war. Kerlerec reported that the Indians "harass us daily, to have supplies and merchandise. They threaten to go over to the English." He also wrote that they "devour the little that remains of our provisions." Agriculture was neglected and the war prevented foreign trade. One of the officials wrote that the colony was "in a state of complete destitution" and that most of the inhabitants were a lazy, insubordinate, drunken lot.

Louisiana Ceded to Spain. By 1756, France was spending over 800,000 livres a year on Louisiana and was re-

Fort at Old Biloxi—model made by eighth grade class, Catholic High School, Baton Rouge, Patrick Kennedy, instructor

ceiving little revenue from it. The colony had never been profitable. Altogether, between seventy million and eighty million livres had been invested with comparatively little return, and expenses were mounting each year. The colony had a total population of less than seventy-five hundred people. In 1757 Kerlerec wrote that he had not had even a letter from France for two years, and in 1761 the French ambassador to Spain admitted that France had not sent any supplies to Louisiana for four years.

France was much more interested in saving her West Indies islands than in saving Louisiana, for it had been a costly and unsuccessful colony. Only a few Frenchmen wanted to keep Louisiana, and one of these few, the philosopher Voltaire, wrote that he could not conceive how Frenchmen could abandon "the most beautiful climate of the earth, from which one may have tobacco, silk, indigo, a thousand useful products."

On November 3, 1762, by a secret treaty signed at Fontainebleau, France ceded the Isle of Orleans and the rest of Louisiana west of the Mississippi River to Spain. A few weeks later (in 1763) Great Britain acquired Spanish East and West Florida and the French area north of the Isle of Orleans and east of the Mississippi. It was not until October, 1764, however, that the people of Louisiana found out that they were now Spaniards instead of Frenchmen.

6. ECONOMIC LIFE AND GOVERNMENT IN FRENCH LOUISIANA

Farms and Plantations. The French had little success with agriculture in the early years, for they did not like the hard work it required. It was not until the coming of the German colonists that good farms were established. By the middle 1720's there were many small farms in the vicinity of Mobile, Biloxi, and New Orleans. During good crop-growing years the markets at these towns sold corn, rice, and wheat, and such vegetables as cabbages, peas, onions, sweet potatoes, pumpkins, watermelons, turnips, and greens of all sorts. Fruits included peaches, pears, figs, oranges, and lemons.

On market days and holidays the farmers went to the towns to sell their produce. There was no advertising except by voice, and everywhere men could be heard crying out their wares. Money was scarce and things were more frequently bartered than sold— a pig for so much grain, vegetables for fruits, articles of home manufacture for a chicken or a cow. Everything was labeled "Creole," which meant native to the colony or grown in the colony. There were "Creole" pigs, "Creole"

figs, and "Creole" rice. After all, many of the people were themselves "Creoles," for they had been born in Louisiana.

As time passed larger farms were cleared, and after the coming of Negro slaves, plantations were developed. These farms and plantations usually fronted a river or bayou, and a man was granted or bought so many "arpents" (approximately 182 feet) fronting the stream. His holding was ordinarily forty arpents deep, or "the usual depth" as the French said.

At first not much land was sold, for there were great areas of frontier land which were free to all. By the middle of the second decade, however, a few farms and houses were being bought and sold near the villages. As the population increased there was of course much more buying and selling of land.

At first corn and rice were the most important crops, but it was not long before cotton, tobacco, and indigo were being produced also. Sugarcane was first brought to Louisiana by Iberville, but little was grown until 1751, when a better variety from Santo Domingo was introduced. The cane juice was boiled down into a thick mass, for it would not granulate, and this was used for sweetening purposes and for the making of an alcoholic drink called "tafia." It was not until 1795 that Étienne de Boré succeeded in clarifying and crystallizing sugar in Louisiana.

The farmers and planters had many problems. Heavy rains frequently caused the streams and bayous to overflow, and storms destroyed their crops. Raccoons, opossums, and other animals and insects ate the plants. Weeds were numerous and often grew faster than the cultivated crops.

It was not until the colony had been settled for many years that enough meat was produced to satisfy the needs of the colonists, and sometimes the killing of cattle, sheep, and hogs had to be prohibited in order to save enough animals for breeding purposes. In 1725 cattle sold for 500 to 600 livres each, but the price gradually declined until in 1749 they were worth only about 60 livres. Not many horses were raised, most of them being bought from the Indians or from the Spanish. By the end of the French period there were several *vacheries,* or stock farms, scattered throughout the colony.

Development of Slavery. No one knows the exact date when the first Negro slave was brought to Louisiana. Indian slavery was first tried but was not successful because the Indians did not work well and found it difficult to understand the agricultural practices of the settlers. It is believed that Bienville first brought two slaves from the West Indies about 1708; by 1712 there were twenty slaves in the colony and twenty more were brought in the following year. A small number of slaves were sold during the Crozat period. The Company of the Indies imported many slaves after 1719, and for some time their slave ships arrived nearly every year. In 1724, Bienville enacted a series of slave regulations called the "Black Code." From this time until the time of the Civil War slavery was an important factor in the economic life of Louisiana.

Industry and Manufacturing. There was very little manufacturing in French Louisiana. The population was too small and the people were too busy growing foodstuffs, trading with the Indians, or working at other industries.

Lumbering was important, for the Gulf Coast and Lower Mississippi Valley were filled with good timber. Cordwood was also cut and sold in the towns for fuel. Brickmaking became an important industry, because the dampness of the climate caused wood to rot quickly. The bricks were somewhat larger than ordinary bricks, usually being 12 x 8 x 2 inches in size. The brickyards also made floor and roof tiles and some pottery. Many of these clay products were exported to the West Indies and to Spanish Florida.

Most of the manufacturing was done in the home or on the farm, for

54

the settlers made practically everything which they used, including furniture, clothing, leather goods, utensils, a few articles of iron or steel, and farm tools.

Local Trade. The Mississippi River, with its tributaries, was Louisiana's great artery of commerce. All types of boats were used. There were dugouts made of cottonwood or cypress, which were sometimes fifty feet long, used

sometime in August or September in order to arrive home before winter set in. The boats usually traveled in "convoys," several boats traveling together for better protection against Indian attacks. The government furnished a guard of several men and a leader who commanded the convoy.

Pack trains were used by Indians and British traders east of the Mississippi River. Following Indian and animal trails in regular Indian file, the

An early Mississippi River cargo boat.

sails, and had a rudder. There were flatboats, some of which carried as much as fifty tons. "Broad horns" were flatboats with a sharp bow. Keelboats, large flatboats sixty to seventy feet long and fifteen to twenty feet wide, with a keel, were introduced after 1740.

The Mississippi River trading boats usually left the Illinois country about the beginning of February, when the water was high and the river current was fastest. They generally started the return journey from New Orleans

pack trains moved along at a trot and seldom stopped until nightfall.

From the Illinois country came wheat, corn, lard, salt meat, dried meat, tallow, bear's oil, beeswax, skins and hides of all sorts, lead, and other articles. From New Orleans went rice, indigo, sugar and molasses, tafia, tobacco, manufactured goods which had been received from France or other countries, and trinkets for the Indian trade. The fur and hide trade was very important. By the middle 1740's over

55

fifteen hundred men were engaged in this trade and its annual value totaled thousands of livres. Owing to the wars which France fought with Great Britain, however, the Louisianians were frequently unable to furnish the goods which the Indians wanted in exchange for furs.

Foreign Trade. Foreign trade presented many difficulties. Ships were slow and sometimes badly built so that they sank during storms, and the voyages from the French ports took many weeks and sometimes several months. The poor food and bad water aboard ship caused diseases. Yellow fever sometimes broke out. Goods were often of poor quality, and smuggling of goods from the West Indies, the Floridas, and Mexico was a general practice.

There was considerable stealing and corruption among ship captains and among Louisiana and French officials. Many cargoes were short when they reached New Orleans. One ship on its arrival was short over 60 casks of wine out of a consignment of 170 casks. One ship captain sold his entire cargo for 250,000 livres to a public official who then retailed the goods at a 150,000 livre profit.

Trade with France was the lifeblood of the colony. From La Rochelle, Bordeaux, St. Malo, Rochefort, Nantes, St. Nazaire, Lorient, Brest, and other ports came ships with flour and other foodstuffs, wines, cloth, spices, cutlery, utensils, notions of all sorts, and after

1730 many types of luxury goods. When they returned to France they carried skins and hides, indigo, tobacco, myrtle wax, bear's oil, pitch and tar, lumber, and other products.

St. Denis was the founder of the Mexican trade and he continued this work until his death in 1744. The early trade with Mexico was carried overland by way of Natchitoches, but later most of it went by sea to the Mexican ports on the Gulf of Mexico. By the 1740's the Mexican trade had become a significant source of income for the Louisiana colonists.

Much of the trading with the Spanish West Indies, Mexico, and Florida was done illegally, because the Spanish usually required all trading to be done with Spain, just as France required all trading to be done with the mother country. Sometimes Spanish officials seized ships and cargoes. During periods when France and Spain were at war with Britain, however, the officials permitted trading between their colonies.

The government officials in France did all they could to prevent trade with the British, but Louisiana frequently needed British goods. British ship captains were very adept at making excuses for putting into the Louisiana ports: the ship had "sprung a leak," it had a "broken mast," there was a "shortage of wood and water." In 1735 a captain entered Mobile Bay on the excuse that he had come to collect some debts which were owed him. A ship which arrived in 1759 brought a cargo of dry goods valued at 600,000 livres, and another which arrived the same year brought flour, lard, beer, hams, cheese, iron, cider, and other goods. During times of war, when British vessels blockaded the mouths of the Louisiana rivers and bays, some trade was carried on with pack trains from Charleston, Savannah, and even Virginia and Maryland towns.

Money. During the entire period the colony depended generally upon bills of credit and exchange, Company of the Indies notes, Bank of France and government treasury notes, card money, and other forms of paper money. Gold, silver, or copper coins were always scarce and most of those in circulation came from the Spanish colonies. During the period of the Company of the Indies some copper money was sent from France, but these coins soon found their way back to France again. Between 1740 and 1750 hard currency was more plentiful, but after that time there was little in use.

Barter was the most common method of doing business. Certain goods, as for example bear's oil, tobacco, and corn, had a standard of value which was used as a guide. In everyday matters the people handled their trades so that they came out more-or-less even, or evened matters up when they traded the next time. Ship captains traded their goods for the goods which they wanted and took or paid the difference in bills of exchange.

Laws and Regulations. Simplicity and centralization were the most important features of French colonial government. The Governor, Commissary-Commissioner, two Lieutenant Governors, the Attorney General, and the other members of the Superior Council were the officials of colonial administration. The Commissary-Commissioner was the financial officer and the guardian of the warehouses. He also served as a check upon the Governor, and these two officials frequently quarreled. Bienville had much trouble with the Commissioners during his governorships.

The Commandant of the post or village was the chief local government official. He was sometimes aided by a judge appointed by the Governor.

The laws were the ordinances and edicts of the King, the laws of Paris (called the "Custom of Paris"), and the orders of the French Council of State. These were all "written" laws. "Common," or unwritten, laws were not used in French Louisiana as in the British colonies. Though there was comparatively little crime in the colony prior to 1740, there were many lawsuits over land titles and the settlement of estates.

There were many regulations for everyday living. Landholders along the streams and bayous were required to build roads and levees fronting the waterways. The settlers had to build and maintain small bridges. Food prices were fixed during the times of scarcity. Government officials in towns

French officers and soldiers

and villages inspected the meat and fish offered for sale. The first police regulations for New Orleans were issued by Governor Vaudreuil.

Punishments were very severe, but at the time this was the practice all over the world. Those who violated the laws and regulations were punished brutally according to modern standards. The death penalty was common. Several Swiss soldiers who had killed their captain at Fort Toulouse above Mobile were executed by the Indian method of head crushing.

Ridicule was the usual punishment for small offenses. In 1723, for example, a man who had sold some dog meat to the patients of the hospital was sentenced to be paraded around New Orleans wearing a sign reading: "Master Eater of Dogs and Cats," and with a dead cat hung around his neck.

7. LIVING IN FRENCH LOUISIANA

Farms and Villages. There were few towns in French colonial Louisiana. In 1762 New Orleans was the only important town, while Mobile, Biloxi, Baton Rouge, Natchez, Les Rapides (Pineville), Natchitoches, and Opelousas were only settlements or villages. New Orleans did not extend beyond the limits of the Vieux Carré, and not all of its blocks were filled with houses. There were a few scattered houses along the river front above and below the town, as well as some settlers along Bayou St. John.

58

The Place d'Armes, present-day Jackson Square, was the center of New Orleans, and behind it and fronting the river was the St. Louis Church. To the left of the church was the house of the Capuchin Fathers and to the right was the town jail and the guardhouse, while on each side of the square was a row of soldiers' barracks. Most of the houses and other buildings were made of wood. On each side of the streets was a small ditch about two feet wide and a foot deep, and these ditches had little bridges for the use of the citizens. After 1735 a town ordinance forced the citizens to build these little bridges, or pay a fine of ten livres.

Many Louisianians lived on farms along the Lower Mississippi or other streams, or along the Gulf of Mexico from present-day Bay St. Louis to Mobile. Pole-fenced farmyards held the horses, cattle, or sheep during nights or bad weather, and during the day the animals grazed on pasture land or in the woods and were usually guarded by small boys. A double furrow or ditch separated the farms. Farm tools were simple and primitive. There were wooden plows, rakes, and harrows. Scythes and sickles were used to harvest the grain, while the threshing was done with a long wooden flail. Every farmer had axes, hoes, spades, hammers, hatchets, and other such tools.

Homes and Home Furnishings. Unlike the British colonist, who built his log house by laying the logs one on top of the other, the French settler stood them on end. He called his cabin a *maison de poteaux en terre,* a house of posts in the ground. The spaces between the posts were usually filled with *bousillage,* a mixture of grass and clay; but if a man could afford a better house, he placed bricks between the posts and called it *briquette entre poteaux,* brick between posts. Gradually houses of sawed lumber and of brick began to make their appearance. They were roofed with straw, grass, or wooden shingles, and the floors were of plain earth or roughhewn boards. A few of the houses had glass windows, but most had only wooden shutters called *contrevents.*

Houses were much alike. The smaller ones had only one room, while the larger ones had two, three, or even four rooms. In most cases the rooms were placed end-to-end, with the front doors opening out upon a gallery, or porch. Frequently there was also a gallery at the back of the house and sometimes on all four sides. If the householder was a farmer he had a few other buildings—a stable, a henhouse, a barn for the storage of grain and vegetables, and a few cabins if he had slaves.

The combined kitchen and living room was the most important room in the house. It had a large fireplace equipped with andirons, a pothook, and a spit for roasting meat. Nearby were the frying pan, an iron grill, and several copper or iron kettles and pots. There was a large table in the center

59

A Louisiana house constructed in the manner of the old French Creoles. The structure, which is near Grand Prairie, has been estimated to be almost two hundred years old.

of the room and around it some straight chairs. Against the walls were a few benches and large chests which held the family's clothing and other belongings and which also served as seats. The mantel held some of the family's prized ornaments and trinkets.

On the wall hung a picture of the Virgin Mary, perhaps the parents' marriage certificate, and the father's musket, powder horn, and bullet pouch.

The bedroom was sometimes partitioned off into several smaller rooms. The beds were frequently six or more feet square, held straw mattresses or feather ticks, and were covered with buffalo hides, bearskins, or heavy woolen blankets. The beds were sometimes curtained with hangings of red or green serge or other heavy materials. If the family did not have enough beds, the children slept on cots or on the floor on pallets.

Food was eaten from earthenware or pewter dishes; glassware was expensive and so was not widely used. Forks were usually of steel or iron, while spoons were made of pewter. Knives were not generally used by the mother or children, the father cutting the meat with his hunting knife. When the fire in the fireplace was low or the weather was warm, the family used crude iron lamps or candles made from the wax of the candleberry myrtle.

Travel. Most people traveled from place to place in some kind of boat, for all of the Louisiana settlements could be reached by waterways. During the period before 1732 there were few roads in the colony, but in that year Governor Périer ordered every man who owned land along the Mississippi to build a road in front of his property, and this law was soon applied to most of the streams and bayous in the colony. After this time more people began to travel in two-wheeled carts, wagons, and even some carriages, but the roads were still in such bad condition that most land travelers rode horseback. In New Orleans there were chaises drawn by two horses, and coaches to which four horses were hitched.

But throughout the French period, boats were the commonest method of travel, and most families had a pirogue or two as well as a small, flat-bottomed boat or skiff called a *chalan*. Even water travel was difficult, however, for the streams and bayous carried floating trees, had sandbars, and few good campsites. The travelers often suffered from excessive heat or cold, heavy rains and storms, from the scarcity of drinking water and food, and from flies, gnats, and mosquitoes.

Clothing. Imported clothing was expensive, so most of the family's wearing apparel was made at home from imported wool, cotton, or other material, for spinning wheels and looms were uncommon in French Louisiana. The men and boys wore knee-length pants and loose-fitting shirts. In summer they went barefoot, but when the weather was cold they wore long stockings and soft-soled shoes somewhat resembling Indian moccasins. Some of them owned a knee-length coat, with a sash and a hood, called a *capot*. Over their heads they tied a large handkerchief or wore a tasseled cap.

The women and girls wore ankle-length skirts and short-sleeved blouses. In winter they added shoes and stockings, a bodice over the blouse, and perhaps a heavy *capot*. When they went to church or to a party they put on their bright-colored costumes— "bodices of red and blue stuffs, waists of flowered muslin, skirts of scarlet drugget [a coarse cloth] and printed calico, and starched white caps." The smaller children were dressed just like their older brothers and sisters and fathers and mothers.

The families of army officers, government officials, and wealthy planters and businessmen imported their clothing from France or bought the cloth and had it made up by tailors or dressmakers in the colony. When one Commandant died in 1737, the Governor wrote of him as a "poor man." His clothing, however, included eighty-five "new, trimmed men's shirts," thirty muslin shirts, twenty-five ordinary

61

French Louisiana lady and gentleman

shirts, twelve pairs of silk and cotton stockings, numerous pairs of pants and dress coats, and one "great coat" trimmed with "gold lace and buttons."

Food. After general farming began, most people had plenty to eat, but there were many times during the early years when the citizens of Mobile, Biloxi, and New Orleans went hungry, for they depended upon France for much of their food supply.

Bread was baked out of doors in large, rounded clay ovens. Butter was usually made by whipping the cream with a spoon, for there were very few churns in French Louisiana. Wild

honey instead of sugar was generally used for sweetening. Meats were boiled, roasted over open fires or in the ovens, or fried in hog lard or bear fat. Meats also were salted, smoked, dried, or partially cooked and put into large jars and covered with hot fat.

During periods when food was scarce, the most common diet was *gru* and wild meats, or *sagamite*. *Gru* was simply boiled corn meal seasoned with a little fat, while *sagamite* was corn meal, fat, and meat all cooked together. For many of the common people the usual diet was rice, corn, and beans.

The larger villages and towns had open-air markets, where during good seasons all kinds of vegetables, fruits, meats, and fish were sold. The Germans who had settled above New Orleans took their produce there on Sundays and sold it near the St. Louis square. At various times food prices were fixed by the government.

Religion. The Roman Catholic religion was the universal religion in French Louisiana. It is believed that the first church was built in 1699 by Father Paul Du Ru near the junction of Bayou Goula and the Mississippi. All of the towns and a few of the villages had churches, and there were a few priests who traveled about or acted as missionaries to the Indians.

More than twenty-five Holy Days besides Sundays were celebrated each year. On some of these days the Blessed Sacrament (consecrated bread, consecrated Host, placed in a sacred vessel called a "monstrance") was carried along the streets and everyone knelt as It passed. Sometimes the Blessed Sacrament was carried to the levee to aid in turning back a flooding river or to a burning building to assist in putting out the blaze.

The church bell was rung on every occasion. It announced each church service and was rung at births and marriages and tolled at funerals. When the bells rang for the Angelus early in the morning, at noontime, and in the evening, the people would pause at their work, bow their heads, and recite a prayer called "the Angelus."

Christmas was celebrated with much revelry. The midnight Mass on Christmas Eve started the holiday, after which the people went to different homes for Christmas breakfasts. On Christmas morning followed another Mass and afterwards dinners and parties in the evening. On New Year's Eve many people dressed in costume, put on masks, and, led by a man playing a violin, paraded through the village. *Le Père Noel* (Santa Claus) visited the children on the Twelfth Night and left gifts, and the next morning everyone had a holiday breakfast and then went visiting his friends and neighbors.

The Catholics of Louisiana were under the jurisdiction of the Bishop of Quebec, who until 1722 permitted the Jesuit, Carmelite, and Capuchin orders to operate churches and missions wherever they chose throughout the entire Mississippi Valley. In that year, however, he assigned the Jesuits the area north of the Ohio River and east of the Mississippi, the Carmelites the country east of the Mississippi between the Ohio and the Isle of Orleans, and the Capuchins the Isle of Orleans and all the territory west of the Mississippi.

This arrangement worked well until the 1750's, when a quarrel broke out between the Capuchins and the Jesuits, who had been permitted to establish a plantation and build a small chapel near New Orleans. The Jesuits were banished from the colony in 1763. Their plantation and 140 slaves were sold at auction, their chapel ornaments and sacred vessels appropriated by the Capuchins, and their chapel "razed to the ground." Father Dagobert, a Capuchin, was appointed Vicar-General soon afterwards.

Until about 1730 the members of the various orders were active in their missionary work among the Indians, but after this time they lost their enthusiasm for this difficult task. At the end of the French period there were many rural areas, small settlements, and villages which were without the services of a resident priest.

Education. It is believed that Father Raphael de Luxemburg, a Capuchin priest, opened the first school in Louisiana in New Orleans in 1725. It was for boys only. About a year later the Ursuline nuns agreed to come to Louisiana to educate the girls, and early in 1727 eleven of them sailed from France, reaching New Orleans after a long and tiresome voyage. Bienville's house was given to them and here they established their school, remaining there until 1734, when their new home was completed. There were few private schools and no public schools in Louisiana during the French period.

Medicine and Health. Yellow fever, malaria, smallpox, mumps, tuberculosis, and disorders of the stomach or intestines were the most common diseases in French colonial Louisiana. On several occasions yellow fever and smallpox epidemics broke out and carried off hundreds of settlers.

There were few doctors or hospitals in the colony throughout the French period. The Ursuline nuns established a hospital in 1734, and two years later Jean Louis, a sailor, willed a small sum of money to be used to found another hospital, which is today the Charity Hospital of Louisiana. But these facilities were all small and poorly equipped. Drugs were scarce and expensive and most of them were brought from France or the West Indies. Quinine, rhubarb, spirits of wine, ammonia, and sarsaparilla were the most common drugs used. The people made home remedies of various kinds and used many different types of charms.

When someone died the funeral was held at the church, where a Mass was said for his soul. His casket was then carried on the shoulders of several men along the streets to the cemetery. Once the men started from the church they never stopped until they reached the grave, for it was believed that death would visit any house in front of which they halted.

Amusements. The typical French settler was a gay, spirited person, carefree, kind, and good-humored. He did not read much even if he was able, for he had little desire for learning. He danced on Sunday after Mass, played card games and billiards, gossiped, hunted, fished, and sang. He organized a *fais-do-do* (country dance) or a party or dinner at the slightest opportunity.

The wealthier classes were much more formal in their amusements. They gave balls, masquerades, and banquets. When Governor Kerlerec arrived in New Orleans to succeed Governor Vaudreuil, he gave an elaborate banquet to which two hundred guests were invited. After dinner there was a display of fireworks, during which two fountains flowed with wine. The dancing then began, and lasted the rest of the night.

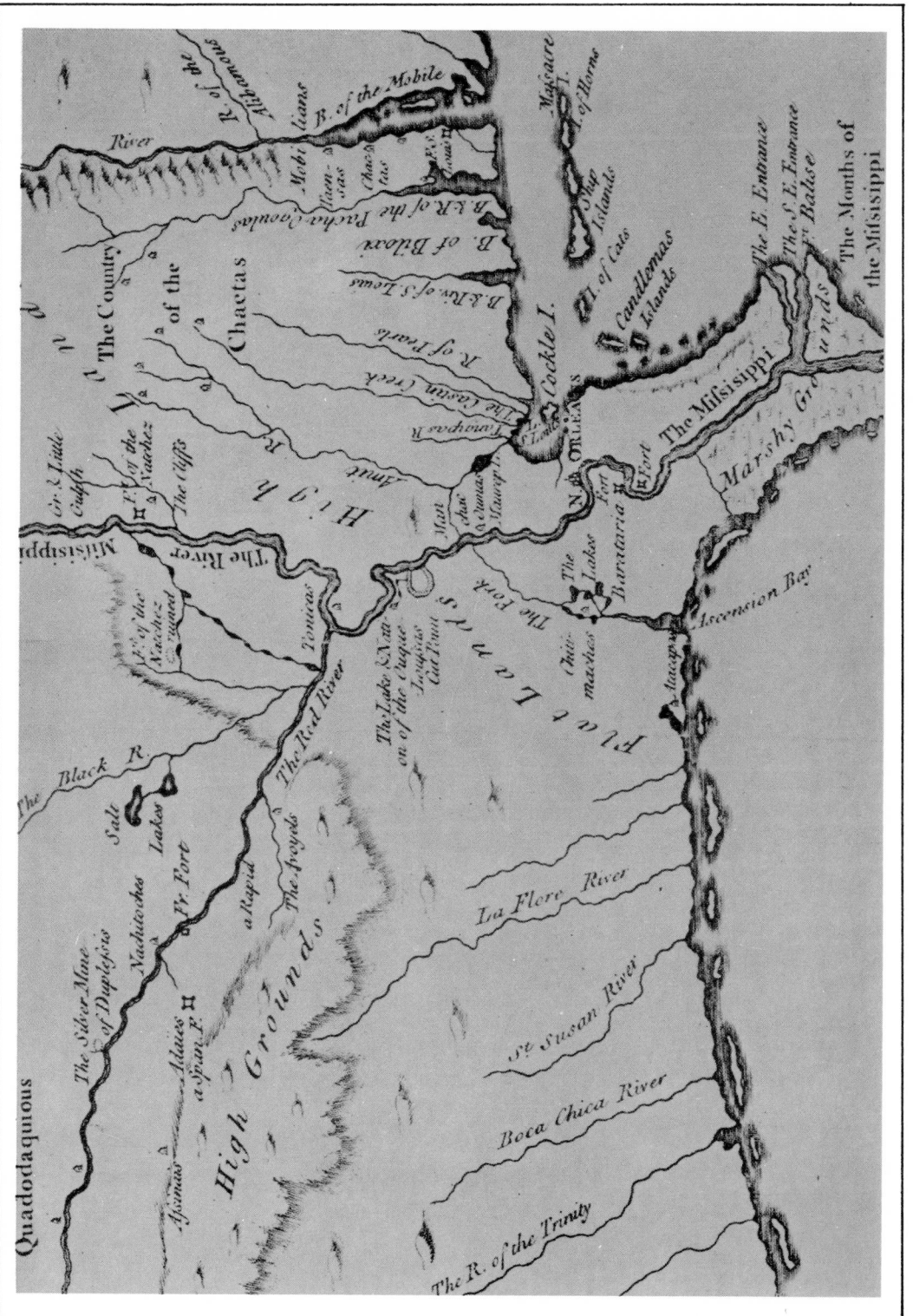

Louisiana at the end of the French period

Acadians on a Louisiana bayou.

PART THREE
Spanish Louisiana, 1762–1803

8. ESTABLISHMENT OF THE SPANISH REGIME IN LOUISIANA

The Spanish did not take Immediate Possession of Louisiana. French Governor Kerlerec continued to act as Governor of Louisiana after the colony had been given to Spain in the fall of 1762. Spanish Governor Don Antonio de Ulloa did not arrive until March, 1766. Meanwhile, the British acquired Spanish East and West Florida and all of French Louisiana east of the Mississippi River and north of the Isle of Orleans.

After Louisiana had been given to Spain, Kerlerec continued to act as Governor. These were troubled days in Louisiana. General economic conditions were bad. Trade and commerce had declined, and the paper money which had flooded the colony had decreased in value until it was practically worthless. The farmers and planters could not sell their products. The Capuchin and Jesuit priests quarreled. The Commissary-Commissioner accused Governor Kerlerec of stealing money from the treasury and of being a dictator, and Kerlerec accused the Commissioner of theft and of neglecting his duties.

Finally, in 1763, Kerlerec was recalled to France and thrown into prison, and a new French Governor, Jean Jacques d'Abbadie, was sent to Louisiana. The new Governor, describing his colony in a report, said that Louisiana had been in a state of disorder since about 1737 and that its financial condition was bad. The people were lazy and insubordinate, they drank too much, and about three-fourths of them were bankrupt. However, D'Abbadie wrote back to France that "everything will again be set to rights," and he immediately went to work. Although he had an army of only about three hundred men, he strengthened the defenses of the colony. He permitted British ships to go up the Mississippi to the British ports of Manchac (which was at the mouth of Bayou Manchac), Baton Rouge, St. Francisville, and Natchez. Soon conditions grew better as the ships brought trading goods and the French were permitted to do business with them.

In September, 1764, D'Abbadie received word that Louisiana had been given to Spain and that a Spanish Governor would soon arrive to take possession of the colony. He was ordered to return to France with his records and those soldiers who did not wish to remain in Louisiana, and to inform the people that they now lived under Spanish rule. The colonists received

the news with dismay, for Louisiana had been a French colony for over sixty years and they considered themselves just as much Frenchmen as if they had lived in Paris. They had lived under pioneer conditions which allowed a considerable amount of personal freedom and they had heard that Spain governed her colonies with a tight rein.

Jean Milhet Sent to France. A group of colonists living in New Orleans and its vicinity held a mass meeting and decided to send a messenger to France to appeal to the King to take Louisiana back again. Jean Milhet, the wealthiest merchant of the colony, was appointed to carry the message, and he immediately set out for France. About this time Governor D'Abbadie died, and Philippe Aubry, the senior captain of the army, became Acting Governor. Milhet proceeded to Paris and went to see Bienville. The former Governor had not been in Louisiana since the end of his term in 1743, but he still loved the colony, and he and Milhet tried to see the King. But Louis XV would not receive them. Finally they were granted an interview with the Duke de Choiseul, the prime minister. Bienville made an impassioned appeal, but the Duke would not alter his resolution concerning the colony, and after remaining in France for some time, Milhet returned sadly to Louisiana.

At first the people would not believe him when he told them that France

Don Antonio de Ulloa

would do nothing for them. Then they became angry. The streets hummed and throbbed with the sounds of marching and shouting citizens . . . they had been loyal subjects of France . . . the King did not know what he was doing . . . his advisers had kept him in ignorance of conditions in Louisiana.

Governor Ulloa. In July, 1765, a letter arrived from Havana. Don Antonio de Ulloa wrote that he had orders to come to Louisiana and take possession of the colony for Spain. But the months passed and he did not appear. A small group of men began to make plans for a rebellion against Spanish authority.

Governor Ulloa finally arrived in March, 1766, nearly three and a half years after Louisiana had been given to Spain. He was a small, thin man with an excitable, nervous temperament. He was certainly not impressive in appearance, although everyone knew that he was one of the greatest scientists of Europe. He had founded

69

an astronomical observatory and established a laboratory for the study of minerals, but he was a scholar rather than a practical-minded man.

Ulloa brought with him only two companies of soldiers, totaling about ninety men. Did these few soldiers represent the great power of Spain? The rebels became more confident.

Ulloa made many mistakes during the two and one-half years of his governorship. He showed little respect for the Superior Council and insulted the French soldiers, so that they refused to enlist in the Spanish service when their term of enlistment expired. He would not attend the social functions which the people of the colony planned for him. When his bride-to-be, the young and beautiful Marquesa d'Abrado, arrived from Peru he went down to the Balize to meet her and had their wedding ceremony performed there by his private chaplain. This made the colonists furious, and when he and his bride returned to New Orleans the wives of the leading citizens refused to call on their Governor's new wife. Having been cut by society, she kept to her home and even attended Mass in a private chapel. Meanwhile, the leaders continued to plot their rebellion.

Ulloa tried to be a good Governor, although he did not publicly assume the authority of one. Aubry still performed many of the duties of Governor, but he carried out Ulloa's orders in the name of the King of Spain. Meanwhile, Ulloa did what he could to help economic conditions. He made

tours of inspection, tried to improve the paper-money problem by paying more for it than had been paid by the French, and prevented overcharging by the merchants. He helped immigrants by giving them land, livestock, tools, and supplies. In general, he tried to carry out his instructions "not to change existing conditions in Louisiana," but to improve its economic life.

Then, in the spring of 1768, instructions came from Spain ordering the people of Louisiana to use only Spanish ships in their commerce and restricting their trade to only Spanish ports. Those who had been plotting against Spain believed that the time for an uprising had come.

Governor Ulloa Leaves Louisiana. In October, 1768, the plotters called a convention to meet in New Orleans. This convention passed resolutions condemning Ulloa, declared him a usurper of power, and ordered him to leave the colony. The Superior Council supported the actions of the convention, though Aubry protested to its members. Aubry did not know what to do. Some months before, he had written back to France: "My position is most extraordinary. I command for the King of France and at the same time I govern the colony as if it belonged to the King of Spain."

A few days after Aubry's protest, the Superior Council declared his protest null and void and ordered Governor Ulloa to leave the colony within three days. Fearing for his life, Ulloa went aboard a ship lying at the wharf.

For years the loyal Frenchmen of Louisiana told this story of Ulloa's departure from New Orleans. On the night of November 1, 1768, a group of citizens who were returning home from a wedding went to the wharf. They sang French songs. They yelled: "Long live the King! Long live Louis-the-Well-Beloved! Long live the wine of Bordeaux! Down with the fish of Spain!" Then a man cut the mooring cables of Ulloa's ship and it drifted down the Mississippi. For a long time the historians believed this story, but it is now thought to be only a legend.

Aubry in Control. The rebel leaders and their friends rejoiced when Ulloa departed. They had succeeded! They shouted: *"Vive le Roi! Vive Louis! Vive la Louisiane! À bas Ulloa! À bas les Espagnols!"* (Long live the King! Long live Louis! Long live Louisiana! Down with Ulloa! Down with the Spanish!). The King had not heard Milhet, but now he would listen to the Louisianians. A member of the Superior Council was sent to France. He carried with him a copy of the decree expelling Governor Ulloa and a memorial of the "Inhabitants and Merchants of Louisiana" swearing loyalty and allegiance to France.

Aubry was now in a trying position. Should he support the revolutionists, whose rebellion against Spain had apparently been successful, or should he support Spain? After all, Spain might send another Governor with sufficient forces to put down the rebellion and

establish Spanish power. Aubry tried to carry water on each shoulder. He sent a report to France blaming Ulloa for what had happened, but he also stated that "it is no pleasant mission to govern a colony which undergoes so many revolutions."

A short time later he wrote to the Spanish Captain General at Havana that he hoped Ulloa had reported the services which he had performed for Spain: "No one venerates the Spanish nation as I do. . . . This revolution dishonors the French in Louisiana. . . . The leaders should be punished as they deserved to be."

Governor Ulloa had gone. Aubry was still at the head of the Louisiana colony. Had the Louisiana rebellion succeeded? What would Spain now do?

Governor O'Reilly. On August 17, 1769, a large Spanish fleet, carrying more than two thousand troops, arrived at New Orleans. The expedition was commanded by Lieutenant General Alejandro O'Reilly, who had been appointed the new Governor of Louisiana. O'Reilly was a man far different from Ulloa. A native-born Irishman who had settled in Spain, he was a professional soldier, and at this time was Spain's best military commander. Suave, courteous, and mild of manner, he was nevertheless a man of iron. He had orders to put down this Louisiana rebellion and he was prepared to carry them out.

At five o'clock the following afternoon a signal gun was fired and with military precision the Spanish troops

General Alejandro O'Reilly

landed. The batteries of artillery and companies of infantry moved to the Place d'Armes and ranged themselves about the square in front of the church. The sailors and the troops shouted, *"Viva el Rey! Viva el Rey!"* (Long live the King! Long live the King!). The guns of the ships roared out a salute, which was answered by the fifty cannon of the batteries. Clad in bright uniforms, O'Reilly and his staff came ashore and with great pomp marched to the square, where Aubry awaited them at the flagpole from which fluttered the flag of France. The French flag came down and up went the flag of Spain, to the roar of *"Viva el Rey!"* and the booming of another cannon salute. Then O'Reilly went into the church to receive the blessing of the Vicar-General.

The rebellion had failed. What chance had a few hundred Frenchmen

against the armed might of Spain? O'Reilly had taken the first step in establishing Spanish authority. He had "displayed most effectively the military force under his command, and through the pageantry of his dramatic entry had inspired the respect of the colonists."

Trial of the Conspirators. On August 21, O'Reilly arrested the leaders of the rebellion. They were informed that they would be tried without delay for having led the people of Louisiana in rebellion against Spanish authority. Later in the day O'Reilly issued a proclamation of amnesty, stating that the majority of those who had participated in the rebellion had been "seduced by the intrigues of some ambitious, fanatic, and evil-minded men, who had the temerity to make a criminal use of the ignorance and excessive credulity of their fellow-citizens. These men alone will answer for their crimes, and will be judged in accordance with the laws." Three days later the people of New Orleans and vicinity were ordered to take the oath of "fidelity and obedience to His Catholic Majesty."

When O'Reilly asked Aubry who had been the leaders of the rebellion, he named them, further stating that they had plotted "to send away the governor, and to free themselves from the Spanish domination." The Spanish law read: "He who labors by deed or word to induce any people, or any provinces, under the domination of the King, to rise against his Majesty,

DE PAR LE ROI,

DON *ALEXANDRE Ô REILLY*

Commandeur de Benfayan dans l'Ordre de Alcantara, Lieutenant-Général & Inſpecteur-Général des Armées de Sa Majeſté Catholique, Capitaine·Général & Gouverneur de la Province de la Louiſianne.

EN vertu des Ordres & Pouvoirs, dont Nous ſommes muni de Sa Majeſté Catholique, déclarons à tous les Habitans de la Province de la Loüiſianne, que quelque juſte ſujet que les Événemens paſſés ayent donnés à Sa Majeſté de leurs faire ſentir ſon indignation, Elle ne veut écouter aujourd'hui que ſa Clémence envers le Public; perſuadée qu'il n'a péché, que pour s'être laiſſé ſéduire par les intrigues de Gens Ambitieux, Fanatiques & mal intentionnés, qui ont témérairement abuſé de ſon ignorance & trop de crédulité; ceux-ci ſeuls répondront de leurs crimes & ſeront jugés ſelon les Loix.

Un Acte auſſi généreux doit aſſurer Sa Majeſté, que ſes nouveaux Sujets s'éforceront chaque jour de leur vie de mériter par leur fidélité, zéle, & obéiſſance la Grace qu'elle leur fait, & la Protection qu'elle leur accorde dès ce moment.

A la Nouvelle Orléans, le vingt-un Aouſt mil ſept cens ſoixante-neuf.

Alexandre ô Reilly

O'Reilly's proclamation of amnesty for the innocent citizens of Louisiana.

is a traitor." The punishment for a traitor was death. There was no question but that the leaders had tried to free Louisiana from the rule of Spain.

The trial was conducted in strict conformity with Spanish laws and lasted about three weeks. The verdict of the court sentenced six of the most important leaders to be put to death by hanging. Several of the others were given prison sentences. The property of all of the men was confiscated.

On the morning of October 25, 1769, the town criers of New Orleans went through the city reading aloud the death sentence, and at about three in the afternoon, five of the men were executed by a firing squad (a hangman could not be found). One of the men had died in prison before the execution day.

A short time later Aubry slipped aboard a ship and sailed for France. It was said by some that he carried a fortune with him, but near the coast of France the vessel ran into a heavy storm and sank, and Aubry was not among the few survivors. No one in Louisiana mourned his death.

O'Reilly's Reorganization of the Colony. O'Reilly had turned his attention to the political and economic reorganization of the colony even before the trial of the conspirators was held. He fixed food prices in order that the merchants could not make excessive profits. He reorganized the government of the colony, wherever possible permitting the French officials to continue to hold their offices. He assisted in reviving trade and commerce. He appointed Frenchmen as Lieutenant Governors of the Natchitoches and Illinois districts. He ordered the abolition of Indian slavery, visited the Indian tribes and signed treaties with them, and licensed only those Indian traders who had good reputations.

In December he sent most of his army back to Havana and organized thirteen militia companies under the command of native Louisianians. He recommended that the Church send more priests to the colony. He aided the farmers by establishing land titles and creating a system of "homesteading" land. In all these reforms, he insisted that the old customs of French Louisiana be kept as much as possible.

By the spring of 1770, O'Reilly had completed the reorganization of the Louisiana colony. In March he departed for Havana, leaving Colonel Luis de Unzaga y Amézaga in charge as Governor.

O'Reilly's Place in Louisiana History. What is O'Reilly's true place in Louisiana history? Most Louisiana historians have condemned him for his punishment of the leaders of the Rebellion of 1768, and some of them have called him "Bloody O'Reilly." The French Creoles never forgave him. But it must be remembered that O'Reilly was a soldier, accustomed to the discipline of a soldier. He had been ordered by his King to punish, "in strict conformity to the laws," the leaders of the rebellion. He carried out his orders, and in so doing only five men were executed, which at this time in history was a mild punishment for a colony which had rebelled against authority.

It must also be remembered that just as Iberville was the founder of French Louisiana, so O'Reilly was the founder of the Spanish regime. His

Map 11—North America in 1763

governmental and economic reforms paved the way for the steady growth and progress of the Louisiana colony, which prospered much more under the Spanish than it had under the French. The Spanish, not the French, were the real makers of colonial Louisiana.

Unzaga as Governor. Unzaga had come to Louisiana with O'Reilly. While O'Reilly was the Governor, Unzaga's commission to succeed to the governorship had already been issued. O'Reilly was to turn the colony over to him just as soon as the rebellion had been put down and order restored. This was done on December 1, 1769, several months before O'Reilly left the colony. After this date O'Reilly acted only as a military commander, though everyone knew that Unzaga was under his orders.

Colonel Unzaga had served more than thirty years in the Spanish army and had fought in Spain, Italy, and Africa. He had lived in Spain's American colonies for twenty-five years and knew well the problems of colonial administration. Older than O'Reilly, with a mild, easygoing nature, he liked the French Creoles and felt that he would have little difficulty in reconciling them to the rule of Spain.

Unzaga continued O'Reilly's policy of appointing Creoles to governmental positions. He explained the code of laws which O'Reilly had drawn up for the colony. Everyone began to realize that Spain wanted Louisiana to be a strong, contented, and prosperous colony, and that there was no desire to oppress the citizens.

It was not long before the Creoles in governmental service were promoted to more responsible positions. As the French and Spanish mixed more socially, the French discovered that the Spanish officials were usually men of merit, good birth, and high moral character. Marriages were arranged between young Spanish officers and the daughters of prominent Creole families. Governor Unzaga himself married a daughter of the St. Maxent family. The Creoles became contented with the new government, even though they would give up neither their language nor their social customs.

Unzaga did his best to promote the welfare of Louisiana. He winked at the illegal trade which was being carried on with the British of West Florida, for the colony needed the British goods. He used government money to purchase the colonists' tobacco, and soon tobacco plantations were springing up throughout Louisiana. He granted land to immigrants, asking only that they obey the laws of the colony, and he organized the first public school in Louisiana. If Unzaga made mistakes, many of the people said, he made them only on the side of kindness.

However, the Governor had many problems to solve. When the Spanish Capuchins arrived and tried to secure the dismissal of the French priest Father Dagobert, he sided with the French. He strengthened the militia when it was rumored that the British were planning to attack Louisiana, and the companies drilled enthusiastically for the defense of their homes and farms. He made treaties with the Indian tribes and licensed traders at the various trading posts, and when the American Revolution began he quietly aided the American colonists by sending them the supplies he could spare.

But by 1776, Unzaga was ready to retire. He was not a young man any more and he wanted to return to his native Malaga in Spain. His requests for retirement were refused, however, and instead he was promoted to be the Captain General at Caracas, Venezuela. He turned the government of Louisiana over to the young colonel of the Louisiana Regiment, Don Bernardo de Gálvez, in January, 1777. The following March he sailed for Caracas.

Unzaga had reconciled the French Creoles of Louisiana to the rule of Spain. A just administrator, he had constantly promoted the public welfare, thereby winning the respect and affection of the people.

9. LOUISIANA AND THE AMERICAN REVOLUTION

Bernardo de Gálvez. Although only in his late twenties, the young colonel who succeeded Unzaga had already proved himself a brave and excellent soldier. Born of a politically important Spanish family, he had entered the army in his teens and won a lieutenant's bars in a war with Portugal. He had served with distinction in Mexico, campaigning along the Rio Grande against the Apache Indians. He carried the scars of several battle wounds. In one fight he had been "struck in the arm by an arrow and with two lance thrusts in the chest." He had returned to Spain, later serving in North Africa, where he had received another severe wound. He was then sent to Louisiana.

Gálvez as Governor. As was customary, Gálvez received an elaborate set of orders. He was to take a census of Louisiana and prepare a statement of the yearly expenses of the colony. He must welcome foreigners on the condition that they become Catholics and take the oath of allegiance to Spain.

He was to encourage agriculture and take especial care to see that slaves were humanely treated. He was to promote commerce but to take strong measures against smuggling. The friendship of the Indians was to be cultivated. He was specifically ordered to watch the British in West Florida and to reorganize and improve the discipline of the Louisiana militia. And he was to make carefully prepared reports on practically everything—roads, money, the people, mines, the religious situation, and many other things.

Gálvez plunged into his work. He reduced the export duty to 2 per cent and permitted trade to be carried on with the British. He called a meeting of farmers and planters to discuss agricultural matters, and as farm labor was short, he permitted slaves again to be imported. His census revealed that out of a total population of nearly eighteen thousand almost half were slaves.

Perhaps his greatest interest was the encouragement of new immigrants to the colony. Gálvez gave to each settler five arpents of land fronting a stream and extending as far back from it as the man would clear his land. He also gave to each family an ax, a sickle, a spade, a hoe, two hens and a rooster, two pigs, and enough food for the first year. It was not long before word of Gálvez' generosity spread beyond Louisiana.

Soon hundreds of Spaniards began arriving, as did *Isleños,* settlers from the Canary Islands. A few Germans from Maryland had come to Louisiana as early as 1774, and now, with Gálvez' encouragement, many more settled along the Mississippi. British and American refugees from the American Revolution also arrived, and some of these settlers founded, a few miles from the mouth of Bayou Manchac, a town to which they gave the name Villa de Gálvez (Galveztown). They asked the Governor not to change the name for it was an indication of their gratitude to him. Francisco Collell, the Commandant of the settlement, wrote Gálvez that "they asked me to give each one of them a Spanish name." So Davis became Deves, Riley became Reeli, Morris became Moris, and so on.

Despite their many duties, Gálvez and his officers and officials had time for social life, and more Spaniards fell to the charms of the French Creole girls. Don Estevan Miro, an army officer and future Governor of Louisiana, begged Gálvez to secure the King's permission for him to marry Marie Celeste Elenore de Macarty. The King approved the match. Jacinto Panis, another officer, won Margarethe Wiltz, the widow of Joseph Milhet, who had been executed by O'Reilly. Gálvez himself fell in love, and petitioned His Majesty for permission to marry Félicie de St. Maxent d'Estréhan, a young and beautiful widow. Their marriage was a happy one and the Governor's wife greatly aided her husband not only in Louisiana but in Mexico, where he later became Viceroy.

Gálvez and the American Revolution. The American Revolution began in 1775, but the British of East and West Florida did not join their kinsmen along the Atlantic seaboard, and Louisiana became a center of war activities for both sides. Although Spain was neutral, Gálvez aided the Americans. He helped their commerce and permitted them to go up and down the Mississippi. He sold much-needed supplies to an American agent named Oliver Pollock, and loaned money to the young republic. Spanish guns, powder, and other supplies aided George Rogers Clark in his conquest of the Northwest.

In early 1778 an American named James Willing led a raiding expedition down the Mississippi against the British of West Florida. He either destroyed or captured much of their property between Natchez and Bayou Manchac. While sympathetic to the Americans, Gálvez extended every courtesy to the refugees who were driven from their homes and who sought safety in Louisiana. He offered them land, which many of them accepted. After Willing's raid the British strengthened their forces at Mobile and Pensacola and later reoccupied their towns along the Mississippi.

Gálvez became uneasy for the security of Louisiana. He began to strengthen his military forces, to build gunboats for patrol work on the Mississippi, and to repair the Louisiana fortifications. Then Colonel Alexander Dickson left Pensacola with an army to strengthen the British forts along the Mississippi, and soon Fort Panmure (Natchez), Fort New Richmond (Baton Rouge), Fort Bute (at the mouth of Bayou Manchac), and other military posts were humming with activity.

In May, 1779, Spain declared war against Great Britain. The British immediately planned an attack on New Orleans. A large force was to descend the Mississippi from the Great Lakes region, while another expedition would sail from Pensacola. But Bernardo de Gálvez had not been idle. Louisiana was ready. He would strike a blow before the enemy could put their plans into operation.

Gálvez Plans an Expedition Against Baton Rouge. Gálvez had already planned his campaign against the British in case there was war between the two countries. He kept secret the news of the declaration of war and also his official appointment as Governor of Louisiana. Advertising his work as

Don Bernardo de Gálvez

preparing for the "defense" of New Orleans, he began to gather a fleet of river boats, gunboats, supplies, and munitions, and to equip and drill the white and free Negro militia.

Gálvez set August 23 as the date for the start of a journey up the Mississippi to capture Baton Rouge. On August 18, however, a violent hurricane sank almost all of his boats. This setback would have disheartened most men, but Gálvez feverishly renewed his activities, setting August 27 as the new date of departure. A few days before this date he called a meeting of the people of New Orleans at the Plaza de Armas (the old French Place d'Armes), to tell them that Spain was now at war with Great Britain. He promised to defend the province of Louisiana, but refused to accept the governorship unless the people agreed to help him: "What do you say? Shall I take the oath of Governor? Shall I swear to defend Louisiana?"

Their cheers drowned his words. He took the oath and continued his preparations.

The Capture of Baton Rouge. By August 27 all was ready, and late in the afternoon the little army moved out from New Orleans. It was a small force of only 650 men of many nationalities. There was no engineering officer and the artillery officer was ill. The men were without tents and other much-needed supplies. The roads were in bad condition.

Gálvez hurried on ahead of his little army, calling upon the local militia units to rally to the defense of Louisiana. Soon they began to join him—from the German Coast, from Galveztown, from Opelousas and the Atakapas country, from Pointe Coupee. More than 700 men answered the call, increasing his army to over 1,400 men, but by the time he arrived at Fort Bute the number had dropped to less than 1,000 because of illness and the hardships of the march from New Orleans.

Gálvez knew that most of the Fort Bute garrison had been withdrawn to Baton Rouge, so he immediately assaulted and captured the fort. He rested his men at Fort Bute a few days, then moved on to Fort New Richmond. The fort at Baton Rouge had only recently been built. It consisted of an earthen wall, encircled by a palisade, on the outside of which was a ditch about nine feet deep and eighteen or twenty feet wide. It was garrisoned by about 400 regular soldiers and more than 150 settlers and Negroes, and was armed with thirteen cannon.

Gálvez tricked the British into believing he was placing his batteries in a grove of trees, at which they then fired all night. Under cover of darkness he moved his guns to the other side of the fort, and on the morning of September 21 opened fire. By mid-afternoon Fort New Richmond at Baton Rouge had been surrendered to the British—and with it, Fort Panmure at Natchez.

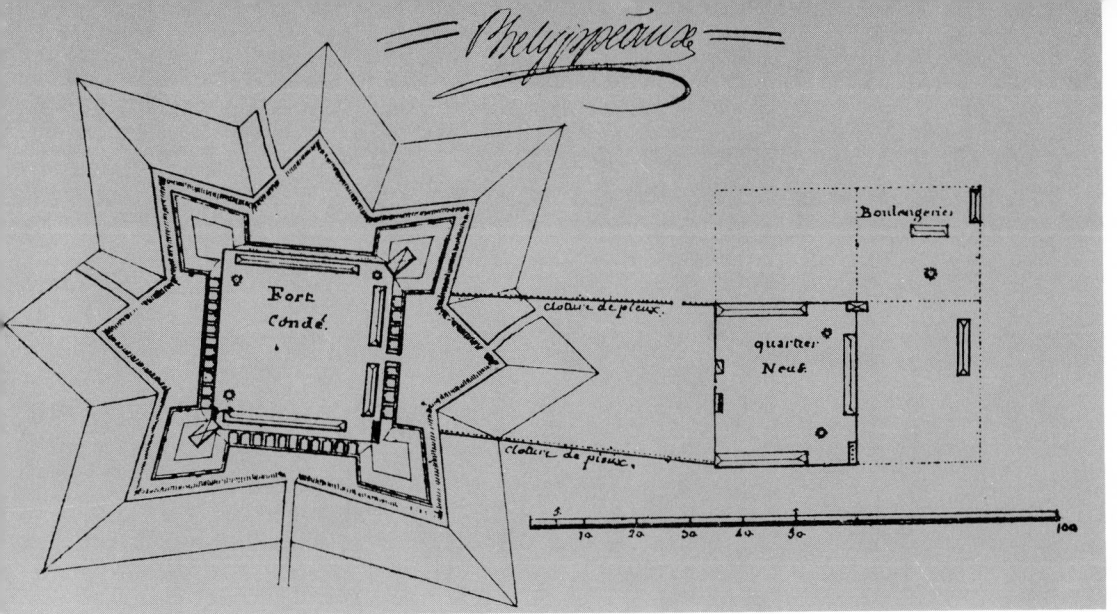

Plan of Fort Charlotte (Conde), Mobile, 1763

This campaign was one of the most significant in American history, for it prevented the British from gaining a secure foothold in the Lower Mississippi Valley. It paved the way for later American occupation. It established Gálvez' genius as a military commander.

Gálvez Captures Mobile. In 1778, Gálvez had sent Jacinto Panis to Mobile and Pensacola to spy on the British, and he had sent back much useful information. After the capture of Baton Rouge, Gálvez began to plan an expedition against these two British strongholds.

Gálvez pushed forward his preparations for an attack on Mobile, and in January, 1780, he embarked 750 regular soldiers and militiamen on a dozen ships and dropped down the Mississippi toward the Balize. Includ-

ing the sailors, he had slightly under two thousand men. After waiting about two weeks in order to get all his ships over the bar, he headed for Mobile Bay, where a few days later the expedition arrived. After many difficulties in landing his batteries of artillery, Gálvez began the siege. They soon had the heavy battery of eight 18-pounder guns in position and began to bombard Fort Charlotte.

The formal surrender took place on March 14. Captain Elias Durnford, the fort's commander, wrote the same day to his superior officer at Pensacola: "It is my misfortune to inform you that this morning my small but brave garrison marched down the beach, and surrendered themselves prisoners of war to General Bernardo de Gálvez' superior arms."

The following days were occupied in repairing the damage to Fort Char-

81

Encounter between a British and a Spanish ship.

lotte. The buildings were restored, the earthworks strengthened, and additional cannon were set in place. The citizens of the region came to Mobile to take the oath of allegiance to the King of Spain. Gálvez had won another significant victory over the British, and had shown courteous regard for the civilians of Mobile. He was

82

promoted to Major General and publicly thanked by the King. The King's Minister wrote him that "the capture of an important town, well fortified and defended with vigor, is an act worthy of praise."

The Capture of Pensacola. Gálvez now turned his attention to the capture of Pensacola, which was the most important objective of his entire Gulf Coast campaign. Knowing that the Pensacola garrison had over two thousand men and that its defenses were strong, he asked that a sizable fleet and a strong army be sent from Havana to aid him. When he failed to get anything but promises, Gálvez went to Havana, and sailed from there in mid-October, 1780, with a large army, artillery, and ammunition, but a storm compelled him to return to port. He sailed again in late February, 1781, and arrived off Pensacola in early March. The larger ships grounded when the fleet attempted to cross the bar of the bay. Gálvez found a deeper channel, but Don José Calbo de Irazabal, the commander of the Spanish fleet, who was aboard the largest ship, the man-of-war *San Ramon,* refused to try it.

Finally Gálvez landed his troops on Santa Rosa Island, to camp there until the fleet could enter Pensacola Bay. A few days later he became impatient and, boarding the *Galveztown,* which was the flagship of the little Louisiana fleet, ordered the ships to follow him. The guns of Fort George began a tremendous fire, but the Louisiana ships went through. Don José, realizing that his reputation was ruined if he did not follow, put his fleet in motion, and it too safely passed the British fort.

Meantime a small force from Mobile had arrived, and a few days after this, Don Estevan Miro came from New Orleans with about 1,350 Louisiana regulars and militia. Gálvez' army now totaled over 3,500 men. He could proceed with the siege of Pensacola. Lines were tightened, batteries of cannon were wheeled into position, and the siege began. Finally General John Campbell sent a flag of truce and asked for surrender terms. The formal surrender of Pensacola and the entire British colony of West Florida took place on the afternoon of May 10, 1781.

The Spanish flag of Louisiana now waved from the upper sections of the Mississippi Valley to British East Florida and westward to the Sabine River. The King had been well pleased with the capture of Baton Rouge and Mobile, but he was particularly gratified with the capture of Pensacola. He issued a Royal Proclamation in which he thanked Gálvez for the "expulsion of the English from the entire Gulf of Mexico." He renamed Pensacola Bay. Henceforth it was to be called *La Bahía de Santa María de Gálvez,* the Bay of Saint Mary of Galvez. He promoted Gálvez to Lieutenant General and gave him the title of "Viscount of Galveztown." Most important of all, he authorized the hero to place on his coat of arms the motto *"Yo Solo"* ("I alone"), in recognition of his having led the Louisiana fleet into Pensacola Bay.

Gálvez and the Rebellion of 1781. The British colonists who lived near Natchez had surrendered at the capture of Baton Rouge and had taken

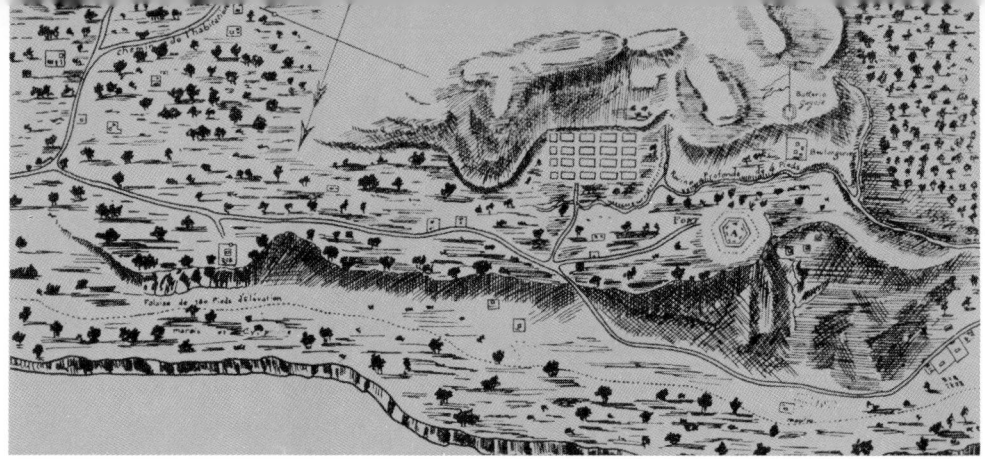

Spanish fort at Natchez

the oath of allegiance to Spain. Just before Pensacola fell it was rumored that Gálvez had been defeated, and without delay they laid siege to Fort Panmure, finally forcing it to surrender. Then they learned that the rumor had been false and that Gálvez had been victorious and had captured Pensacola. Gálvez would now certainly lead an army to Natchez and would punish them just as O'Reilly had punished those who led the Rebellion of 1768. Some of them decided to retain possession of the fort and fight, while the others decided to surrender.

Carlos de Grand Pré, the Commandant of the Natchez-Baton Rouge District, sent a militia captain of the Atakapas District, Roberto de la Morandière, from Baton Rouge to recapture Fort Panmure. He did so, and several of the rebel leaders were sent to New Orleans for trial. The others escaped to Savannah, Georgia. Gálvez was more lenient than O'Reilly had been. The property of twenty-one of the leaders was confiscated and they were imprisoned for about two years, and then released.

Gálvez Leaves Louisiana. After the capture of Pensacola, Gálvez was ordered by the King to lead an expedition against the British island of Jamaica. However, just as his fleet was about ready to sail from Havana, peace was declared between Great Britain and the United States, France and Spain.

Meanwhile the King had joined West Florida to Louisiana and appointed Gálvez Captain General of Cuba and Governor of West Florida and Louisiana. In the late spring of 1785 he was appointed Viceroy of New Spain, which included all of Spain's colonies north of Central America. He and his family arrived in the City of Mexico early in 1786 and were received with "the greatest pomp and jubilee," but he did not live long to enjoy his new honors, for he took a fever and died in the fall of 1786.

Louisianians have never forgotten Bernardo de Gálvez. The French Creoles forgot that he was a Spanish Don, for he worked hard for Louisiana and led its troops to brilliant military victories over the British.

10. GROWTH AND PROGRESS OF SPANISH LOUISIANA AFTER 1785

Spain's Plans for the Future. After the capture of the Floridas from Great Britain, Spain's plans centered around protecting and perhaps enlarging her Louisiana and Florida territories. The northern boundary of East and West Florida had not been definitely located, and Spain hoped to fix this boundary as far northward as possible. She also planned to develop Louisiana into a strong, self-sufficient colony.

From the end of Gálvez' governorship in 1785 until France took possession in 1803, Louisiana was ruled by five governors, each of whom attempted to carry out the plans of the mother country.

Governor Miro. Colonel Don Estevan Miro had been Acting Governor of Louisiana since Gálvez organized his expedition against Mobile in 1780. He became Governor shortly after Gálvez was appointed Viceroy of New Spain. Miro was not as brilliant as Gálvez, but he was an intelligent and mild-tempered man. He was well educated, was acquainted with several languages, and had a high code of honor. Already well known in Louisiana for his tireless industry and strict standards of morality, he was compared to Governor Unzaga by many Louisianians because of his quiet but progressive governorship.

As was usual with Spanish governors, he issued a *Bando de Buen Gobierno* (Proclamation of Good Government), a sort of inaugural proclamation that listed the improvements to be made in the colony, and set forth his civil and police regulations. The people approved, nodded their heads, and said that he would make a good Governor.

New Settlers for Louisiana. Miro's great ambition was to make Louisiana a stronger colony. To do this he had to promote immigration, keep the Indians at peace, and increase trade and commerce. He immediately offered assistance to prospective settlers, and in order that he might locate them properly when they arrived, he took a new census of the colony.

Miro found that the population of Louisiana had more than doubled in the preceding sixteen years. More people had settled in the colony during

An immigrant's cabin.

that period than during all the years of French control. New Orleans was a city of nearly 5,000. The population of the Tchoupitoulas District, which adjoined New Orleans, totaled over 7,000; the German Coast and the area above it, 4,500; and the Balize and Lower Coast, over 2,000. The Pointe Coupee and Natchez districts each had more than 1,500 inhabitants. More than 1,200 persons lived in the Natchitoches area and along the Red River, about the same number in the Opelousas District, and over 1,000 resided in the Atakapas country. Baton Rouge had nearly 300 citizens and the Ouachita country, a few over 200. The to-

tal population of the colony, excluding Arkansas, Missouri, and the Mobile area, was slightly over 29,000. Louisiana was growing up.

Immigrants arrived steadily from France, Spain, and the Canary Islands. Americans received grants of land in the Florida Parishes, in the Opelousas District, and in other sections. The only conditions imposed by the Louisiana government on immigrants were that they swear allegiance to Spain and openly practice only the Catholic religion.

New settlements were soon springing up all over Louisiana. One of these was the "Post of the Ouachita" (later Fort Miro and now Monroe), which was established by Don Juan Filhiol in 1785 and which soon became an important Indian trading post.

Miro's Peaceful Indian Policy. Miro pursued a peaceful policy toward the Indians. He frequently called the tribal chiefs to New Orleans, where he entertained them, gave them presents, and secured agreements for fur and hide trading. Problems arose, however. Sometimes one tribe would raid another, after which an appeal would be made to the Governor for help and for the replacement of lost goods. The tribes quarreled over their hunting grounds. Occasionally a chief would refuse to come to New Orleans. One chief wrote to Miro: "i am willing to come and see you and take you by the hand if you will appoint to meat me at Mobille for if i was to set of[f] to come to Orleans with ten men i should not Get back with five of them alive upon the account of the sickley cuntrey." The chief's spelling and grammar were poor, but his meaning was clear.

But the Indians kept the peace with Miro and caused the settlers little trouble.

Trade and Commerce During Miro's Administration. After the capture of Baton Rouge, Spain had approved Gálvez' recommendations for the promotion of trade and commerce. Louisianians were to be permitted to trade with France for a period of ten years.

Don Estevan Miro

They were also to be allowed to trade with the islands of the French West Indies. They might purchase slaves free of duty for ten years and duty-free ships for two years. All exports and imports were to be taxed only 6 per cent. Plans were to be made for the building of a customhouse at New Orleans.

These regulations went into effect shortly before Miro became Governor, and greatly aided him in the promotion of trade and commerce. It was not long before the Louisiana trading posts were making a good profit and New Orleans was a busy port city. All kinds of goods came down the Mississippi from the St. Louis region and the Ohio River country. Miro re-

St. Louis Cathedral, about 1794.

ported that as many as forty river boats at a time could be seen at the New Orleans landing.

Important Events During Miro's Administration. On Good Friday, March 21, 1788, a lighted candle in the private chapel of the treasurer of the colony, Vicente José Nuñez, fell against the lace draperies of the altar. In a few moments the house was in flames. Because of a very strong wind, the fire spread rapidly throughout New Orleans. Many of the French Creoles could not understand the directions for fighting the fire for they were given in Spanish. As a result, over eight hundred buildings were burned, including the town hall, the guardhouse, the church, the arsenal, the prison, and the Capuchin convent.

The next morning one of the citizens wrote, "In the place of the flourishing city of the day before, nothing [remained] but rubbish and heaps of ruins."

Miro immediately went to work to rebuild the city, securing financial assistance from a wealthy citizen, Don Andres Almonester y Rojas. The Church of St. Louis was rebuilt, as were the Cabildo, arsenal, military hospital, customhouse, and other public buildings. A new Governor's house was erected. In the space on the lower levee side in front of the Plaza de Armas, sheds were built for those who sold fruits, vegetables, meats, and other foods. This was the beginning of the present-day "French Market."

The new buildings had high-ceilinged rooms, arched windows and doorways, balconies, courtyards, and much handmade ironwork. Many of them were constructed of brick and stone rather than of wood. A few of these buildings still stand today, reminding us that the architecture of the Vieux Carré is really Spanish and not French in style.

About this time a Capuchin priest in New Orleans named Father Antonio de Sedella was appointed the representative of the Inquisition, which was a Catholic Church court for the seizure and trial of heretics. Governor Miro soon received a letter from him saying that it might be necessary, in carrying out his work, to have some guards or soldiers placed at his command. "On reading the communication," wrote Governor Miro, "I shuddered." And he added that "the mere name of the Inquisition" would keep prospective immigrants from coming to Louisiana and might even drive out some who had already arrived. So he bundled Father Antonio aboard a ship which sailed away from Louisiana the next morning.

In 1788, Governor Miro took another census. He found that during the past three years the population of Louisiana had been increased by some 5,000 persons. More than 34,000 people lived within what is now the limits of Louisiana. In 1791 a slave revolt broke out in Santo Domingo, and many white and free Negro artisans, shopkeepers, and planters came to

Louisiana. A small number of them were able to bring along some wealth and a few slaves.

Miro had asked several times to be relieved of his governorship so that he might retire to Spain. Alternatively, he would have liked a position there, where his knowledge of American affairs would have been useful to the government. He was a tired man. For some time the Americans of the Ohio River country had been causing him considerable trouble, and some of them had been threatening to invade Louisiana. The growth of Louisiana had greatly increased the duties of the Governor. He was satisfied with his army rank, for in 1789 he had been promoted to Brigadier General.

Finally, the Spanish government recalled him to Spain, where he later rose to the rank of Major General. On December 30, 1791, Don Francisco Luis Hector, Baron de Carondelet, succeeded to the governorship.

Carondelet and His Reforms. Carondelet was a prudent, firm man of great administrative ability. Short and plump, with a somewhat thin face, he could be short tempered when things did not go well. But ordinarily he was in good humor, and he quickly became a well-liked and highly respected Governor. At the time of his appointment he was serving as the Governor of San Salvador.

Early in 1792, Carondelet published his inaugural proclamation. He divided New Orleans into four wards,

in each of which was to be a combination fire and police chief whose duty was to preserve order in his ward, keep a record of small debts, and in case of fire, to take charge of the fire companies.

In 1796 he organized a regular police force for New Orleans. There were to be thirteen *serenos,* or watchmen, who would patrol the city at night and see that order was kept. At the same time he ordered eighty lamps to be placed along the streets. To meet the costs of the watchmen and the street lights, a "chimney tax" was levied upon every chimney in the city.

Carondelet continued the Spanish government's policy of encouraging American trade with Louisiana, and New Orleans grew in trading importance. All types of river boats came down from the Ohio and Upper Mississippi River country. Merchants arrived from Philadelphia and the other American cities. Young men came to represent manufacturing or mercantile houses or to make quick fortunes in this land of opportunity.

Carondelet and the French Revolution. The French Revolution, which had started in 1789, caused some of the French Creoles to hope for a revolution in Louisiana. They marched through the streets of New Orleans yelling "Liberty, Equality, and Fraternity" and singing the "Marseillaise," the "Ça Ira," and other French revolutionary songs.

In 1793 the French Revolutionists

Don Francisco Luis Hector, Baron de Carondelet

beheaded Louis XVI and Spain declared war on the new French Republic. Carondelet immediately issued a proclamation forbidding Louisianians either to discuss or to read aloud any printed matter concerning political affairs in France. Those guilty of so doing would be sent to prison at Morro Castle, a great fort in Havana. Anyone who permitted "meetings, gatherings, or conversations of this nature" was to be fined two hundred pesos. Some of the Creoles violated the proclamation, but only about seventy of them were expelled from the colony and only a half dozen were sent to Morro Castle for a year's imprisonment.

Carondelet also strengthened the defenses of his colony. He built Fort St. Philip down the river from New Orleans, repaired the fortifications of New Orleans, and reorganized the militia companies.

Carondelet and the Americans. The Governor had considerable trouble with the Americans, many of whom at this time wanted to secure Louisiana for the United States. They plotted

91

to start a revolution in Louisiana or, if this failed, to organize an expedition on the Upper Ohio River to invade and capture the Spanish colony. As a defensive measure, Carondelet built a small fleet of river boats to patrol the Mississippi River as far north as the mouth of the Ohio.

In 1795 the United States and Spain signed a treaty which settled many of their differences. One section of it fixed the northern boundary line of that section of Louisiana east of the Mississippi. This line today is the northern boundary of the Florida Parishes. The troubles came temporarily to an end.

Everyday Events During Carondelet's Administration. In a New Orleans courtyard, on the afternoon of December 8, 1794, some boys started a small fire which spread to a feed store next door where some hay was stored. There was a brisk wind blowing, and despite the efforts of the firemen the blaze roared across the city. In about three hours over two hundred buildings, many of which had been built since the fire of 1788, burned. There was great distress in New Orleans. Carondelet sent to Havana and Vera Cruz for supplies and started to rebuild the city. He wrote that the houses had formerly been "covered with roofs of shingles, and when they take fire they spread it to buildings sometimes very distant." He ordered future buildings to be constructed of

brick or adobe and roofed with tile.

Also in 1794, Étienne de Boré began planting sugarcane on his plantation near the present Audubon Park in New Orleans. The planting of cane had been largely abandoned in Louisiana after 1766, because the Louisiana sugar could not be made to granulate. All the neighbors laughed at De Boré, but he replied that his sugarhouse was about completed and that "I am convinced that I am right and that I shall succeed." The next year his sugar did granulate and he made a profit of $12,000. It was not long before his neighbors stopped laughing and planted sugarcane themselves, using his methods.

Carondelet watched the actions of the commandants at the various posts throughout Louisiana very carefully, and if they did not perform their duties efficiently he replaced them with men who could do better. Laws were enforced throughout the colony and violators were brought to justice and punished. The Governor continued Miro's mild Indian policies and became friends with many of the chiefs.

In 1797 the Baron de Carondelet was promoted to a high position in the Spanish government at Quito, Ecuador. The people of Louisiana regretted to see him and his baroness leave their colony, for he had protected their rights and had treated everyone fairly. He had conducted a strong and businesslike administration and was one of the greatest of Louisiana's colonial governors.

Three Spanish Governors: Gayoso de Lemos, Casa Calvo, Salcedo. Carondelet was succeeded by Don Manuel Gayoso de Lemos, the Commandant of the Natchez District, whose governorship was marked by wisdom and moderation. His biographer has written that he "won more friends to the Spanish monarchy than any other Louisiana governor." Friendly and completely honest, he was respected and loved by the people. He died of a fever in the summer of 1799.

His successor was the Marquis de Casa Calvo, who was sent to Louisiana from Havana to serve as Acting Governor from the fall of 1799 to the early summer of 1801. Casa Calvo was Governor when Louisiana was again acquired by France through the Treaty of San Ildefonso in 1800. Brigadier General Juan Manuel de Salcedo served until November 30, 1803, when he officially turned Louisiana over to the French.

During the governorship of Gayoso de Lemos, Casa Calvo, and Salcedo there was much unrest throughout the colony. Disagreement existed with the United States over the navigation of the Mississippi River. Many Americans living west of the Appalachian Mountains would have liked to conquer Louisiana for the United States, and some of these people even wanted to secede from the Union and organize a new country which would include Louisiana. Commerce and trade were in bad condition.

Spanish Accomplishments in Louisiana. When Spain acquired Louisiana in 1762 it was a small, unprofitable colony of less than 7,500 inhabitants. Apart from New Orleans, there were only a few small villages along the Mississippi and other streams. The farms and plantations were centered along the Mississippi above and below New Orleans. At the end of the Spanish regime Louisiana was a large and prosperous colony with over 50,000 inhabitants, over 30,000 of whom lived along the Lower Mississippi and in New Orleans.

Economic progress had been slow prior to 1762. The Louisiana colonists had of necessity used paper money which quickly went down in value, and trade had not been permitted with other colonies or countries. Some of the French governors had been more interested in making fortunes for themselves than in providing good government. The French had scattered their settlements too widely, and their administration of justice had been poor.

In contrast to the French, the Spanish had introduced sound currency into Louisiana. In spite of the fact that Spain had imposed many trade restrictions, she had permitted Louisianians to trade with other countries. The Spanish governors had generally been hard-working, intelligent, and honest, and the Spanish systems of government and administration of justice had been efficient and fair to all. Under Spanish rule settlers from many countries had established farms and villages and towns in Louisiana, and better means of communication had been organized.

From a weak French colony in 1762, Louisiana had grown into a strong and prosperous Spanish colony forty years later. While the French in Louisiana never adopted Spanish ways and customs, they owed a greater debt to Spain than they did to their mother country.

11. ECONOMIC AND GOVERNMENTAL LIFE IN SPANISH LOUISIANA

Immigration. Despite the efforts of the French to promote agriculture, there were periods as late even as the 1750's when the people of New Orleans went hungry. There were simply not enough farmers to raise the staple necessities during years when harvests were poor. The Spanish remedied this situation by rapidly settling much of Louisiana's unoccupied land.

Governor Ulloa offered land to Maryland farmers who wished to leave their British colony. Many British settled in the Florida Parishes in the 1760's and 1770's when this section was owned by Great Britain. During the 1770's numerous immigrants from the Canary Islands arrived and established farms below New Orleans, along the Amite River, in the upper areas of the Isle of Orleans, and along Bayou Lafourche. During the 1780's several hundred Pennsylvanians came to Spanish Louisiana.

A constant stream of Acadians arrived after 1764. The Acadians were French Canadians whose ancestors had settled the province of Acadia, or Nova Scotia, early in the seventeenth century. Great Britain acquired Nova Scotia in 1713, but the Acadians never became loyal British subjects, refusing to adopt different customs and to obey the laws. Finally, in 1755, the British lost patience, deported several thousand Acadians, and scattered them among their Atlantic seaboard colonies, after confiscating their lands and burning their homes and barns. A few Acadians reached Louisiana between 1756 and 1764, but the great Acadian migration to Louisiana began in 1765. More than 1,500 arrived in 1786.

The Spanish governors were sympa-

94

British soldiers forcing the Acadians onto ships for deportation

thetic and kind to the Acadians, gave them land, tools for their fields, supplies, and some money. Governor O'Reilly complained: "The settlement of these poor families is very costly." Their chief areas of settlement were the Lower Mississippi section above the German Coast, which they called the Acadian Coast, and the Opelousas, Atakapas, and Lafourche districts, though many settled in small groups in other sections. They were hardworking farmers, herdsmen, and fishermen, extremely conservative and religious, and became good citizens. Some four to six thousand of them came to Louisiana during the Spanish period.

Several large land grants were made by the Spanish during the 1790's. The Marquis de Maison Rouge was given a large tract on the Ouachita River near the present city of Monroe, and the Baron de Bastrop received over thirty square miles of land north and northeast of Monroe. The Baron agreed to settle four hundred families on his land, but was unable to do so.

There were many hardships involved in moving to Louisiana. An uneducated Carolina farmer wrote to Governor Miro explaining that he would have to travel through "a howling Wilderness of 200 Miles, infected by hostile Hords and Savages & through a perillous, & irksome River-navigation of nearly 1,800 Miles, which is yet before me."

But, unlike the French, the Spanish found many new settlers for the rich lands of Louisiana. Those who came established farms and plantations and made the colony self-sufficient through their agricultural products.

Agriculture. Governor Ulloa encouraged the raising of wheat for flour and in 1768 he asked the government to send six horse-drawn mills and six water-driven mills to Louisiana. He stated that there were only two horse-drawn mills in the colony, at Opelousas and Natchitoches, and that they were crude mills and ground only four bushels of flour per day. Wheat production began to improve.

Indigo had become an important product during the French period and it continued in importance until worms appeared which destroyed crop after crop. The farmers and planters then turned to tobacco. Governor Gálvez called a meeting of the tobacco farmers, at which they fixed the price and established a system of grading, packing, and shipping the tobacco. The Governor then agreed to purchase the entire tobacco crop. One of the planters wrote that Louisiana had a better tobacco-producing climate than Maryland or Virginia and that the colony could "furnish the world with tobacco." In 1790 the Pointe Coupee District alone produced nearly 75,000 pounds of tobacco.

After Étienne de Boré granulated sugar, the planters began to clear more land, acquire more slaves, and build sugar mills, so that they could produce large quantities of sugar. By the end of the Spanish period there were many sugar-producing plantations in the colony.

General farming, however, was the common practice. The farms and plantations produced hogs, cattle and sheep, corn, rice, wheat, vegetables of all kinds, and different varieties of fruits. These foodstuffs were produced in all sections of Louisiana, and even during periods of drought or too much rain there was enough food for all, with some left over for export. However, there were many agricultural problems. Cold weather sometimes killed the plants. In the winter of 1784, for example, the temperature went below zero and blocks of ice drifted down the Mississippi as far as New Orleans. Storms and hurricanes destroyed entire crops. Insects and wild animals were troublesome. Another problem, particularly in western and southwestern Louisiana, was the stealing of livestock. Despite the fact that the cattle were branded, many were stolen, killed, butchered, and the meat sold.

Agricultural labor was difficult to secure. There were never enough slaves to supply the demand, and white men were hired by the month, most of them living in the homes of their employers. Wages were about twelve dollars a month, and board, which was estimated at six dollars. Parents sometimes signed a contract whereby their sons or daughters worked for farmers for a period of years. In 1796, for example, ten-year-old Alexis la Montagne was contracted to William Walker for ten years. Alexis was to be given a heifer and a mare, and a brand for them. He was to be the owner of their increase and was to be housed, clothed, fed, and "treated as a son."

Slaves and Free Negroes. Slavery had existed in Louisiana since early in the French period, but the slave system increased in importance during the Spanish years because of a general advance in economic conditions.

The importation of slaves increased, but Governor O'Reilly ordered that they be brought only from Africa. He believed that African slaves worked better than West Indian slaves did, and he strongly opposed the West Indian practice of voodoo. But West Indian slaves were smuggled into Louisiana throughout the Spanish period.

As the plantations increased in number and grew larger in size and as the slaves gradually developed into skilled laborers, the slave labor system developed in economic importance. Slaves became more valuable, for they became carpenters, blacksmiths, mechanics, ironworkers, and brickmakers and learned other trades. The Louisianians imported more and more slaves. The Black Code of the French, which had been issued in 1724, became out-of-date. In 1792, therefore, Governor Carondelet issued another code.

The two codes offered rather broad areas of protection to the slave, and they represented the least harsh regulations of that time. Slaves should be adequately housed, fed, and clothed. They should not work on Sunday unless they were paid for their labor. They should not be required to work before sunrise or after sunset. They could sue in the courts, could be baptized in the Church, and their marriages were legally recognized.

Some Louisiana slaves were permitted to earn their freedom. Slaves, along with free Negroes, fought in the militia companies under Bernardo de Gálvez at Baton Rouge, Mobile, and Pensacola. Several were decorated by the Governor for their bravery.

But unless he could somehow purchase his own freedom, the slave was bound for life. He was subject to the abuse of a cruel owner. He was still subject to being chained or flogged. Although the slave system was widely used throughout the world at that time, it was already being attacked as an oppressive labor system.

By 1790 there were about fifteen hundred free Negroes in Louisiana. During the next fifteen years many others arrived, some of them with their wealth and slaves from the West Indies. They acquired plantations and other property. Many of this group were well educated and cultured people. They established an economic, social, and cultural group of their own in New Orleans. They built nice homes and furnished them well. Some sent their children to France or Spain to be educated. By 1860 their descendants had raised black culture to its highest level in the world.

Industry and Manufacturing. There had been little manufacturing in

Reconstruction of an Acadian kitchen, at the Longfellow-Evangeline State Park, St. Martinville, Louisiana.

French Louisiana, but the production of manufactured goods increased during the Spanish period. Sawmills grew in number; brickyards were soon scattered throughout the colony; indigo was processed; hides were tanned and mills began making flour and corn meal. Candles were made from tallow and myrtle wax, while pitch and tar were produced as a by-product of the timbering business. Tobacco was processed and packed for export. Syrup was

boiled, and considerable amounts went into the making of tafia. But most of the manufacturing continued to be the production of articles needed in the home: furniture, leather goods, clothing, utensils, and various tools and other implements made of iron.

The Mississippi River and Local Trade. Trading in the villages and towns was usually done in open-air markets or in the public squares, as in

98

Artist George Caleb Bingham's "The Happy Flatboatmen."

the French period, but every village or town now had a few shops. The market in New Orleans was the largest in Louisiana and carried all types of goods. There were three kinds of merchants at this time: first, the merchant who had a shop; second, the peddler who traveled the bayous and streams in a trading boat; and third, the peddler who traveled on foot, on horseback, or in a hack or carriage. Most of this trading was done by barter, and there was much haggling over the value of the articles to be traded.

Prices were cheap as compared with modern prices. In 1769 fresh beef and pork cost about six cents a pound; fresh butter, about twenty-five cents; and a jar of bear's grease for frying or seasoning purposes, about thirty cents. A jar of milk cost twelve cents and a barrel of kidney beans $3.75. Other items were in proportion. By 1797 prices had risen slightly. Sugar was thirty cents a pound, meat seven to ten cents a pound, and a hat or a pair of shoes cost two dollars.

After 1784 the Spanish tried to close

the Mississippi to American traders, but the need for their goods was too great. The trade continued but was subject to close regulation. Though the keelboats, flatboats, scows, and other boats kept coming down the river loaded with flour, whiskey, bacon and salted or smoked meats, furs and hides, bear's oil, corn, butter, and a wide variety of manufactured goods, the trade caused much trouble between the United States and the Spanish governments.

Foreign Trade. Foreign trade presented as many difficulties as it had when Louisiana was under the French. Spanish Louisiana needed to sell its goods and it needed supplies of all kinds, many of which Spain could not supply. In 1769, O'Reilly wrote to a Spanish official: "Your Excellency is well aware that this province cannot live without commerce." The Governor then listed the goods which Louisiana needed, and those which she produced, then suggested trade regulations which, in general, were followed throughout the rest of the Spanish period.

Most of Louisiana's foreign trade during the time of Ulloa and O'Reilly continued to be with the West Indies and British West Florida. Later, however, trade increased with Mexico and even with Texas, despite the fact that Mexico wanted this trade for herself. On several occasions, particularly during the American Revolution, trade was permitted with France.

Trade with the United States increased rapidly after 1790.

There had been considerable corruption in regard to trade during the French period, but most of the Spanish officials were honest and forced ship captains to account for all of their shipments There was little personal graft, and no official permitted his wife to engage in business or establish monopolies, as Madame Vaudreuil had done. Luxury goods were imported into the colony at an ever increasing rate, for the colonists, by producing more themselves, had more money to spend. Life was much easier in Spanish Louisiana than it had been under the French.

Money. When Louisiana was ceded to the Spanish, there were over seven million livres worth of French paper money being circulated in the colony at but a fraction of its normal value. The Spanish fixed the trading value of this paper money at one-fourth of its face value in gold or silver. Soon a stream of Spanish gold and silver money came pouring into Louisiana from the Spanish colonies and, as trade developed, from the American colonies and from the countries of Europe.

Thus, French paper money quickly disappeared and Spanish gold and silver took its place. This proved to be a great blessing to the colonists, for the hard money did not depreciate in value as the paper money had done.

The Cabildo. The original building was constructed in 1770, burned in 1788, was rebuilt but burned again in 1794. The present Cabildo was completed in 1795.

Laws and Regulations. In 1769, O'Reilly abolished the French colonial government and created a Spanish political unit called the Province of Louisiana. At the same time he issued a code of laws for the people and a list of rules to be followed by Spanish officials. The Code of 1769 was issued in the form of two ordinances, or proclamations, written in French and in simple form so that the people could understand them. They followed the various laws then in operation in Spain and her other colonies.

101

The change in government was a drastic one. The French had been lax in their enforcement of the laws. Now the French Creoles saw that the Spanish intended that their laws should be observed. By the end of 1769 the Spanish laws and courts were functioning, and the French Creoles had realized their value. O'Reilly wrote that his political government had been well received and that a favorable impression had already been made "on the minds of the people."

Government. Under the Governor there was an Intendant, who was in charge of the treasury and the revenues. Two Lieutenant Governors were located in the Illinois and Natchitoches districts. There was an Auditor, who also served as assessor, and a Surveyor General. Other officials performed special duties.

O'Reilly organized a *Cabildo,* which was a town council for New Orleans composed of two alcaldes (judges), a prosecuting attorney, a sheriff, and several other members. The *Cabildo* met every Friday and the Governor presided at the meetings. But the *Cabildo* was more than an ordinary town council. In addition to governing New Orleans, it advised the Governor, made suggestions concerning the general public welfare, and acted as a court of appeals for the entire colony. It was a dignified and efficient body.

Of course, money was needed to run the government. The colony's expenses were largely paid from taxes on ships and from the duties on exports and imports. Local governmental expenses were paid from the taxation of chimneys, inns, billiard halls, taverns, butcher-shops, liquors, from the rental of government buildings and land, and from the collection of fees and fines by local officials. In 1769 the total income of New Orleans was about two thousand dollars, and O'Reilly wrote that this sum paid for the city's *fiestas* and for other unusual expenses.

The colony was divided into twelve districts. each of which was governed by a Commandant. The number was increased as the population of Louisiana grew, but they were too large and parishes then became the units of local government. The Commandant of a district had many duties. He preserved order and examined the passports of all travelers. He registered titles to lands, witnessed contracts, took inventories of property, and acted as the sheriff of his district. He was a judge in all cases which did not involve more than twenty dollars. He performed marriage ceremonies. By the time of Carondelet, justices of the peace were needed, and these officials, whom the Spanish called "Syndics," were appointed.

The citizens had to build and keep the roads, levees, and bridges in good condition. Sometimes they protested. In 1792 Governor Carondelet ordered the people of the Baton Rouge District to rebuild their levees. They protested to Alexander Patin, their local Syndic, saying that their levees were already high enough, that they were busy with their farming, and that there had been "no breaks or crevices." However, they were forced to comply with the Governor's orders.

Justice was rapid and there was no favoritism. Civil suits were settled, divorces were granted, marriage contracts were witnessed, land titles were made legal, and criminals were brought to justice. Justice was sometimes harsh, torture being permitted as it had been under the French. All the Spanish officials had to keep exact records of what they did. Several copies of each document had to be made for recording by the higher officials.

Indian Affairs. The Spanish had little trouble with the Indians. Through a system of councils and gifts and efficient trading methods there was generally peace with the various tribes. Indian slavery was forbidden by O'-Reilly, and the Indian was given justice in the courts. In 1783, for example, when Henry Bradly "borrowed" a canoe from an Indian to go to New Orleans and did not return the canoe, he was ordered to pay twenty dollars to the owner.

Occasionally there were complaints about Indian activities. In 1782, Antonio Maxent wrote to Governor Miro from Galveztown saying that there were over four hundred Choctaw Indians there and about fifteen hundred more expected to arrive on their way to New Orleans. He was having to feed these Indians and they were stealing from the settlers. They had broken into his warehouse and had stolen more than twenty barrels of corn and forty barrels of potatoes. At another time a report came from what is now Sabine Parish, where the Indians had eaten all the corn crop and had consumed almost all the beans, pumpkins, and watermelons. Sugar was getting short because the Indians found it "most pleasing to their appetites."

But the Indians kept the peace because trading was good and because the Spanish gave them many presents each year. At Natchitoches in 1787 the presents included gunpowder, shot, muskets, kettles, rifle flints, beads, knives, mirrors, needles, shirts, blankets, ribbons, small bells, scissors, combs, lace, vermilion dye, and many other items.

It was not without reason, then, that an old chief named Franchmastabbia called himself a friend and brother of Governor Gayoso. He painfully wrote: "Old Friend and Brother This Comes to Let you no that I am well and hope this will find you in the Same This is to Let you no that I am a man of Strate hart and one talk and dont want to tell you lyes nor to hid any talk from you—I Believe in you and you Believe in me Our Acquaincence is Small but the Chaine of our Frindship is Grate We are bound to hid no bad talks from Each other."

12. SOCIAL AND CULTURAL LIFE IN SPANISH LOUISIANA

French Creoles Never Became Spanish. The Spanish period of colonial Louisiana began with a rebellion against Governor Ulloa and the Spanish government. The execution of the rebel leaders by O'Reilly caused Louisiana to hate Spain and the Spanish, but O'Reilly and the succeeding governors were men of ability, honesty and extreme tact. They appointed French Creoles to high positions in the army and in the government. They permitted the French to hold most of the local offices, generally to govern themselves, and to continue speaking French.

After a time the hatred for the Spanish began to disappear, and although the Louisianians would have preferred to have remained Frenchmen, they could see the many benefits of the Spanish regime over the old French government. The French who came to Louisiana from Santo Domingo after the slave insurrection of 1791 had no such hatred, and as many of them were wealthy and cultured they immediately took a high place in the society of the colony. However, the Louisianians would not speak Spanish.

French was the language of the people. Even in the homes of the Spaniards who had married French women the children frequently did not know a word of Spanish. In this way, the Spaniards left few traces of their period of colonial rule. However, they did leave the spirit of chivalry, many of their laws and legal customs, and a few geographic names.

The French of Louisiana did not forget that their life under the Spanish had been peaceful and happy. When Pierre Clement de Laussat denounced the Spanish government in 1803, they answered him: "We should be unworthy of what is to us a subject of so much pride . . . if we did not acknowledge that we have no cause of complaint against the Spanish government. We have never groaned under the yoke of an oppressive despotism. . . . We have become bound together by family connections and by the bonds of friendship."

Where the People Lived. When Spain gave up control of Louisiana, most of the area within the limits of the present-day state was occupied. There

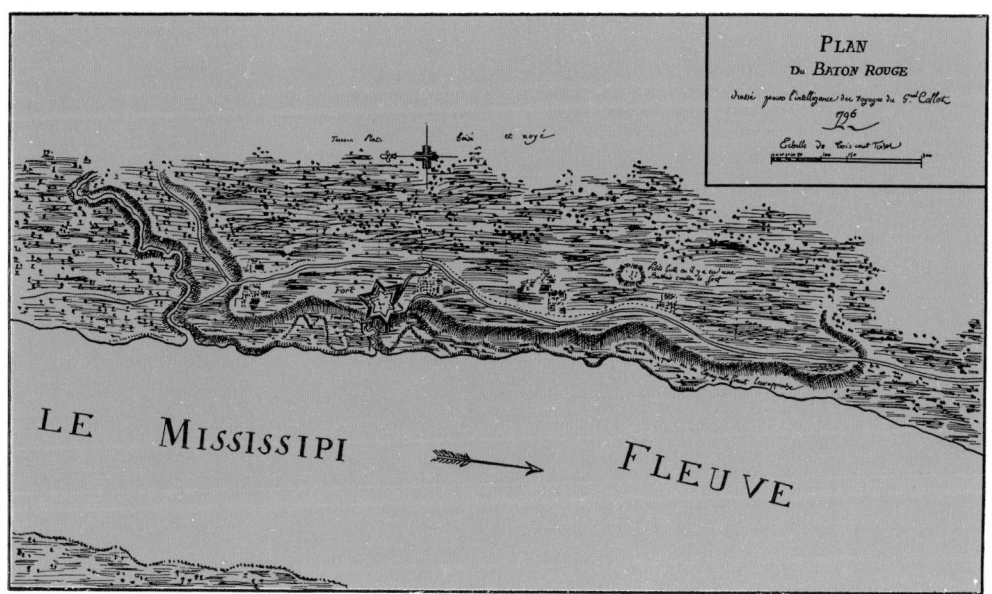

A plan of Baton Rouge as it looked in 1796.

were over fifty thousand people in the colony. New Orleans was, of course, the most important city; but Natchitoches, Fort Miro (Monroe), Baton Rouge, Opelousas, and several suburbs of New Orleans were growing towns. Villages had been founded throughout the colony.

New Orleans grew rapidly after the Spanish acquired Louisiana. By 1771 it had 3,200 inhabitants and by 1785 nearly 5,000. At the end of the Spanish era its population had increased to nearly 10,000. The rural areas had also gained in population. Farms and plantations lined the Mississippi and most of the bayous in the southeastern section of the colony. There were a few settlers living along the Ouachita. The

Red River area was settled as far as Natchitoches. Only in the southwestern, western, and northern sections were the settlers widely scattered and few in number.

The People and How They Lived. The inhabitants of Louisiana at the end of the Spanish period numbered about 50,000. Roughly half were freeborn and slave blacks, including many from Santo Domingo. Fewer than half of the whites were of French ancestry. There were many other nationalities, including Germans and Swiss, whose ancestors came during the French period, as well as Englishmen, Scots, and Irish. Americans who had migrated by riverboats or wagons

105

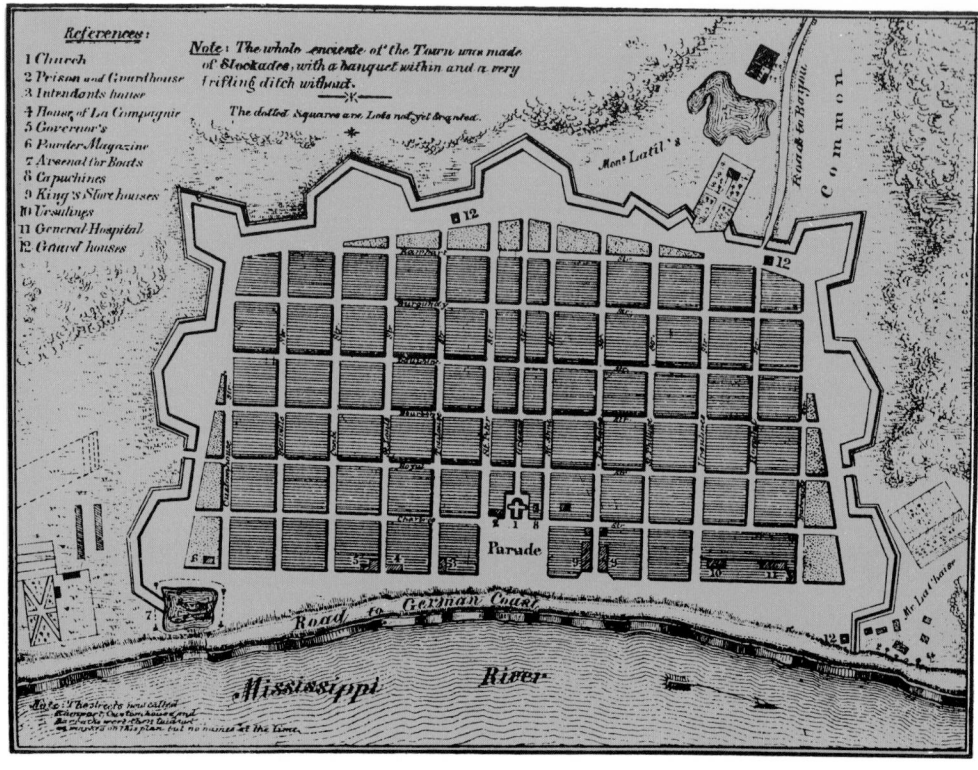

References:
1 Church
2 Prison and Courthouse
3 Intendants house
4 House of La Compagnie
5 Governor's
6 Powder Magazine
7 Arsenal for Boats
8 Capuchines
9 King's Store houses
10 Ursulines
11 General Hospital
12 Guard houses

Note: The whole enceinte of the Town was made of Stockades, with a banquet within and a very trifling ditch without.

The dotted Squares are Lots not yet granted.

Map 12—New Orleans, about 1770

from Pennsylvania, Virginia, the Carolinas, or other states were settled in towns or in rural areas. A few Scandinavians lived in North Louisiana, and, according to one traveler who visited Louisiana about this time, there were even a few gypsies.

New Orleans had been rebuilt following the fires of 1788 and 1794, and in 1803 was a comparatively new city, with well-built houses constructed according to the Spanish style. The city was surrounded by an earthwork and palisaded walls. Five forts, which

had been allowed to run down during the previous few years, offered some protection in case of attack. Facing the river upstream was Fort San Luis. Directly behind it on the far corner was Fort San José. Facing the river downstream was Fort San Carlos and behind it was Fort San Juan. Between Fort San José and Fort San Juan on the side directly behind the Cathedral was Fort San Fernando. Three gates opened out of New Orleans, the upper-river or San Luis Gate, the lower-river or Gate of France, as the French Cre-

106

Plantation homes near New Orleans often resembled those in the West Indies.

oles called it, and the Bayou Gate which was directly behind the town.

A traveler up the Mississippi passed first the Tchoupitoulas Coast, then the First German Coast, the Second German Coast, the First Acadian Coast, and the Second Acadian Coast. Eastward from the mouth of Bayou Manchac was Galveztown. Farther up-river were settlements at Baton Rouge, Thompson's Creek, Pointe Coupee, and Bayou Sara (St. Francisville). Fort Miro was on the Ouachita River, and up the Red River was El Rapido (called Les Rapides by the French, modern Pineville) and the old French town of Natchitoches, the oldest town in Louisiana and in all of the Louisiana Purchase.

Southward from El Rapido were the villages of Opelousas and Atakapas (St. Martinville). On down Bayou Teche was a growing Spanish settlement called New Iberia, which means

107

New Spain. There were no sizable villages along Bayou Lafourche or the other bayous in this section, but along all these waterways were farms and plantations, livestock ranches, truck farms, and the homes of hunters and fishermen. Outside New Orleans and the larger towns, life was much like it had been under the French, for the French influence was very strong. Houses and clothing were French, and most of the customs of the people had been inherited from the days of French rule.

But New Orleans was a Spanish town as far as its houses and other buildings were concerned. The wrought ironwork was just like it was in Havana or the City of Mexico, even though it had been hammered out by slaves who spoke only French. Many of the houses were built of brick, with flat roofs of tile supported by heavy cypress timbers which had been cut, according to the Spanish regulations, only during certain phases of the moon. No house was complete without its patio, or courtyard, in the back. The houses were built flush with the street and the sidewalk was right against the front wall.

Most Louisianians now had better household furnishings, for they were more prosperous; except for the houses of the Spanish officials, most of the furnishings were French in style. If the family was wealthy, the home was filled with French furniture, tableware and dishes, linens and chests, and French-style clothing. If the family was poor, the furnishings were homemade, without style or ornamentation.

Most small farmers could be compared with Gidgeon Walker, who lived near the Avoyelles Post about 1799. Walker's farm was six arpents wide and forty arpents deep and was valued at $125. It had a house sixteen feet wide and about twenty-five feet long, covered with split shingles and with a gallery all around it. There was a small barn behind the house. The farmer owned two horses worth $36, an unbroken horse valued at $15, six cows and calves worth $36, and ten or twelve head of cattle in the woods. Walker's tools, household furnishings, and clothing included: three chairs and a table, a chest, a bed, a mirror, several spreads and blankets, some family clothing, an ax, a brace and bit, a file, a pressing iron, a pair of scissors, a Spanish saddle and bridle, a large bucket, a grinding stone, two knives, three hoes, and a spade. Plantation slaves lived in even smaller cabins, furnished with about the same amount of crude, homemade furniture.

There was little traveling about the colony, as in the French period. But there were more villages and towns, and people who lived in the vicinity usually went to town on Saturday afternoons. They traveled along the poor roads on horseback or in wagons or carts. If they wanted to travel any distance they still used some type of boat on one of the many waterways.

The Spanish brought the early sugar-making process from the West Indies.

Religion. The Spanish were Catholics, just as the French were, but to them religion was a much more serious matter. The French were inclined to an easygoing practice of faith.

Governor O'Reilly, immediately upon his arrival, reorganized the Catholic Church in Louisiana. Since Louisiana had only eight parishes, including two in the Illinois country, O'Reilly ordered the establishment of new parishes throughout the colony.

The Spanish were very critical of the French Capuchins. Father Cirilo de Barcelona criticized them in reports to his superiors in Havana. They wore a "watch in a fob," had a clock in the dining hall which cost $270, had silver spoons and "smaller ones to take coffee with." They "ruled teal duck as fish and ate it on fast days."

It will be recalled that Father Antonio de Sedella had attempted during the time of Governor Miro to establish the Inquisition and that Miro had quickly sent him out of the colony and spared Louisiana the persecutions of that institution. Later Father Sedella returned to Louisiana under the name of Father Antoine and spent the rest of his life in New Orleans. He became one of the most beloved priests in Louisiana history, and when he died at the age of eighty-one in 1829, Protestants and Catholics alike mourned him.

The stern, Puritan-like Spanish Catholicism did not appeal to the French, and the Spanish constantly found fault with them. In 1792, Governor Carondelet criticized the religious practices of the French and of the French priests and pleaded for more non-French but French-speaking priests to be sent to

109

Spanish architecture did not extend much beyond New Orleans; the French influence remained strong elsewhere. In 1765 Chevalier de La Houssaye built this house which can be seen at the Longfellow-Evangeline State Park in St. Martinville.

Louisiana so that "our religion then will be loved, respected, and generally followed."

Time has, however, proven that the French Creoles are better Catholics than the Spaniards realized. The French Creoles possessed a quiet brand of faith, but it was strong and true.

Amusements. Despite their religious severity, the Spaniards were a fun-loving people, and they joined the other nationalities living in Louisiana in en-

joying a full social life. They had a good time on Sunday afternoons and on feast days; Christmas, New Year's, and the various Saints' Days were opportunities for celebrations. A *fiesta,* or party, was *made,* as the Spanish said, whenever possible. Everyone—French, Spanish, Acadian—was invited. On one occasion, after the feast was eaten, the Spaniards drank a toast "To Spain—Land of Queen Isabella, who made possible the discovery of the New World." The Frenchmen drank "To

France—Land of Louis XIV, the Grand Monarch." The Acadians drank "To Acadia and Grand Pré—birthplace of the exiles." Then, all of them drank "To the Acadian Country, the Golden Coast—the adopted homeland of all." And the dancing began.

Those were happy days, those days of Spanish Louisiana. Times were good. The country was growing up, and providing opportunity for all.

Education. Although a few of the wealthy Creole families educated their sons in France or the United States and an even larger number provided tutors to teach their children to read and write, the majority had little interest in education. The Spanish government projected a public school system in 1771 and sent Don Manuel Andres Lopez de Armesto to New Orleans as director. Armesto thus has the distinction of being the first city school superintendent in the United States. But he accomplished little: the people simply refused to send their children to public or Spanish-language schools.

The Ursulines continued their educational work, largely for the training of girls and young women. They disliked Spanish regulations, however, and opposed the receiving of "Spanish subjects ignorant of French." By 1788 there were eight private schools or academies in New Orleans with a total enrollment of about four hundred pupils.

In 1803, Louisiana was still an educationally stagnant colony, in which it was estimated that only a few hundred persons were able to read and write well.

Medicine and Health. Spanish Louisiana was, of course, subject to the same diseases that attacked French Louisiana. Epidemics appeared from time to time and there were the usual cases of smallpox, mumps, and stomach disorders. The old home remedies continued to be relied upon, for there were few doctors. Organized medicine, however, appeared during the Spanish period. By 1770, before a man could practice medicine he had to show the records of his study as well as his books and instruments and submit to an examination before the Spanish King's physician. In addition he had to prove that he was of high moral character and a good Catholic.

One of the most noted doctors of Spanish Louisiana was a Scotsman, Dr. Robert Dow, who left a rather large number of records including medical bills. He was a genial, kindly man and it has been written that "no member of his profession ever acquired more popularity." The inventory of Dr. Joseph Dorquiny illustrates that physicians of the period dressed well, for he possessed numerous pairs of stockings, waistcoats, satin trousers, a "cravat buckle set with stones," and a silver-trimmed sword. By the end of the Spanish period there were practicing physicians living in most communities.

111

Culture. There had been little culture in colonial Louisiana prior to 1762; no printing, no literary or musical activities, no painting, no sculpture. The colonists were too busy clearing forest lands, draining swamps, and planting food crops to permit time for such things. In 1763, Denis Braud was granted the right to set up the first printing press in Louisiana, and the same year he printed a proclamation for a British general who was stationed at Mobile. The proclamation carried the line "Published in Mobile." Shortly after this Braud began his Louisiana printing career, preparing broadsides and handbills.

It is said that the first Louisiana newspaper, called *Le Courier du Vendredi (The Friday Courier)*, was printed in New Orleans in 1785. This cannot be proved, however, for no copies exist today. During the 1790's a refugee from Santo Domingo named Louis Duclot arrived at New Orleans and in 1794 he began the publication of *Le Moniteur de la Louisiane (The Louisiana Monitor)*. This was the first newspaper in Louisiana of which copies still exist. By 1797 *Le Moniteur* had become the official paper of the government, and in it are found many of the official governmental documents of that time.

Louisiana literature may be said to have had its beginnings in 1777, when two short unsigned poems were published. One of them congratulated Gálvez on recovering from an illness, and the other heaped a great deal of outright flattery upon him. Two years later, in 1779, Julien Poydras, who was later to become a wealthy merchant, published a long epic poem on Gálvez' capture of the British fort at Baton Rouge. Amateur theatricals gradually increased during the Spanish period. The first record of a music teacher in Louisiana was during the late 1780's or early 1790's. Organized musicales and music organizations had to await the American period.

Society. Society flourished in Louisiana after the American Revolution, for the country settled down to peaceful pursuits and its wealth grew rapidly. The middle and upper classes wore fashionable clothes, and they frequently attended festive balls and dances.

The letters of the Spanish officials reveal both their friendship with the citizens of the colony and something of society in general. Carlos de Grand Pré, then Commandant of the Natchez District, once wrote to Governor Miro: "Permit me to place myself at the feet of your wife, to whom I offer my respect and obedience, and to whom my wife offers her affectionate expressions of love and friendship, as well as to Your Lordship. I hope to have the honor of seeing her soon in the company of Your Lordship, whose life I pray the all-Powerful to lengthen the many years I desire.... I Kiss Your Lordship's hands."

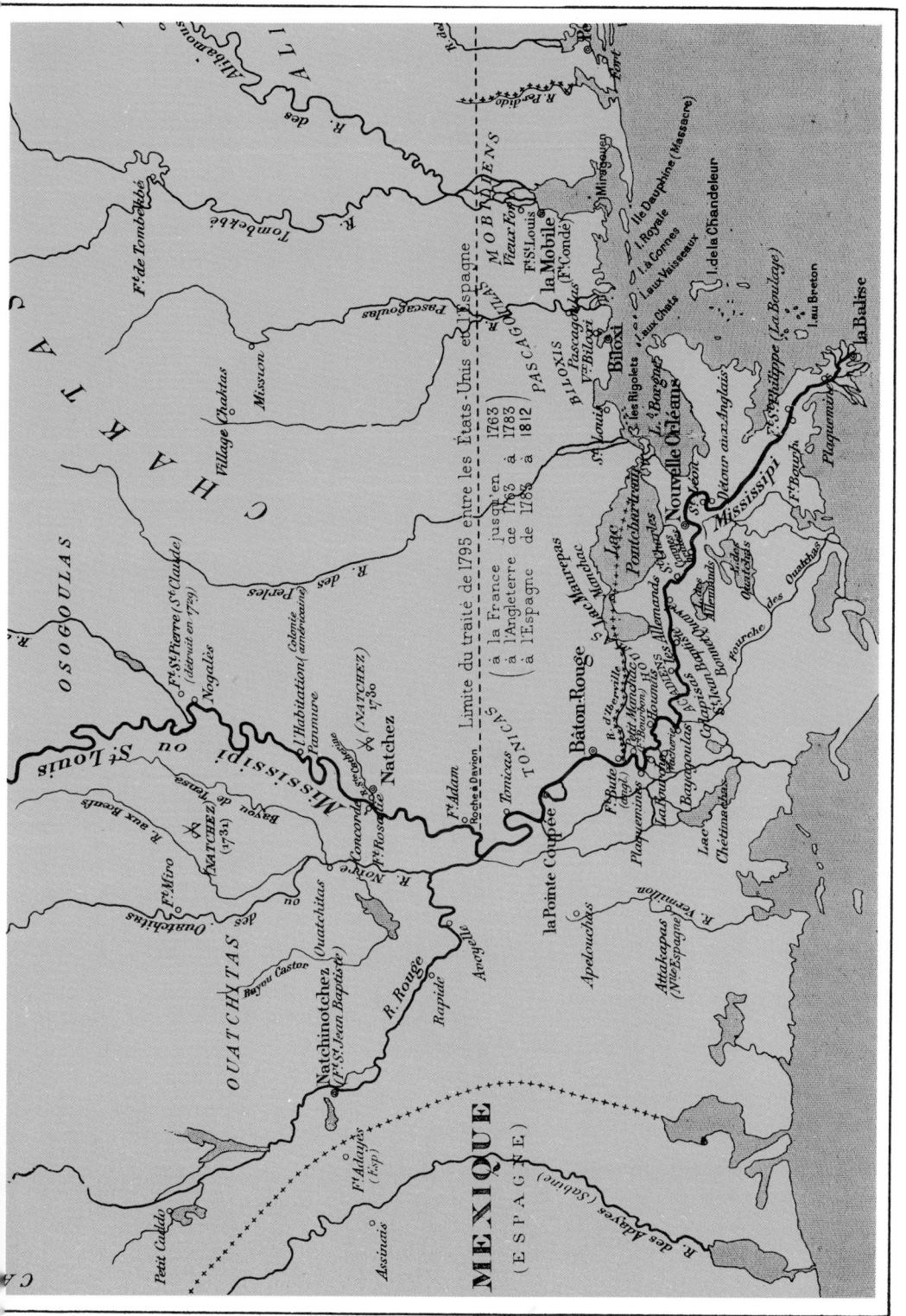

Map 13—Louisiana at the end of the Spanish period

Andrew Jackson at
the Battle of
New Orleans

PART FOUR
Early Years of
The American Regime,
1803–1815

13. THE LOUISIANA PURCHASE, 1803

The United States and the Land West of the Mississippi River. During the American Revolution, Richard Henry Lee of Virginia wrote a letter to Samuel Adams of Massachusetts in which he said that the young republic must always have a strong navy. He believed that two things were necessary to make the navy really strong— the development of fisheries and the control of the Mississippi River. In a similar letter to Henry Laurens of South Carolina, he wrote: "These, sir, are the strong legs on which North America can alone walk securely in Independence." Thereafter, American statesmen dreamed of the day when the land west of the Mississippi would belong to the United States.

After the Revolutionary War, the Americans pushed west of the Appalachian Highland and settled the areas of Kentucky, Tennessee, and

Ohio. By 1790 there were more than 100,000 people in this region who needed markets for their surplus pork, wheat, corn, and other products. The easiest way to reach these markets was to send the goods down the Mississippi to New Orleans and there transfer them to oceangoing ships.

In 1795 Spain agreed to give the Americans the right to transport goods down the Mississippi River to New Orleans and to deposit them there until they could be loaded onto ships. The treaty was to be in effect for three years and could be renewed. This treaty also secured for the United States undisputed title to all lands north of the thirty-first parallel and east of the river.

The Mississippi River trade prospered, but after 1798 the western settlers had many difficulties with the Spanish over this trade and the right of depositing goods at New Orleans. They complained to President John Adams and at times angrily talked of organizing an army and capturing New Orleans and Louisiana.

Spain Cedes Louisiana Back to France. In spite of Louisiana's prosperity during the late 1790's, the colony was costing the Spanish government over $300,000 a year. This was a serious problem, for Spain at this time was not a wealthy country.

France had been making plans to rebuild her colonial empire since 1798, and early in 1800 Napoleon

Bonaparte began to put pressure upon Spain to trade Louisiana and Florida to France. He argued that France could better protect these colonies against the Americans and the British than could Spain. However, while Louisiana had not been acquired by Spain until 1762, Florida had been originally settled by the Spanish, and they would not consider giving it up. Louisiana was a different matter, about which one of the Spanish officials wrote that "it costs us more than it is worth." Louisiana under the French would serve as a strong barrier for Spanish Texas against the British and Americans.

The power of Spain had been declining for a number of years. If Spain had held her former strength, she would never have given up the Mississippi Valley. A Spanish writer explained the situation by saying that if Spain refused to give Louisiana back to France, France might declare war against her; and while Spain and France were fighting, the United States would be free to capture Louisiana. In either case, Louisiana would be lost to Spain.

At this time Napoleon was making plans for a new French Empire which would include Louisiana and the Caribbean island of Santo Domingo. France began to negotiate with Spain, and on October 1, 1800, Louisiana was returned to France by the secret Treaty of San Ildefonso. The treaty was not made public until about two years later.

Settlement in the Pineries

The French Commissioner Arrives in Louisiana. On March 26, 1803, Pierre Clement de Laussat, a French colonial official, landed at New Orleans to make arrangements for the official transfer of Louisiana back to France. Laussat announced that he had been ordered to make preparations for the arrival of General Claude Victor, who had been appointed the new French Governor. When General Victor arrived France would take official possession of Louisiana. The Spanish Governor declared that everything was ready for turning the colony back to France.

A short time later over a hundred Louisianians presented to Laussat an address in which they thanked the French government for taking Louisiana back again. They said that they had been citizens of Spain for over forty years but that during all this time they had remained loyal sons of France. They were happy at becoming French citizens again.

117

Thomas Jefferson

Most of the French Louisianians, however, showed little enthusiasm over becoming Frenchmen again. The Spanish government had been more efficient and more honest than the government under France had been, and Spanish silver money was much more stable than the French paper money. The merchants, planters, and farmers feared new French commercial regulations. Louisiana had never really prospered under France; it had prospered greatly under Spain.

The United States Plans to Acquire Louisiana. The Louisianians did not know that at this time negotiations were going on between the United States and France for the American purchase of Louisiana.

The United States government had heard that France was about to regain Louisiana. In 1801, Rufus King wrote to President Thomas Jefferson from London that he feared that "Spain is ceding Louisiana to France, an inauspicious circumstance to us."

The American government did not want France to secure possession of Louisiana. France and Great Britain were now at peace, but everyone realized that they would soon be at war again. The British might then capture Louisiana, and the United States did not want Louisiana to become a British possession.

American newspapers began to argue that since New Orleans and the Mississippi River were very important to the people of the west, the United States should organize an expedition to capture New Orleans. President Jefferson wrote to Robert Livingston, the American Minister to France, in 1802, that the cession of Louisiana to France "works most sorely on the United States." He also wrote that "every eye in the United States is now fixed on the affairs of Louisiana. Perhaps nothing since the revolutionary war has produced more uneasy sensations through the body of the nation."

Jefferson believed that if France secured Louisiana, she would soon afterwards capture the Floridas from Spain. Canada already bounded the United States on the north. If Louisiana and Florida became French the American nation would be hemmed in on the west, the north, and the south.

The United States Tries to Buy Louisiana. Robert Livingston was an old man, deaf, and not considered a good diplomat, even though he was the American Minister of France. He had secured the appointment because he was a member of one of New York's old wealthy families and was a good friend of President Jefferson. Jefferson ordered Livingston to talk to the French officials about the possibility of the United States buying Louisiana.

Livingston wrote back that Napoleon was the dictator of France. "There is no people, no legislature, no counsellors. One man is everything. He seldom asks advice, and never hears it unasked. His ministers are mere clerks, and his legislature and counsellors are parade officers." Livingston promised to do the best he could.

In January, 1803, Jefferson appointed James Monroe as a special representative of the United States to help Livingston in trying to buy Louisiana. It took Monroe three months to reach Paris. Meanwhile, the negotiations between Livingston and the French officials moved forward with incredible swiftness.

The Purchase of Louisiana. During the early months of 1803, Napoleon realized that he would have difficulty in protecting Louisiana from the British, with whom France was about to go to war. It was rumored that Great Britain was already making plans to send a large fleet to capture the colony just as soon as the war started. Napoleon finally decided to sell Louisiana to the Americans. He said: "I already consider the colony as entirely lost." He sent for François Barbé-Marbois, his Minister of the Treasury, ordering

119

Robert R. Livingston

him to begin negotiations with Livingston.

Many Frenchmen did not want to relinquish Louisiana, for they had hoped that France would rebuild her old colonial empire. One day Joseph and Lucien Bonaparte, two of Napoleon's brothers, visited him. Napoleon was taking a bath. They followed him into the bathroom, where they argued with him not to sell Louisiana, but Napoleon became angry and hurled his snuffbox at them.

Barbé-Marbois and Livingston began their negotiations, at first making rapid progress, for the rumors of the British fleet were indeed true. "They have twenty ships of war in the Gulf

of Mexico," said Napoleon. "I have not a moment to lose in putting it [Louisiana] out of their reach." However, Barbé-Marbois was a shrewd diplomat and he argued over the selling price. On April 12, Livingston lost patience and wrote Jefferson: "Only force can give us New Orleans. We must employ force. Let us first get possession of the country, and negotiate afterwards."

Monroe arrived in Paris that night, and he, Livingston, and the French officials spent most of the next day working on a purchase treaty. Late in the afternoon the basic problems were settled, but it took three weeks to work out all the details. The Louisiana Purchase Treaty was officially dated April 30, 1803.

When Napoleon was informed that the work had been completed he said: "This accession of territory affirms forever the power of the United States, and I have just given England a maritime rival that sooner or later will lay low her pride." His prophecy came true during the War of 1812.

The Americans were well satisfied with their bargain. After they had signed the agreements, Livingston said: "We have lived long, but this is the noblest work of our whole lives. . . . From this day the United States will take their place among the powers of the first rank. . . . The instruments which we have just signed will cause no tears to be shed; they prepare ages of happiness for innumerable generations of human creatures."

Who was responsible for the purchase of Louisiana? Credit should be given to President Jefferson, Secretary of State James Madison, Minister Livingston, and Monroe, but Livingston earned most of the credit for the negotiations. He had proven to be a discreet and zealous diplomat, and one of the French ministers said that he was the most persistent negotiator he had ever met. The man really responsible for the Louisiana Purchase, however, was Napoleon, for his decision to sell had made it possible.

The news of the purchase of Louisiana reached the United States on July 3, 1803. It was a good Fourth of July present for the young republic.

The Cost of Louisiana. The United States agreed to pay France 60,000,000 francs, or about $11,250,000, for Louisiana. In addition, the United States promised to pay the claims which certain of her citizens held against France, these claims to be limited to 20,000,000 francs.

The United States did not have the $15,000,000 needed to pay for Louisiana in its treasury, for its total annual income at this time was only about $10,000,000. Jefferson and the other officials, therefore, arranged to borrow the money from a British banking firm and from a Dutch banking firm, the rate of interest being fixed at 6 per cent. One-third of the principal was to be paid in 1819 and the remainder the two following years. Including the interest, the total cost of Louisiana was nearly $27,000,000.

France in Possession of Louisiana. It will be remembered that Laussat had already come to Louisiana to take possession for France. Although it had soon become known in Louisiana that the colony had been purchased by the United States, Laussat decided that France should take possession of Louisiana, even if it would be for only a short period.

The summer of 1803 passed and fall came. The cane-grinding season started. Finally Laussat and the Spanish officials agreed that France should take formal possession of Louisiana on November 30.

At noon on this day the Spanish

Governor took his place on a platform in the council room of the Cabildo at New Orleans. The legal documents were read and signed, and the keys of the city and of the forts were handed to Laussat on a silver platter. Then the officials went to the balcony and watched the Spanish flag being hauled down and the flag of France take its place.

Laussat immediately destroyed all traces of the Spanish government. He abolished the *Cabildo* and removed all the Spanish officials from their offices. He restored the laws of France and appointed Louisiana French Creoles to all the offices throughout the colony.

On December 1 Laussat gave a great fete "in honor of the French flag." A banquet was served to some seventy-five French, Spanish and American guests. Toasts were drunk to France, to Spain and to the United States. A final toast was drunk to the ladies present. Then the dinner guests went into the ballroom where over two hundred people waited for the dancing to begin.

During the next twenty days banquet followed banquet and ball followed ball. One of the banquets is supposed to have lasted for about twelve hours and during it more than twenty different kinds of gumbo were served.

The United States Takes Possession of Louisiana. President Jefferson selected General James Wilkinson and Governor William C. C. Claiborne of Mississippi Territory to take posses-

sion of Louisiana for the United States. General Wilkinson spent several weeks gathering a small military force at Fort Adams, in the southwestern corner of Mississippi. The American troops finally arrived outside New Orleans on December 17, and after several conferences with Laussat, December 20 was fixed as the date for the transfer of Louisiana to the United States.

The American troops marched into the city to what is now Jackson Square and stood fronting the Cabildo, where the ceremony was conducted with great pomp and military display.

Laussat later wrote a description of the scene: "The beautiful women and fashionable men of the city adorned all the balconies of the square. The Spanish officers were distinguishable in the crowd by their plumes. . . . The eleven galleries of the city hall were filled with beauties." The various formalities and the signing of documents took place in the council room of the Cabildo, after which the officials stepped onto the balcony and watched the French tricolor slowly lowered. The striped and starred American banner rose in its place. The audience was silent and nothing was heard but the deep rolling of drums. When the American flag reached the top of the flagpole the American soldiers broke forth with wild cheers, while the cannons roared and the rifles cracked out in salute.

Late that night William C. C. Claiborne wrote to President James Madison: "The Standard of my Country was this day unfurled here amidst the

The United States takes possession of
Louisiana.

123

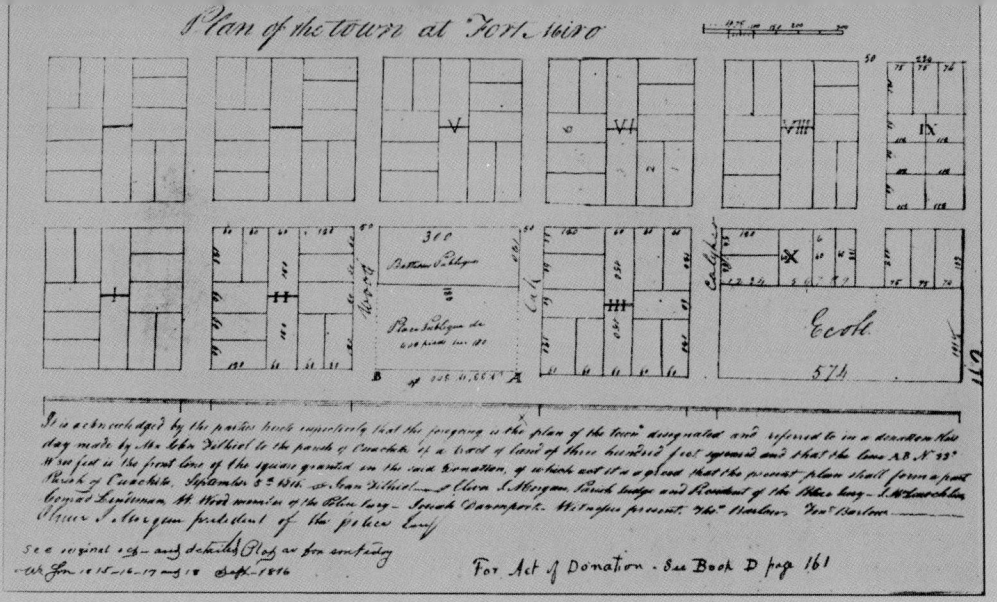

Plan of Fort Miro (Monroe) at the end of the Territorial period

reiterated acclamations of thousands. ... the Government of the United States is received with joy and gratitude by the people."

Attitude of the French Creoles Toward the Purchase. Many of the French Creoles had shown little enthusiasm when their colony was returned to France; more of them showed even less enthusiasm when they heard that Louisiana had been sold by France to the United States. Americans were strangers to them. They spoke another language and had different social and political customs. It would be many years before the American form of democratic government and American ways of life would become really appreciated by them.

French and Spanish Officials Remain in Louisiana. Laussat remained only about four months after the United States took possession of Louisiana. During this period he was occupied with listing and selling the property that belonged to France.

Some of the Spanish officials also remained in Louisiana, including former Governor Casa Calvo. Governor Claiborne feared that they planned to stir up trouble along the western border of Louisiana and finally ordered them to leave. In February, 1806, Claiborne sent Casa Calvo a passport with "best wishes for the health and happiness of the nobleman whose presence has become so unacceptable." Casa Calvo left Louisiana, so it was said, "full of wrath and indignation."

14. FROM TERRITORY TO STATE

Louisiana in 1803. The purchase of Louisiana almost doubled the land area of the United States. At that time the young nation totaled a little over 900,000 square miles. The purchase added another 875,000 square miles of territory, an area which included the entire western side of the Mississippi Valley and the Isle of Orleans. It was larger than the combined countries of Great Britain, Germany, Italy, Portugal, and Spain and was seven times the size of Great Britain and Ireland.

It was one of the richest areas in the entire world, with agricultural and ranching lands, large tracts of timberland, and stores of minerals, oil, and natural gas. While many of these natural resources were not known at that time, everyone realized the value of Louisiana. Laussat had written back to France that the Americans "would have given $50,000,000 rather than not possess it." He prophesied that within a few years much of the area would be in a state of cultivation and that New Orleans would have grown into a port with a population of from 30,000 to 50,000.

At that time the population of the area of present-day Louisiana was only about 50,000. New Orleans, the largest city, had some 10,000 people, of whom nearly half were free Negroes or slaves. The rest of the Louisiana Purchase territory had comparatively few inhabitants, and most of these people lived along the Mississippi, Missouri, or other rivers.

New Orleans then still did not suggest the great city of our own day. The city extended only a short distance above and below what is now the Vieux Carré section, which had a combination earth and wooden palisade wall around it. There were five forts, one at each corner and one in the center of the side opposite the river. The walls and the forts, however, had not been kept in repair and were in bad condition. The rusty guns were mounted on dilapidated wooden carriages and the sentinels stood guard at hingeless gates. During the winter of 1803-1804, when the season was exceptionally cold and firewood scarce and expensive, the poorer citizens almost demolished the wooden portions of the fortifications.

The drainage ditches on either side

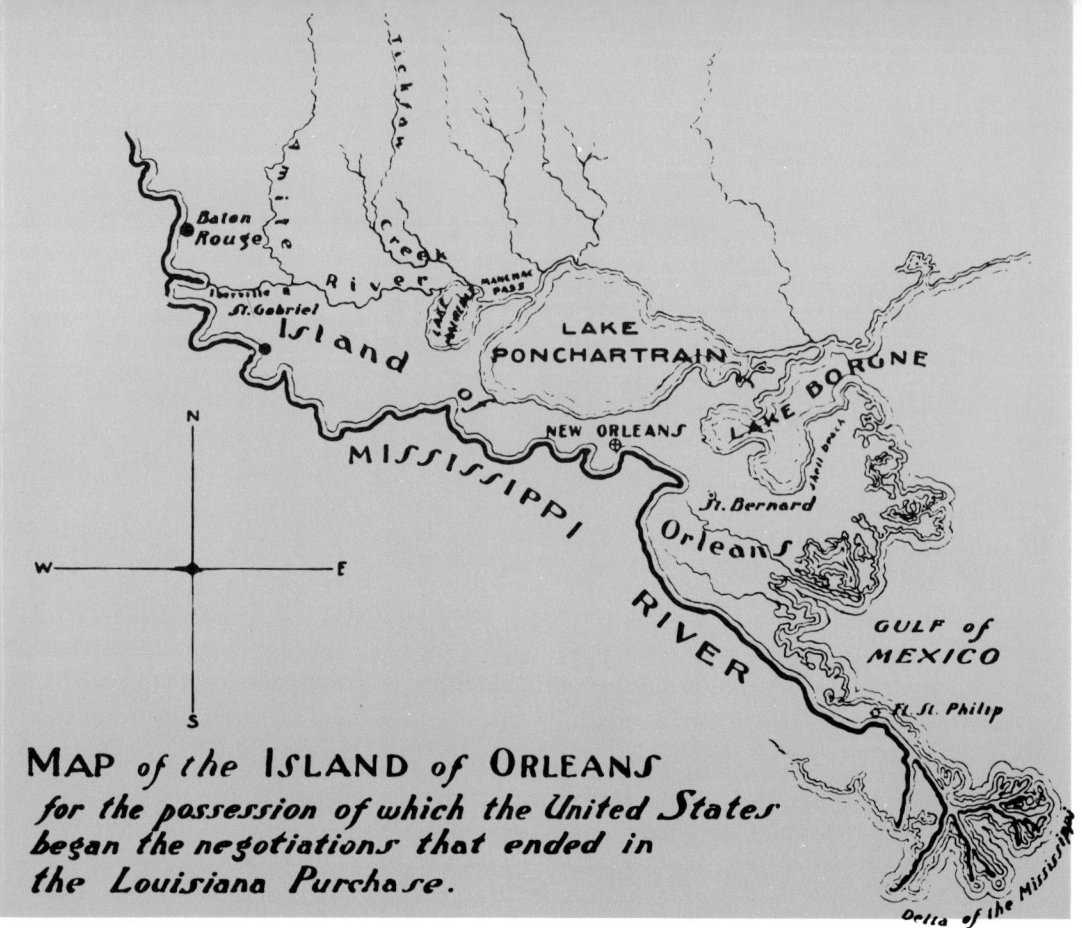

MAP of the ISLAND of ORLEANS
for the possession of which the United States
began the negotiations that ended in
the Louisiana Purchase.

Map 14—The Isle of Orleans. From an
old map.

of the streets had partially filled up
with dirt and rubbish and the little
bridges across them were in bad condition. The streets were unpaved and
were littered with trash and garbage,
and the air reeked with foul odors.
The wooden buildings and the
wooden doors and window shutters of
the brick houses and stores were generally unpainted. Despite its appearance, however, New Orleans compared
favorably with most Latin American,
French, or Spanish towns of its size at
this time.

There were only a few business
houses. These included four or five
general stores, a trio of Scottish banks,
one German business firm, and eight
or ten commission houses which had
been opened by Americans from New
York, Philadelphia, and Baltimore.
However, the people of New Orleans
enjoyed many luxuries, despite the
fact that they lived in a small city. The
shops carried quantities of Malaga,
Bordeaux, and Madeira wines, olive
oil, liqueurs, and such items as
brandied fruits, anchovies, raisins,

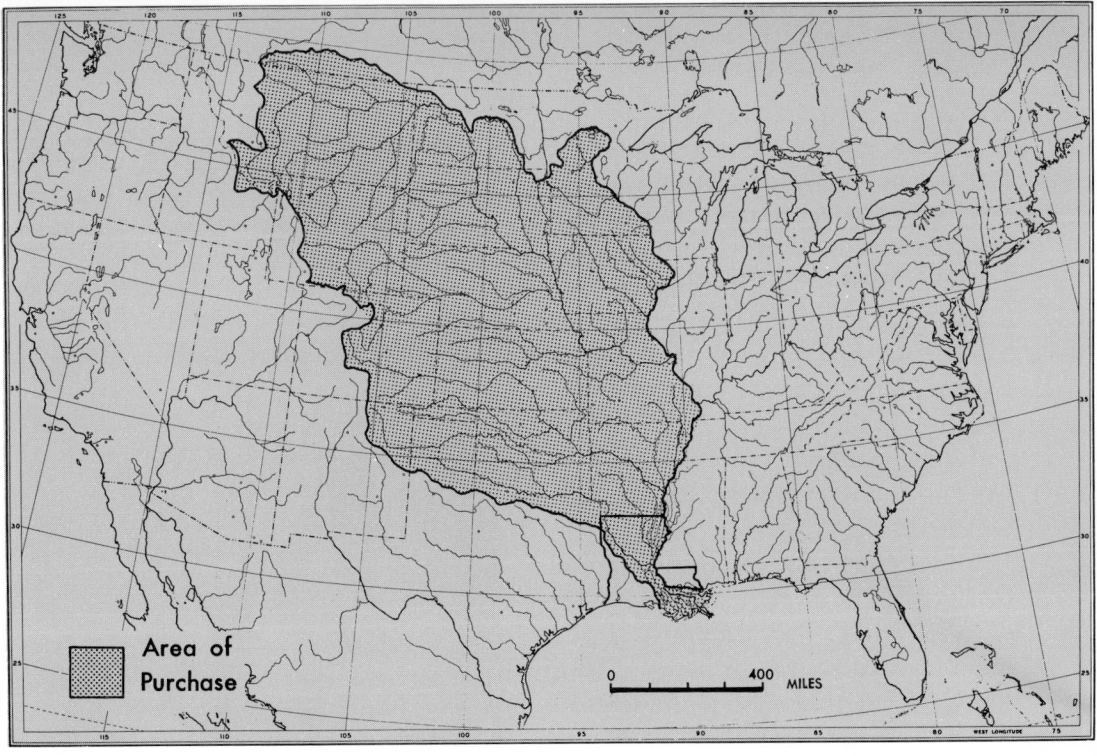

Map 15—The Louisiana Purchase,
1803

cheese, sausages, prunes, and almonds. Various types of expensive clothing materials could be purchased, as could home furnishings, jewelry, and other personal accessories. The women wore silk for balls and similar social occasions and brightly colored calicoes and muslins for everyday wear. The men wore the heavy clothing of Europe, with their "heads sunk in high collars, arms and hands lost in long sleeves." Their chins were buried in triple cravats and their legs were encased in high boots. Just as in Spanish or French colonial days, the children were dressed like their parents.

There were only a few other towns in Louisiana proper, and these were very small. Among them were Natchitoches, Opelousas, Baton Rouge, St. Martinville, and Monroe. Most people lived in what is now the southeastern one-fourth of the state. Only hunters, trappers, and a few pioneer farmers lived in the other sections, except for those planters and farmers who lived in the vicinity of Monroe and Natchitoches.

The people of Louisiana were of many nationalities. As well as the French and Spanish Creoles, there were Germans who lived along the Mississippi above and below New Orleans. The Acadians lived along Bayous Lafourche, Teche, Vermilion, and in other scattered places. *Isleños* from the Canary Islands made a living from fishing and trapping in South Louisi-

127

ana, from east of the mouth of the Mississippi to Bayou Teche. Americans were concentrated in New Orleans and in the vicinity of Opelousas and Fort Miro. French refugees from the West Indies had been given grants in northeast Louisiana and along Bayou Teche. Many farmers, planters, and city dwellers owned Negro slaves, and a large number of free Negroes lived in the towns, especially in New Orleans.

The French and Spanish Creoles looked with disfavor upon these other peoples. They were Catholics, while the majority of the Americans and British were Protestants. The Creoles spoke French and Spanish, while the Americans and British spoke English, and the Creole folkways and habits of living were quite different. They were very proud, enjoyed their leisure time, were carefree and easygoing. Governor Claiborne wrote that the planters were wealthy and had "luxurious and expensive" tastes. He also wrote that many of the Creoles were "deplorably uninformed" because the Spanish and French governments had not encouraged public education. The Americans and British were much more democratic, more aggressive in economic matters, and had a bustling enthusiasm.

A few years after this time, when young Alexander Porter planned to move to Louisiana to practice law, he met General Andrew Jackson. The General advised him: "And remember, Alick, you are going to a new country. . . . You will find a different people from those you have grown

William C. C. Claiborne

among, and you must study their natures, and accommodate yourself to them." Not all Americans who came to Louisiana during those early years had this good advice, and many of them were convinced of the backwardness and stupidity of the native Louisianians.

William C. C. Claiborne. William C. C. Claiborne had been one of the two commissioners who took possession of Louisiana for the United States. From

December 20, 1803, until March 26, 1804, he was in charge of the civil affairs of the colony while General James Wilkinson was in command of the army.

During this period President Jefferson gave much thought to whom he should appoint as first Governor when Louisiana was made into a territory. He seriously considered the Marquis de Lafayette, the French nobleman who had so greatly aided the United States during the Revolution. Lafayette, however, was not able to accept the position, so Claiborne was named the first Governor of Louisiana.

Like his predecessors, Claiborne faced many problems. The French and Spanish Louisianians were not acquainted with democratic government and had to be educated to its principles. The old French and Spanish customs must be changed slowly, however, for people do not change their political habits quickly. Many Creoles did not like the Americans, their ideas of government, or their customs. About this time, for example, a small earthquake interrupted one of the New Orleans balls. An old Creole gentleman remarked sarcastically, as he glanced at the Americans present: "It was not in Spanish times or the French that the amusements of the ladies were interfered with."

However, Claiborne was able to write to Jefferson that the people were doing their best to understand the Americans and that the various problems could be solved.

Government of Territorial Louisiana. From March 26, 1804, until March 2, 1805, Louisiana was an "unorganized" territory of the United States. It was called the Territory of Orleans. The rest of the Louisiana Purchase was called the District of Louisiana.

Claiborne was appointed Governor by the President for a three-year term. He commanded the militia, granted pardons, and appointed all local officials. The President appointed a Secretary of the Territory for a four-year term, and he also appointed a thirteen-member Legislative Council, a federal District Judge, and three judges of the Superior Court.

On March 2, 1805, Louisiana was made into an "organized" territory. Under this new form of government a Legislature was added, which was composed of a Legislative Council of five members appointed by the President and a twenty-five-member lower house elected by the people. This form of government lasted until Louisiana became a state in 1812.

Claiborne was Governor during the entire period.

Local Government. At the first meeting of the Legislative Council in 1804, Louisiana had been divided into twelve counties. They were Acadia, Atakapas, Concordia, German Coast, Iberville, Lafourche, Natchitoches, Opelousas, Orleans, Ouachita, Pointe Coupee, and Rapides. In 1806 the territorial Legislature also divided the Territory of Orleans into nineteen parishes. These first parishes were

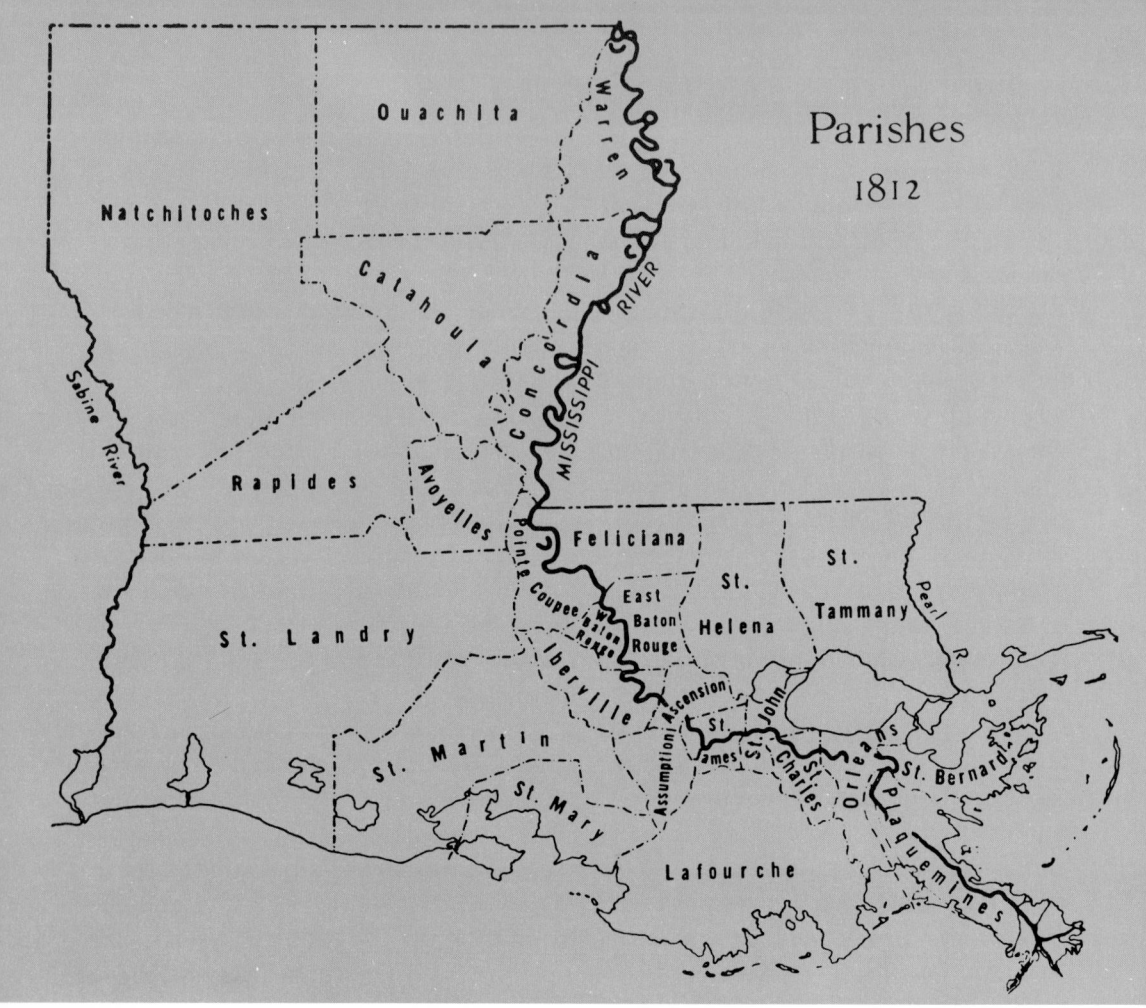

Map 16—Louisiana parishes, 1812

Ascension, Assumption, Atakapas, Avoyelles, Baton Rouge, Concordia, Iberville, Lafourche Interior, Natchitoches, Orleans, Ouachita, Plaquemines, Pointe Coupee, Rapides, St. Bernard, St. Charles, St. James, St. John the Baptist, and St. Landry. The term "parishes" was used because it was the old Spanish custom. Both counties and parishes were in existence in Louisiana local government until

1845, when the counties went out of existence. All the other states are divided into counties instead of parishes.

The parishes had several local officials such as judges, sheriffs, coroners, clerks, treasurers, and justices of the peace. They had Police Juries, which were called by this name because they had twelve members as do ordinary juries. At first the Police Juries only advised the parish judges, but in 1811 they became the governing bodies of the parishes and the members were elected by the people.

The parish officials handled most local governmental problems. They collected taxes and spent the monies collected, built roads and levees, and kept peace and order. As time passed the people of territorial Louisiana, who had never before had a part in their local government, began to learn how to govern themselves. Louisiana would soon be ready for statehood.

Territorial Law. Claiborne kept in force most of the old Spanish laws which were not in conflict with those of the United States. In 1805 the territorial Legislature passed a law which defined various crimes, but a code of criminal law was never passed. A code of civil law was adopted in 1808.

All laws of territorial Louisiana were written in both French and English, and all the business of the courts was conducted in these two languages. The membership of the juries had to be divided among those who spoke French and those citizens who spoke English.

Problems of Governor Claiborne. Claiborne was only twenty-eight years of age when he became Governor, but he had sound and mature judgment. In his first speech to the people of Louisiana he promised that he would promote their general welfare and work for the good of the Territory.

The western part of Louisiana caused Claiborne much anxiety. The western boundary of the Louisiana Purchase had not been definitely fixed, and the Spanish in Texas considered it to be somewhere east of the Calcasieu River. Americans claimed the Sabine River as the boundary. The disputed land between the Sabine and the Calcasieu rivers became generally known as the Sabine Strip, although it was sometimes called the Neutral Ground. Its northeastern limits ran north-northwestward from the source of the Calcasieu a few miles west of Natchitoches to Bayou Pierre, and up that bayou to the 32nd parallel. The northern boundary was the 32nd parallel.

The Spanish kept an army in eastern Texas and held their Louisiana settlements, which were only a few miles west of Natchitoches. The largest of these posts, Los Adaes, was the tip of the wedge which they thrust into Louisiana. Sometimes their army patrols came to the very outskirts of Natchitoches.

The Sabine Strip became a kind of "No Man's Land," and to it went large numbers of lawless people. The region became unsafe for traders on their way to Texas or on the return trips to Louisiana—robberies and even murders were frequent.

It was not long before the United States established a military post at Natchitoches to patrol the area and to keep the Spanish from further penetrating into Louisiana.

The Indians who still lived in northern and western Louisiana constituted another problem for Claiborne. In

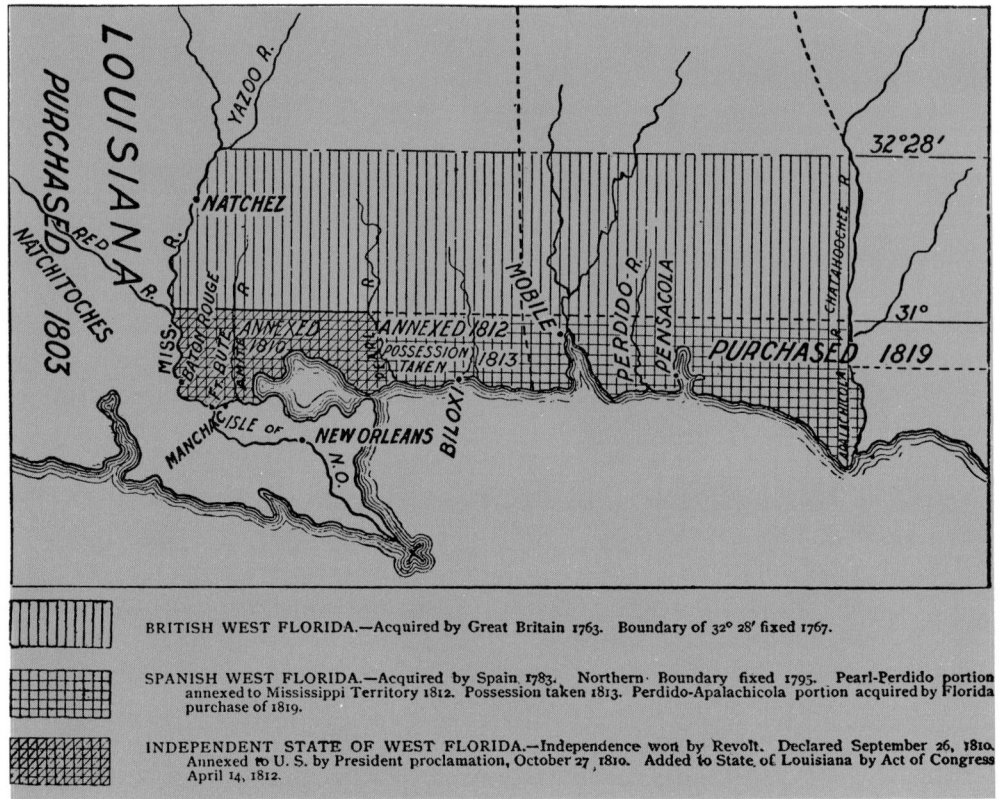

BRITISH WEST FLORIDA.—Acquired by Great Britain 1763. Boundary of 32° 28' fixed 1767.

SPANISH WEST FLORIDA.—Acquired by Spain 1783. Northern Boundary fixed 1795. Pearl-Perdido portion annexed to Mississippi Territory 1812. Possession taken 1813. Perdido-Apalachicola portion acquired by Florida purchase of 1819.

INDEPENDENT STATE OF WEST FLORIDA.—Independence won by Revolt. Declared September 26, 1810. Annexed to U. S. by President proclamation, October 27, 1810. Added to State of Louisiana by Act of Congress April 14, 1812.

Map 17—West Florida. The extent of the areas controlled by Britain, Spain, and the boundaries of the Independent State of West Florida.

1805 the United States appointed Dr. John Sibley as the Indian agent. He had settled in Natchitoches two years before and had become well acquainted with the Indians of that area. Dr. Sibley held many conferences with the various chiefs, helped them in their trading operations, and prevented white men from taking unfair advantage of them.

At various times before 1812 several Americans planned expeditions to invade Texas and take it from the Spanish. This was against American law, so it was Claiborne's duty to prevent such expeditions from being organized. Only a few of them succeeded in crossing the Sabine River and none of them was successful in capturing Texas.

Many of the land titles which had been granted by the French and Spanish were not clearly written or did not give exact boundaries. This was a serious obstacle both for the native Louisianians and the Americans who were coming into Louisiana.

In 1806 and 1807 it was rumored in Louisiana that Aaron Burr, a former Vice-President of the United States, was conspiring to start a revolution in the western part of the country. For some months everyone in Louisiana was much excited about this plot, but finally Burr was captured near Natchez, Mississippi. He was tried for treason, but acquitted.

Keeping order in Louisiana was another difficulty. In 1806 a police force, called the *garde de ville,* or city guard, was organized for the City of New Orleans. The men were armed with short spears and heavy swords when they patrolled the streets.

The West Florida Revolution, 1810. What is now the Florida Parishes was not then a part of Louisiana. This region still belonged to Spain, but the people, who were mostly Americans and British, wanted a more democratic government. In 1810 they revolted against Spain, captured the Spanish fort at Baton Rouge, and organized a republic. The Free State of West Florida existed for only a few weeks, for the Florida Parishes were soon occupied by the United States.

Economic Life. When the people of the United States learned that Louisiana would be admitted into the Union after it had sufficient population and when the Creoles had learned the ways of democratic government, many of them moved to Louisiana. Soon Louisiana agriculture, business, trade, and commerce were booming. New Orleans and the other towns began to grow and new towns, such as Donaldsonville, were organized.

The Mississippi River was soon filled with boats of all descriptions carrying goods down to the people of Louisiana or carrying Louisiana's products upstream. The first river steamboat arrived in New Orleans in 1812, beginning the age of the great Mississippi steamboats. Foreign trade also increased, for the United States did not impose restrictions such as had been set forth by the French and Spanish.

The improved economic conditions created a need for banks, so the Bank of Louisiana was organized in 1805, and the Bank of Orleans and the Planters' Bank in 1811.

New roads became necessary. Although these roads were only narrow dirt trails winding through the swamps and forests, filled with holes and tree stumps, they greatly aided the people in traveling and in hauling their products. One of these roads ran from Madisonville, opposite New Orleans on Lake Pontchartrain, to Natchez. Two roads ran to Texas. One of these, sometimes called the Texas Road, went west from Vidalia through

Alexandria and Natchitoches. The other, called the Nolan Road, went westward from Alexandria. Other shorter roads followed the rivers and streams or cut across the country to various towns and villages.

Mail service was irregular, at first being carried by men on horseback and later by stagecoaches. Advertisements in the newspapers or handbills usually announced the departure of the mail. In 1808, for example, it was announced: "An express will leave this office for Natchitoches (via Lafourche) on Thursday next, the 16th inst. at 8 o'clock A.M. The citizens are requested to have their letters in the Post-Office on Wednesday next at Sun set, at which time the mail will close. Post Office, New Orleans, March 7, 1808." By the end of the territorial period mail routes had been established throughout Louisiana.

Growth of Culture. Just before the United States took possession of Louisiana, President Jefferson sent a description of Louisiana to Congress. In it he said: "There are no colleges, and but one public school, which is in New Orleans." He proceeded to say that there were only a few private schools, where the pupils were taught only in the Spanish language. He said that not more than half the people could read and write and that not more than two hundred could do it well. But he explained that the Louisianians were "endowed with a natural genius" and that they had "an uncommon facility

of learning whatever they undertake."

The Louisiana Creoles, however, did not favor public education. Most of them were Catholics and they preferred schools operated by their church. They did not agree with the American ideal of the separation of Church and State, so public education made little progress during the territorial period.

Governor Claiborne believed in public education, for he saw that the private schools had not educated a large enough percentage of the people. He said that there should be "a school in every neighborhood" and that it should be supported by public tax money. In 1805 an act was approved which provided for a system of secondary schools, and the next year a parish school system was authorized. In 1811 money was appropriated to each of the parishes for the purpose of organizing a public school, but by 1812 only three schools were in operation. Many years passed before public education became a reality in Louisiana.

The College of Orleans was authorized in 1805 and began operation a short time later. It was not really a college, as there were few courses of college grade. Boys were enrolled at the age of seven as "boarders" or as "day scholars." The historian Charles Gayarré has given a fascinating account of his education at the college and some good descriptions of the people there. Bruno was the Negro servant who at six o'clock every morning

Many Louisiana settlers rafted down
the Mississippi.

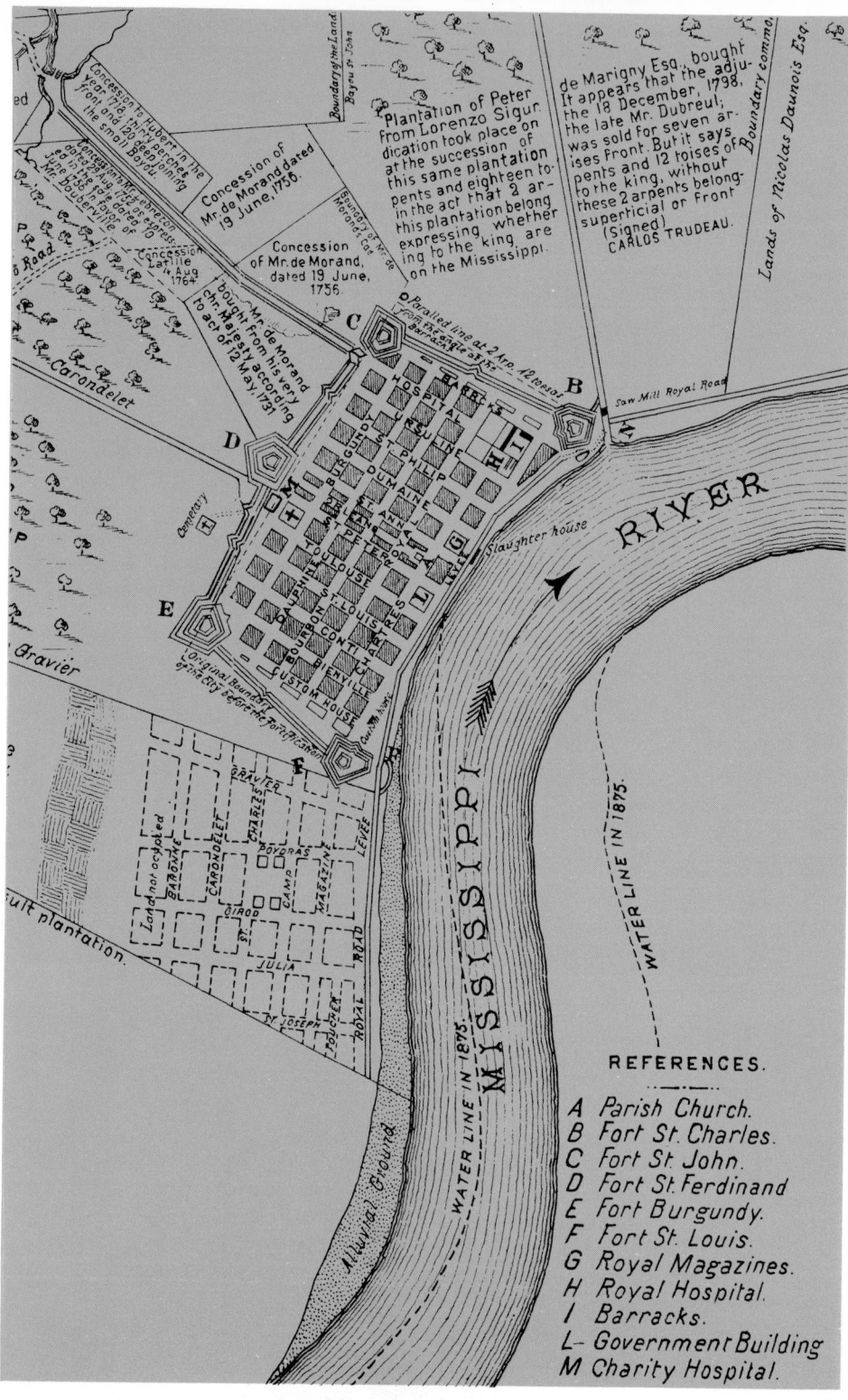

Map 18—New Orleans at the beginning of the American period

REFERENCES.

A Parish Church.
B Fort St. Charles.
C Fort St. John.
D Fort St. Ferdinand.
E Fort Burgundy.
F Fort St. Louis.
G Royal Magazines.
H Royal Hospital.
I Barracks.
L Government Building
M Charity Hospital.

handed to each boy his breakfast of a cup of coffee and a piece of dry bread. Vincent, the doorkeeper, had a crooked neck and a doleful face. Marengo, the cook, was ugly and ferocious in appearance.

The first newspaper of which there are copies still in existence, *Le Moniteur de la Louisiane*, had been established during the late years of the Spanish period. The second newspaper was *Le Télégraphe,* founded in 1803. *La Lanterne Magique (The Magic Lantern)* began publication in 1808 but lasted hardly a year. Printed in both French and English, it criticized the newly established American government. The first English-language newspaper was the *Louisiana Gazette,* which began publication in 1804 and had for its motto "American Commerce and Freedom."

Amateur theatrical performances had been given in Louisiana during the Spanish period, but it was not long after the arrival of the Americans that theatrical societies and several small theaters were established. Plays and various other forms of entertainment were presented infrequently, many of them for charitable purposes. In 1812, for example, the *Louisiana Gazette* announced the presentation of a play titled *The Weathercock.* Box seats cost $1.50, while seats in the pit and the gallery were $1.00. The doors opened at 5 P.M. with the "curtains positively to rise at 6 o'clock."

Social Life. Social life continued much as it had during the French and Spanish colonial periods, for the Creoles loved social gatherings and entertainments of all kinds. They particularly loved their balls and for a short period believed that the Americans would stop them, but Governor Claiborne announced that the balls would continue. There were some problems, however, for the Americans wanted American music, while the Creoles wanted French or Spanish music. It soon became the custom for the musicians to alternate "Hail Columbia" with Creole songs, and after each number the Americans would yell, "Hurrah for the United States," while the Creoles would yell, "*Vive la République.*"

Louisiana Admitted as a State. Before Louisiana was purchased, President Jefferson had written to a friend telling of his plans for Louisiana. "Our policy will be, to form New Orleans, and the country on both sides of it on the Gulf of Mexico, into a state." This became the official American policy toward Louisiana.

Early in 1811 a Federal law authorized the Louisianians to draft a state constitution. Delegates to a constitutional convention were elected.

The convention met at Tremoulet's Coffee House in New Orleans in November, 1811. Julian Poydras, now an influential New Orleans merchant, was elected president of the convention. The new state constitution was approved by Congress in April, 1812.

135

After the Louisiana Purchase, wagon trains rolled into the new lands in increasing numbers. From an old print.

Many of the newly arrived Americans in Louisiana hoped that the new state would be named after Thomas Jefferson. But Louis de Blanc de St. Denis, a member of the convention from Atakapas, said that if this were done he would "arm himself with a barrel of powder and blow up the con-

136

vention." Nothing further was said about the matter.

William C. C. Claiborne was elected Governor and Louisiana was admitted into the United States as the eighteenth state on April 30, 1812, the ninth anniversary of the Louisiana Purchase.

15. LOUISIANA AND THE WAR OF 1812

The War of 1812. Thirty-two days after Louisiana was admitted into the Union as a state, President James Madison recommended that the Congress of the United States declare war against Great Britain. Congress debated the question for a little over two weeks; then, on June 18, the act declaring war was passed and signed by the President.

Great Britain had not treated the young Republic as an equal nation after the American Revolution. Her ships stopped American merchantmen on the high seas and took American sailors from them. She kept military posts on American soil near the Great Lakes, blockaded American ports, and urged the Indians to make war upon the western settlers. She hindered American trade with France and other European countries. On the other hand, many Americans, who were called War Hawks and who were interested in the development of western lands and in securing Canada for the United States, wanted a war with the British.

At this time the United States was not prepared to fight a war. The country had only a small army. The people were not unified, for many citizens of New England and New York opposed the war. The national treasury did not have enough money to furnish the necessary funds.

The war on land went against the United States. General Isaac Hull surrendered Detroit, and the garrison at Fort Dearborn (Chicago) was massacred when it tried to evacuate the fort. An attempt to invade Canada near Niagara Falls failed, as did the attempt to capture Montreal. In 1814 the British invaded the Chesapeake Bay region and captured Washington, D. C., where they burned the capitol, the White House, and many other buildings.

It was a far different story on the sea. The American navy was young and its ships small, but the ships were fast and the seamen fired their cannon with deadly accuracy. During the early months of the war the navy won many victories and captured many British ships.

Louisiana and the War. Soon after the declaration of war, Governor Claiborne reorganized the Louisiana state militia. He traveled over the state getting better acquainted with the Creoles and urging their loyalty to the United States. It was not long before the Louisianians began to strengthen the white and free Negro militia companies for the defense of the state.

The British blockaded the mouth of the Mississippi River with two warships, which prevented merchant vessels from entering or leaving the port of New Orleans.

Encouraged by the Spanish and British, some of the Southern Indians took the warpath. General Andrew Jackson of Tennessee marched south with a small army to punish them and later occupied Mobile.

British agents attempted to secure the cooperation of the privateers who lived at Barataria. They proposed that Jean Laffite and his men join the British, but Laffite refused and sent their messages to Governor Claiborne. The British sent a military force to Pensacola and later attacked Jackson at Mobile. They landed marines and attacked Fort Bowyer from the rear while their fleet bombarded it from the bay, but the attack failed. Although the British lost over 230 men, Jackson lost less than 10. A short time later Jackson captured Pensacola.

British Plan to Attack New Orleans. New Orleans was the key to the entire Mississippi Valley, and if the British could capture the city they would gain control of the entire area. Vast quantities of products of all kinds, particularly cotton, sugar, and tobacco, would be taken. Furthermore, the British might then move northward up the Mississippi and occupy Mississippi Territory and the states of Kentucky and Tennessee. They might even add the territories further up the river to the British Empire. It was a prize worth taking, and the British anticipated little opposition from the Americans and none from the French and Spanish Creoles of Louisiana, who were not expected to fight.

In August, 1814, Colonel Edward Nicolls, the Commander of His Britannic Majesty's forces in the Floridas, issued a proclamation to the "NATIVES OF LOUISIANA." He offered to "liberate" the soil of Louisiana from the "faithless, imbecile government" of the United States. He would stop this "unjust and unnatural" war which Britain was fighting against "those brawlers for liberty." But most Louisianians did not believe Colonel Nicolls, and continued with preparations to defend their state.

The British Expedition. During the late summer and early fall of 1814 the British concentrated a large fleet and a strong army at the island of Jamaica in the West Indies. This fleet of over fifty ships was commanded by Vice-Admiral Sir Alexander Cochrane, while the army of about ten thousand soldiers was led by General Sir Edward

138

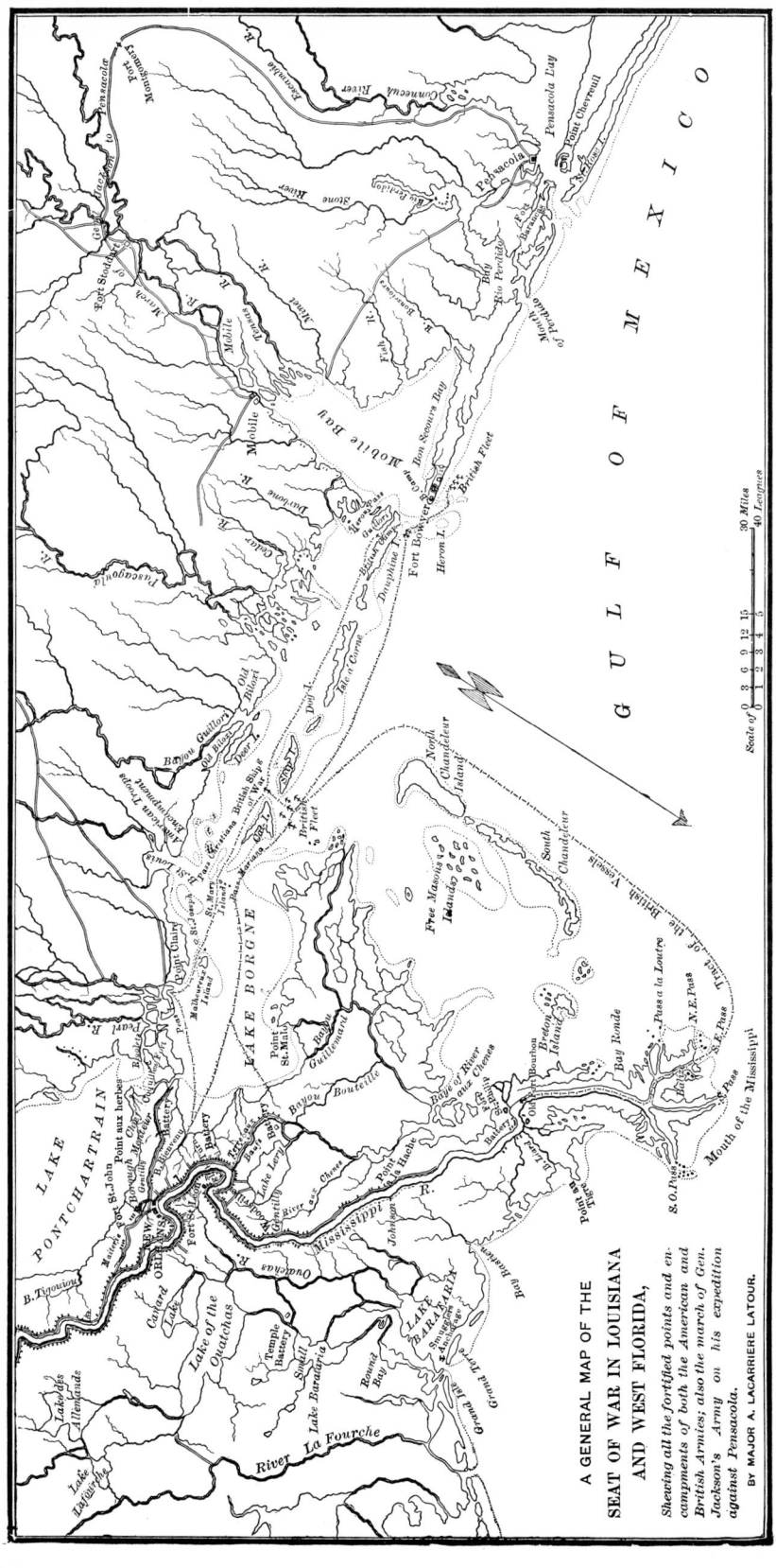

A GENERAL MAP OF THE

SEAT OF WAR IN LOUISIANA
AND WEST FLORIDA,

*Shewing all the fortified points and en-
campments of both the American and
British Armies; also the march of Gen.
Jackson's Army on his expedition
against Pensacola.*

BY MAJOR A. LACARRIERE LATOUR.

Map 19—Seat of war in Louisiana

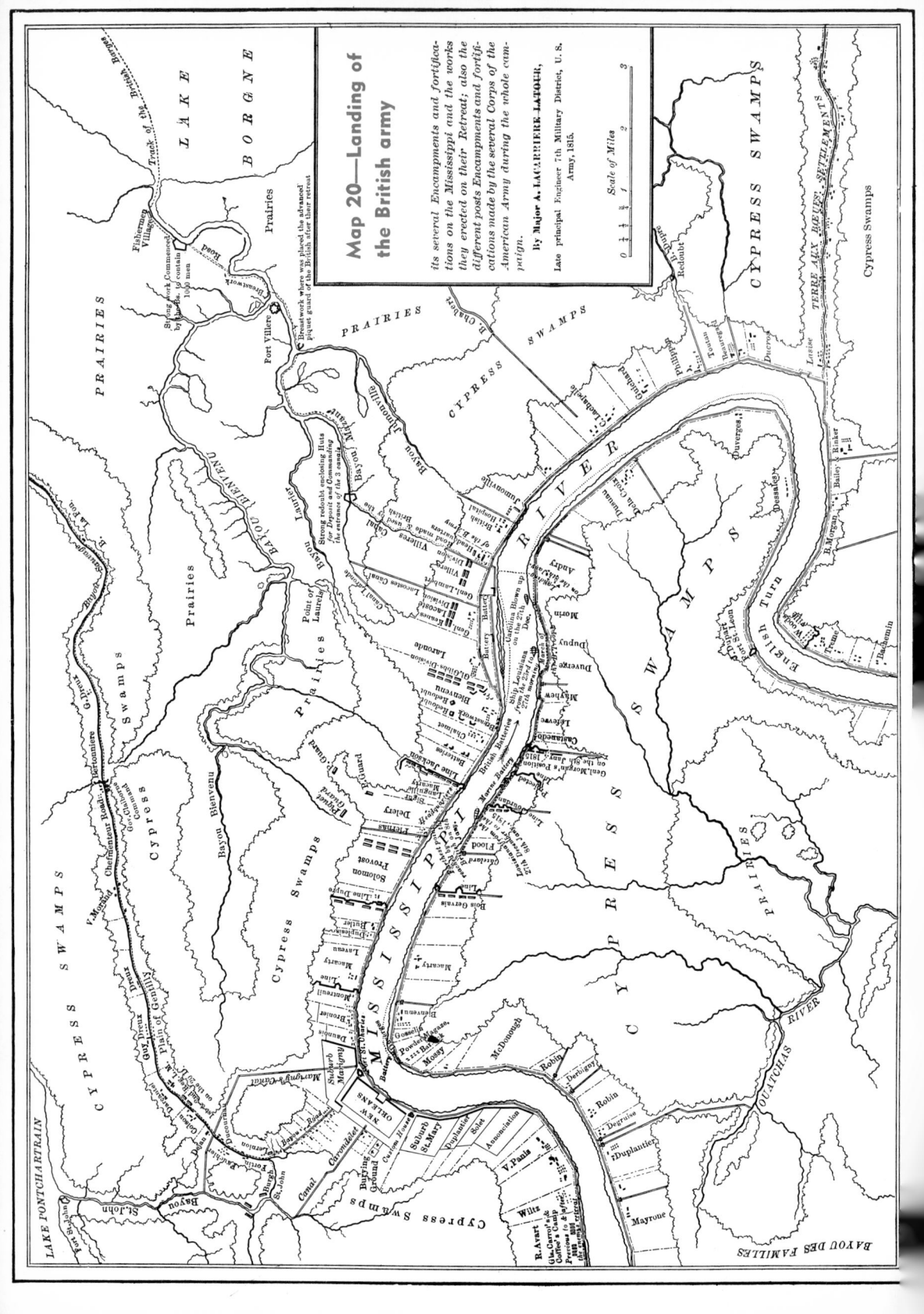

Map 20—Landing of
the British army

its several Encampments and fortifications on the Mississippi and the works they erected on their Retreat; also the different posts Encampments and fortifications made by the several Corps of the American Army during the whole campaign.

By Major A. LACARRIÈRE LATOUR,
late principal Engineer 7th Military District, U. S. Army, 1815.

Scale of Miles

0   1   2   3

Pakenham. The expedition sailed from Jamaica in November, 1814, and the British were very confident of victory.

The British fleet first sailed to Pensacola. One of the Americans there immediately warned Master Commandant Daniel Patterson, who commanded a small American fleet then lying in Lake Borgne, that the British had arrived. He wrote that the object of the British was to capture New Orleans and that they had a strong fleet and a large and well-equipped army.

General Jackson started for New Orleans late in November with only a few men, moving along the Gulf Coast in order that he might "have a view of the points at which the enemy might effect a landing." He arrived at New Orleans on December 1.

Difficulty of Defending New Orleans. The American troops were widely scattered, some were in Alabama, some were in Mississippi, and a small detachment was stationed at Baton Rouge. A strong division of Tennessee militia was on the march and was expected to arrive at New Orleans about December 20. Another group of Kentucky militia would arrive about January 1. Meantime, the British fleet and army were sailing toward New Orleans.

Few preparations had been made for the defense of New Orleans. The Legislature had done very little and its members were quarreling among themselves. Some of the French Creoles had shown little enthusiasm and were distrustful of Jackson. They did not want to join the state militia, swore that they were Frenchmen not Americans, and claimed the protection of the French Consul at New Orleans. There were only small stores of weapons, powder, bullets, and the other supplies of war.

Jackson and Claiborne Work Together. General Jackson immediately went to work. At this time he was in his late forties, tall, lean, and straight of figure. His face was wrinkled and seamed; heavy brows shaded his bright eyes; his iron-gray hair bristled over his head. Although he was exhausted by exposure and he suffered from malaria, his face revealed his restless energy, his strong sense of purpose, and his stern patriotic devotion. He dressed in a small leather cap, a short blue coat, well-worn pants, and frayed, high boots. At first glance he was not imposing to the well-dressed, debonair Creoles, but they soon found out that he was a man of iron.

Jackson inspected Fort St. Philip below New Orleans and the shores of Lake Pontchartrain and Chef Menteur. He rapidly trained the militia units which Governor Claiborne had mobilized, fortified the banks of the Mississippi just below New Orleans, and erected an artillery battery at the Rigolets and another at the mouth of Bayou St. John. Gangs of slaves built earthworks near the city. Jackson and Claiborne accepted the services of the

General Andrew Jackson

Henry Miller Shreve, the founder of Shreveport.

Baratarians and pledged assistance in securing pardons for their past offenses against the government. Henry Miller Shreve, who had come down from Pennsylvania with the steamboat *Enterprise* and who later was to found the city of Shreveport, began to bring supplies to New Orleans from points up the Mississippi.

Governor Claiborne and General Jackson did their work well. Most of the people enthusiastically began to support the preparations for the defense of the state. The militia units drilled with grim purpose. One aged Louisiana mother wrote to the Governor: "My four sons are at the front with Andrew Jackson. I regret having no others to offer my country; I am bent under the load of years, but, if my services in caring for the wounded should be thought useful, command me, and in spite of age and distance I shall hasten to New Orleans." Louisianians soon felt more confident that their state could be defended.

But General Jackson was in a dilemma. Which approach to New Orleans would the British use? Would they approach from Barataria? Would they come up the Mississippi? Would they move by way of the Rigolets and Chef Menteur and then over high ground to the city? It was not long before Jackson knew the answer.

The Battle of Lake Borgne. On December 10 the British fleet sighted North Chandeleur Island, rounded the northern tip, and anchored in the channel between Cat and Ship islands. Here it was discovered by Lieutenant Thomas Ap Catesby Jones, who commanded six small American gunboats with 182 men. Three days later, the British ships sailed into Lake Borgne. The little American fleet stood fast, awaiting them.

The American ships were small and could sail in shallow water, where the large British ships could not follow them. The British therefore sent a squadron of small sloops of war with nearly twelve hundred men against Lieutenant Jones and his little fleet.

The American schooner *Sea Horse* was set on fire and blown up, and the rest of the ships withdrew further westward. Then the wind died and all the vessels became becalmed.

On December 14, 1814, the Battle of Lake Borgne was fought. It began about eleven o'clock in the morning. The British transferred their sailors and marines to boats and barges rowed by oarsmen, which were more maneuverable than the American ships. The American ship *Alligator* was taken; the other vessels fought on, but after a desperate fight they, too, were captured. The British lost about one hundred and seventy-five killed and wounded while the Americans lost six killed and thirty-five wounded.

The Battle of Lake Borgne gave the British control of Lake Borgne but it also delayed their advance upon New Orleans. This gave time for reinforcements to arrive there and for General Jackson to complete his plans for the defense of the city.

The Night Battle of December 23. After the Battle of Lake Borgne the British reorganized their fleet and army at Pea Island, near the mouth of Pearl River. On December 22 about sixteen hundred men, commanded by Colonel William Thornton, rowed across Lake Borgne in barges and the next morning landed at the mouth of Bayou Bienvenu. Thornton sent a detachment up Bayous Bienvenu and Laurier about five miles to the mouth

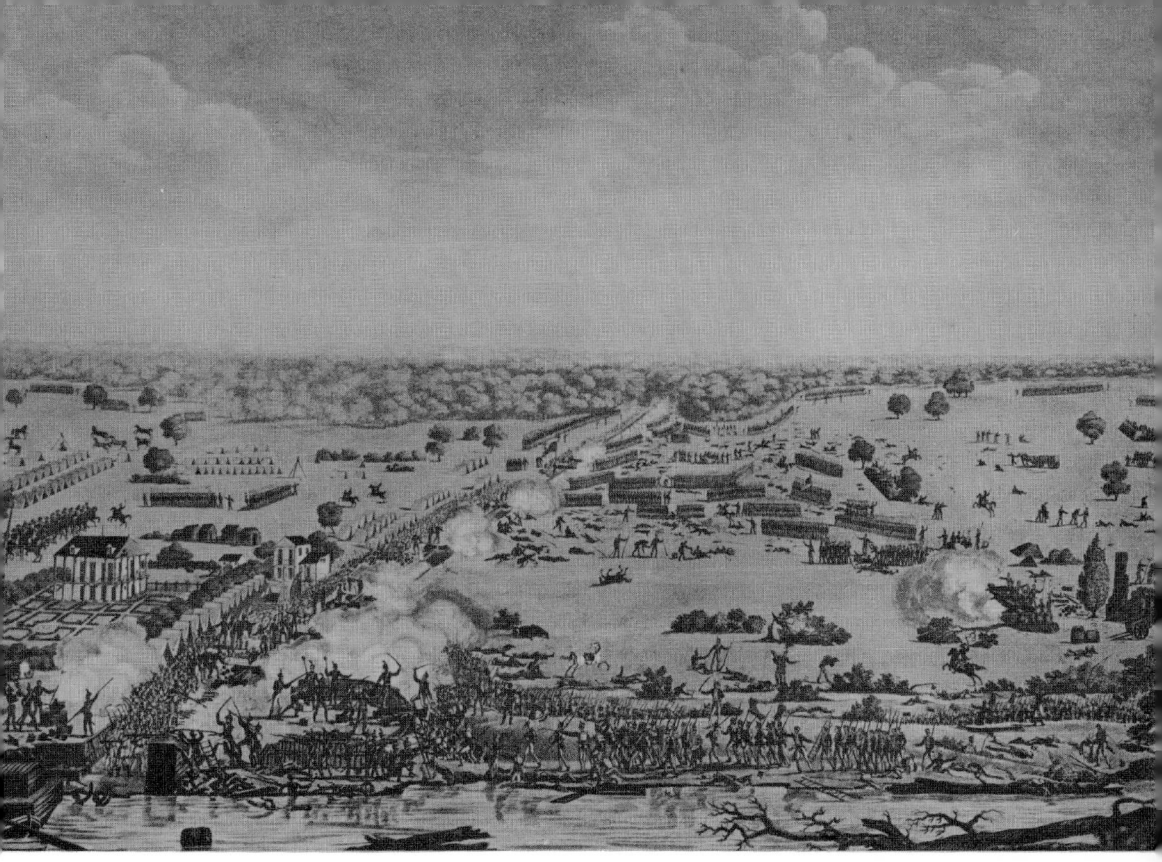

The Battle of New Orleans

FORTIER, **HISTORY OF LOUISIANA**

of Bayou Mazant, and then up this bayou about two miles to the Villeré Canal. The British followed the canal to the Villeré plantation, but Major Gabriel Villeré escaped to New Orleans to warn General Jackson that the British had landed.

The British raised the Union Jack from the treetops at the Villeré plantation, while their bands played "God Save the King." They distributed proclamations throughout the area, giving reasons why the people should withdraw their allegiance to the United States and join the British.

Jackson immediately ordered the American forces in New Orleans to gather at Fort St. Charles and then to march down the river about six miles to a place which had been selected by Major Arsene Latour.

As the Cathedral clock struck three, the American troops poured along the streets of the Vieux Carré singing "Yankee Doodle," the "Marseillaise," and other songs. Women and children crowded the balconies waving their hands while the old men stood on the banquettes waving their hats.

The troops rapidly assembled: the Bayou Sara Mounted Riflemen, Beale's Rifles in their blue hunting shirts, the free Negro militia. The five companies of the Bataillon d'Orléans, which had been stationed at the old Spanish fort out on Lake Pontchartrain, came panting in, after a run of six and a half miles. Major Thomas Hinds's daredevil Mississippi Dragoons followed. After them rode Colonel John Coffee and his Tennessee-Cavalry "dirty shirts," clad in their home-dyed, copper-colored pants, woolen hunting shirts, and coonskin caps, and wearing long knives and tomahawks stuck in their belts. A band of about a hundred Choctaw Indians in their war paint came next, and the regular troops followed. Jackson swung his hat and the army marched off at the double-quick down the river.

The Americans soon reached the place selected by Latour. It was a narrow strip of solid ground about 1,500 yards wide between the Mississippi and the swamp. Across it was an abandoned drainage canal which marked the boundary of the Chalmette and Rodriguez plantations. The soldiers immediately began to throw up a breastwork on the New Orleans side of the canal.

Jackson decided to attack the British, who lay about two miles farther on, that night, saying, "By the Eternal, they shall not sleep on our soil!"

The Americans struck the British outposts at eight o'clock and in a furious attack drove them back. The British became confused and gathered in small groups, where the Americans attacked them with gun-butts, knives, and even fists. At four o'clock the next morning Jackson withdrew to his line of breastworks.

The British lost over 250, killed, wounded, and missing, while the American loss was slightly over 200. Jackson had saved New Orleans from immediate capture by the British, but the danger was not yet past, for the enemy was still landing troops.

The Grand Reconnaissance. For five days the British did not attack. Meanwhile, both armies celebrated Christmas and the British soldiers rejoiced at the arrival of their commander, General Sir Edward Pakenham. He would lead them to victory against the Americans, who were lying so smugly behind their earthworks.

On the morning of December 28, Pakenham ordered his troops forward to feel out the American defenses and if possible to pierce their line and move on toward New Orleans. The British advanced in solid columns, supported by their artillery. The Americans had fewer cannon than the enemy, but they had been strengthened only a few hours earlier by the arrival of "Capitaine" Dominique You, Renato Beluche, and the rest of Jean Laffite's Baratarians. The Baratarians were excellent artillerists.

The British attack failed because of the accurate fire of the American riflemen and artillerists. One of the Englishmen wrote that "the Americans are excellent marksmen as well with artillery as with rifles," and that after the

144

Jean Laffite. From an old drawing

battle the English soldiers felt "both shame and indignation."

Pakenham decided to strengthen his batteries of artillery with naval guns from the fleet before attacking the Americans again.

The Artillery Battle of New Year's Day. The morning of New Year's Day was foggy and, believing that the British would not attack, the Creoles asked to have a grand review of the army. Jackson consented, and the bands began to play and the Americans to parade up and down across the open field. Then the fog lifted and a blast from twenty-four British heavy cannon broke over the line. All was confusion

as the Americans ran back to their breastworks to man their fifteen guns.

A British battery centered its fire against Dominique You and the Baratarians who were manning one battery. You was wounded in the arm by a cannon shot, but he had the arm bandaged, and then yelled, "I will pay them for that!" Soon one of his guns knocked to pieces the carriage of the gun which had wounded him. The fighting had begun about eight o'clock in the morning. It lasted until about one in the afternoon, when the British artillerists abandoned their guns. One of their junior officers wrote: "Never was any failure more remarkable. . . . The sun, as if ashamed to shine upon

145

our disgrace, was slow of making its appearance. . . . Our batteries were all silenced. The American works, on the other hand, remained as little injured as ever, and we were completely foiled."

The Battle of New Orleans. For a week the British landed and moved up reinforcements from their fleet, while Jackson strengthened the American earthworks, and two thousand Kentuckians arrived to reinforce the American army. Three regiments of the Louisiana Militia were stationed just north of New Orleans to guard against a flanking movement by the British. General David Morgan was ordered to cross the Mississippi with about 850 men and nine cannon to protect that side of the river.

So far the British attacks had failed. The American soldiers had defeated them in the battles of December 23 and 28, and the American artillery had won an important victory in the battle of January 1. Pakenham had about 5,300 men to attack Jackson's line, over 1,200 to cross the river to attack Morgan, and about 1,200 men to hold in reserve. Jackson had about 3,000 men on his line of earthworks, with about 1,000 in reserve. Morgan had about 850 men on the other side of the Mississippi. Pakenham had less than a dozen cannon in fireable condition, while Jackson now had twelve guns behind his line and nine with Morgan across the river which could help cover the area near the river in front of Jackson.

After some hesitation Pakenham finally decided to attack Jackson and Morgan at the same time. The main attack would, of course, be against Jackson. One British division would attack Jackson along the river, while the main attack would be against the left side of Jackson's line. Pakenham foresaw the risk of making a frontal attack upon the American line, but Admiral Cochrane said, sarcastically: "If the army shrinks from the task, I will fetch the sailors and marines from the fleet, and with them storm the American lines and march to the city. The soldiers can then bring up the baggage."

The citizens of New Orleans were fearful during that Saturday night of January 7, 1815. The morning of January 8 broke with a heavy fog, and about six o'clock the British columns moved forward in solid ranks. The American batteries opened fire. On the British came, advancing to within 150 yards of the American line, then 100 yards. At this point the American riflemen opened fire, not firing in volleys, but each man firing when he had reloaded his gun. The advancing British soldiers fell by the hundreds. Only a few ever reached the American breastworks. General Sir Samuel Gibbs was mortally wounded; General John Keane was severely wounded; General Pakenham was killed. General John Lambert finally stopped the fight— slightly more than an hour after it had started.

As one American historian has described this moment: "From the field

Jackson's triumphal parade in New Orleans.

everywhere shattered and depleted regiments were now retreating in disorder. The proud British army was vanquished; its bugles silenced; its colors trampled in the earth; its guns unable to reply." The blood-soaked Chalmette Plain was covered with dead and wounded British soldiers.

The British lost over two thousand killed, wounded, and missing. The Americans had only seventy-one casualties, of whom only six were killed.

A view of New Orleans, about 1815.
From an old print.

When victory was assured, the white and free Negro militiamen cheered while Jackson paraded the line and congratulated them. The New Orleans and Plauche bands, which had played throughout the battle, continued their playing of martial music. In New Orleans the church bells rang while the people ran and danced in the streets. The celebrations continued for some days. One jubilant American officer, writing to a friend, ended his account of the battle with a brief statement that the body of General Pakenham was put into a hogshead of rum and "sent home to England in good spirits."

After the Battle. As soon as the fighting had stopped at the Battle of New Orleans, Jackson ordered some of his troops forward to assist in burying the dead and caring for the wounded. About four hundred of the wounded were not in condition to be moved far, so they were brought to New Orleans where special hospitals had been prepared for them.

The day following the Battle of New Orleans, the British fleet sailed up the Mississippi and began a nine-day bombardment of Fort St. Philip, but that attack failed.

January 23 was declared a day of prayer and thanksgiving, and ceremonies were held at the Cathedral.

On February 13, Admiral Cochrane wrote Jackson that he had received the news of the Treaty of Ghent, which ended the war with Great Britain. Nine days later, this news was confirmed. But it was not until March 17 that the British fleet sailed away from the shores of Louisiana.

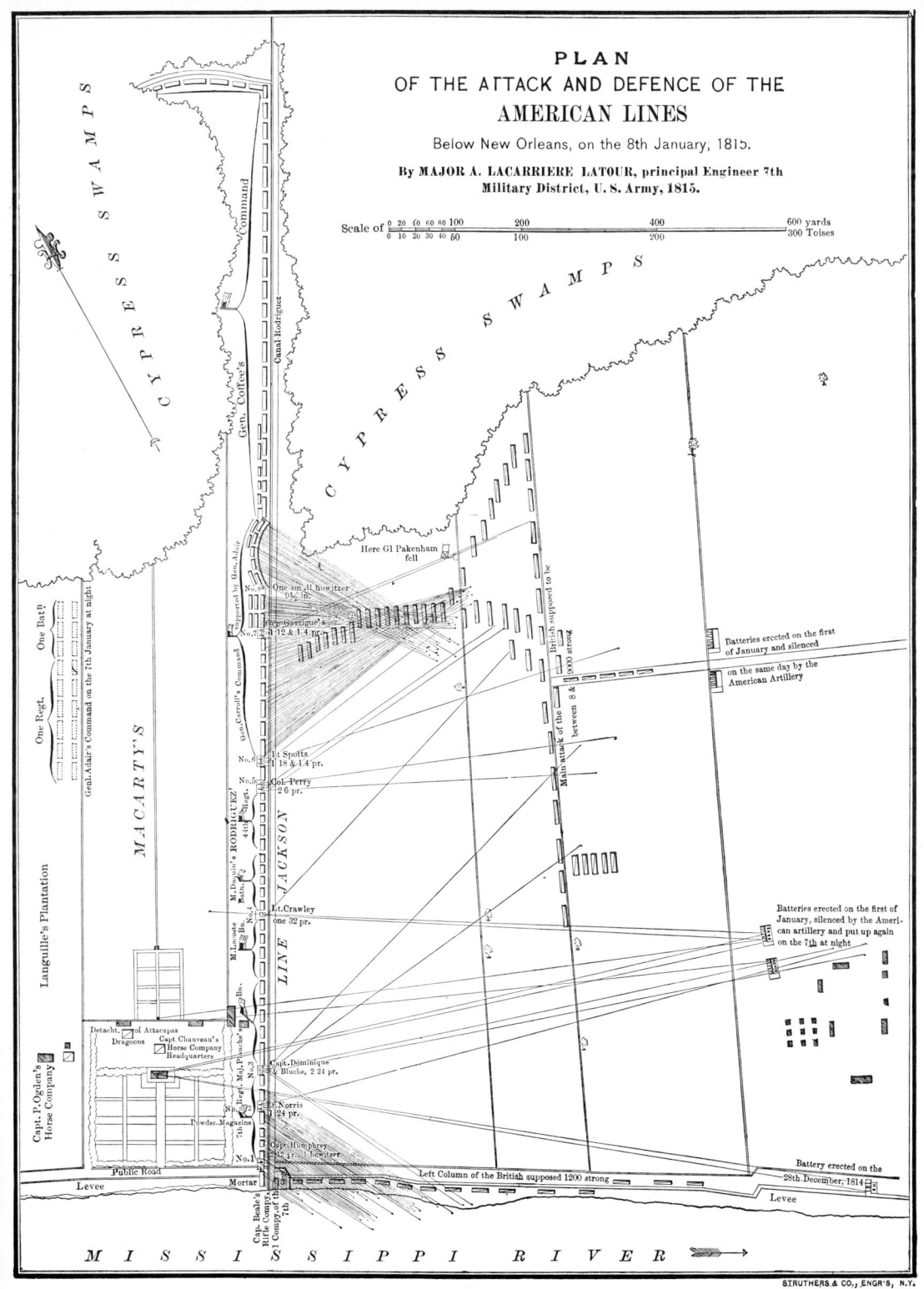

Map 21—Plan of the attack and defense of the American lines

PART FIVE
Antebellum
Louisiana,
1815–1861

16. LOUISIANA GOVERNMENT, 1812–1860

Government of Louisiana Under the First Constitution. As has been mentioned before, a convention met in New Orleans in the fall of 1811 to draft a constitution for the soon-to-be state of Louisiana. It was approved the following April and on April 30, 1812, Louisiana was admitted to statehood in the American Union.

The Governor was to be elected by the Legislature every four years from the two highest popular-vote candidates. He was required to be thirty-five years of age, a citizen of the United

States, a resident of Louisiana for six years, and to own at least $5,000 worth of property. No minister of any religious group was eligible for the office. The Governor had authority to appoint the Secretary of State and the Attorney General with the consent of the Senate, and the State Treasurer with the consent of both legislative houses. He was required to tour the state once every two years to inform himself of "the general condition of the country."

The two-house legislature was called

"A Street in the Faubourg Marigny," New Orleans
about 1821.

the General Assembly. Members of the Senate were elected for a four-year term, while those of the House of Representatives were elected for only two years. Senators must have property valued at $1,000 while Representatives were required to own only $500 worth of property.

The judiciary power was vested in a Supreme Court, having from three to five judges who were appointed by the Governor and confirmed by the Senate. The court was to hold its sessions at New Orleans and Opelousas.

Claiborne the First Governor. Although Claiborne had served as terri-

torial Governor, his election to the first state governorship was not expected. He had been unpopular with the Creoles, and the period of his territorial governorship had been filled with dissatisfaction and controversy. Jacques Villeré, the favorite of the Creoles, was nominated, and it was thought he would win, but when the votes were counted it was found that enough Creoles had voted for Claiborne to secure his election. The good work which he had performed during his nine years as territorial Governor had earned their confidence.

No Governor had to solve more problems, face more opposition, make

"A Street in the Faubourg Ste. Marie," New Orleans about 1821.

GENERAL L. KEMPER WILLIAMS

more important decisions, or meet more threatening dangers than did Governor Claiborne. He was distrusted by many of the Creoles, some of whom refused to serve in the Legislature. The Indians of northwest Louisiana caused trouble, and it was difficult to collect national, state, and local taxes. The privateers of Barataria openly smuggled all kinds of goods into the state, and after the declaration of war, the British blockaded the mouth of the Mississippi. Many Creoles would not support the state militia, and numbers of the newly arrived Americans refused to join the various units if it required leaving Louisiana.

The New Orleans militia units would not be mustered into the service of the United States.

One of the most important of Claiborne's tasks was that of educating the Creoles in self-government, in which they had had comparatively little experience during the territorial period. Many of them did not care for politics, but they learned rapidly and by 1816 were becoming accustomed to taking part in state government.

Claiborne tackled the difficulties with justice and common sense, while meeting the crisis of the British invasion with calm assurance. In his last message to the people as Governor he paid tribute to their "generous character," realizing that he had won the affection of both Creole and American. In 1816 he was elected United States Senator, but he died the following year. Jacques Villeré called him "one of our best patriots, . . . distinguished for his virtues and talents." Louisianians generally praised his qualities of leadership and acclaimed him one of the most important leaders "in what was then the great Southwest."

National Party Politics in Louisiana. Louisianians were not much interested in national politics during the first years of statehood. While the majority of them were Jeffersonian Republicans rather than Federalists, they were not well enough acquainted with national party leaders to become excited during presidential campaigns.

After 1820, Louisiana generally supported Henry Clay or Andrew Jackson. Clay advocated a protective tariff which helped the sugar industry, while Jackson was very popular because of his victory at New Orleans.

After 1830, Louisianians became much more interested in national politics, and though most of them favored the Democratic Party in national elections, the Whigs won numerous local and a few state elections. Occasionally the Governor would be a member of one party while the majority of the members of the state Legislature would belong to the other. After the death of the Whig Party in the early 1850's, the American, or "Know-Nothing," Party became strong for a time, but most of the elections continued to be won by the Democrats.

Occasionally a presidential election caused much excitement in Louisiana. Young Robert Patrick of Clinton recalled that in 1844 "there were barbecues, public speeches made by the leaders, torch light processions, glee clubs, and all that sort of thing." In 1848 the major candidate was a resident of Baton Rouge, General Zachary Taylor, and the voters campaigned throughout the state with great enthusiasm.

During the period several outstanding political leaders were elected to Congress to represent Louisiana. Alexander Porter, Edward Livingston, Pierre Soulé, John Slidell, and Judah P. Benjamin served ably in the Senate and were statesmen of national importance.

Governors and State Politics. Until the election of 1834 the most important issue in state elections for Governor was whether the candidate was "Creole" or "American." During this early period the Americans elected William C. C. Claiborne, Thomas Bolling Robertson, and Henry Johnson, while the Creoles elected Jacques Villeré, Pierre Derbigny, and A. B. Roman.

After 1834 party politics became more important. The Whig Party elected governors in 1834 and 1838, when Edward D. White and A. B.

General Zachary Taylor at his home in
Baton Rouge.

Roman won the elections, but after this all governors were Democrats: Alexandre Mouton, Isaac Johnson, Joseph Walker, Paul Hebert, Robert Wickliffe, and Thomas Moore.

Americans believed that Creoles were "opposed to development and progress," while Creoles considered Americans to be radical in their political thinking. Free Negroes had no political rights, although a few were occasionally permitted to vote for favorite candidates in local, state, and even national elections.

Most of the officeholders and legislators were either Creole or American, but there were also a few Italians and Englishmen plus, as one man wrote, "here and there a Scotchman, with his boat-shaped head and hard common sense."

Campaigns for state offices were usually hard fought, the candidates attracting much attention as they traveled about the state. Frequently they wrote stories or songs about their rivals.

During the election of 1849, for example, the opponent of Joseph Walker sang a song about him to the tune of "Old Uncle Ned," the chorus of which ran:

Take off the saddle from his back,
Pull down the fodder from his rack;
There is no more run in poor old Joe—
Turn him out to grass and let him go.

Occasionally legislators quarreled, and challenged each other to duel. One of these challenges ended humorously. During the legislative session of 1817 the hot-tempered Bernard Ma-

rigny became angry at the remarks of James Humble, by trade a blacksmith, and challenged him. Humble was a giant nearly seven feet in height, while Marigny was a short, thin man. Humble did not want to fight—"I know nothing of this duelling business." His friends argued that no gentleman could refuse a challenge. "But I'm not a gentleman," Humble insisted, "I'm only a blacksmith." Finally Humble gave in but insisted on his own terms: "The duel shall take place in Lake Pontchartrain in six feet of water, sledgehammers to be used as weapons." Marigny's friends laughingly told him that he would have to fight standing on a box, but Marigny declared that it was impossible to fight a man with such a sense of humor.

Major Political Issues. During the early years of statehood governors Claiborne and Villeré were kept busy. Taxation, the Choctaw and Caddo Indians, smuggling along the Gulf Coast, financial distress caused by the War of 1812, and relations between the Americans and Creoles all demanded their attention. It took hard work to get the government of the state running on a sound basis.

After 1820 the major political issues centered round more common matters of state government and the passage of legislation for economic and cultural betterment.

Louisiana's first civil code had been enacted during the territorial period and generally it followed the principles of French and Spanish law. A new civil code was compiled in 1825, and a code of criminal law adopted in 1828.

Throughout the period laws were passed regulating banks and banking and the construction and maintenance of roads, bridges, ferries, and levees. Late in the period, laws were needed for controlling railroads and telegraph lines, which were just beginning to be built. Education required much legislation, as also did the protection of the public health from epidemics and ordinary diseases.

The legislators had considerable trouble with the problem of language, for some of them spoke only English and others spoke only French. Interpreters were constantly needed and the laws of the state had to be published in both languages.

Moving of the State Capital. The first state capital was located at New Or-

The Old State Capitol at Baton Rouge as it looks today.

Jackson Square, 1830's

leans, which had been the seat of the territorial government, but in 1825, after considerable debate, the Legislature voted to move the capital to Donaldsonville.

The Legislature voted $30,000 to build the new "statehouse," fifteen feet wide by one hundred feet long, at Donaldsonville, and here the Legislature met in 1830. But the legislators were "thoroughly disgusted" with the "unsightly and badly constructed" capitol and with its accommodations and, "under the shallow pretext that the roof was leaky, abandoned the place for good and all." The capital was moved back to New Orleans.

However, the agitation to move the capital away from New Orleans continued. In 1846 an act was passed moving it to Baton Rouge and $100,-000 was appropriated for a statehouse. James H. Dakin, a New Orleans architect, drew the plans and became the

contractor. The building was completed by 1850 and the seat of government officially moved when Governor Joseph Walker was inaugurated. The capital remained at Baton Rouge until it was moved to Opelousas during the Civil War.

The Constitutions of 1845 and 1852. The Constitution of 1812 remained in effect for many years, but by the early 1840's the old document was out of date. The Constitution of 1845 abolished the property qualifications for voting or holding office. The Governor lost many of his powers, and the office of Lieutenant Governor was created. The office of State Superintendent of Public Education was approved, and the Legislature was directed to "establish free public schools throughout the state."

The Constitution of 1845, however, did not satisfy all the citizens, many

158

of whom believed that it should have been more democratic. A new convention met at Baton Rouge in 1852 and drafted a new document.

Most of the features of the Constitution of 1845 were retained, but several new liberalizing clauses were added.

Louisiana and International Problems. During the antebellum period there were many international problems in which Louisiana was involved. These included piracy on the Lower Mississippi and the Gulf of Mexico, filibustering expeditions against various Spanish colonies and Latin American countries, the western boundary dispute, the Texas War for Independence, and the war with Mexico.

After the War of 1812 some of the Baratarians continued to capture and rob ships in the Gulf of Mexico, and from time to time pirates captured river boats along the Lower Mississippi. By the middle of the 1820's, with the aid of the United States government, they were finally driven from Louisiana.

During the period several expeditions were organized in Louisiana to assist the Texans, Mexicans or other Latin Americans in winning their wars of independence from Spain or to fight in rebellions against existing governments. These were called filibustering expeditions. The headquarters of these movements were generally Turpin's Coffee House on Marigny Street, Maspero's Exchange on Char-

tres Street, Banks' Arcade on Magazine Street, or other cafes in New Orleans. Dr. James Long led expeditions to Texas in 1819 and 1821, but each was defeated.

Until the middle 1820's adventurers and fugitives from justice continued to settle in the Sabine Strip and it became noted for its "robberies, murders, and other crimes of an infamous and astounding character." The Florida Purchase Treaty of 1819 finally fixed the boundary at the Sabine River, and in 1823 the United States built Fort Jesup, a few miles northeast of present-day Many. The army soon brought law and order to the Sabine Strip, and Fort Jesup remained an important military post until the late 1840's.

After the Texas War for Independence began in 1835, the New Orleans *Bee* headlined an article: "AMERICANS TO THE RESCUE!" Hundreds of Louisianians joined military companies to fight for Texas or gave money and supplies. Banks' Arcade and the Rising Sun Tavern on Old Levee Street were the headquarters of those who wished to aid the Lone Star Republic. After the war had been won Louisianians recited:

On San Jacinto's bloody field
Our drums and trumpets loudly pealed
And bade a haughty tyrant yield
*   To Texas Chivalry.*

Ten years later the Mexican War began. Soon six regiments of some

159

An old drawing showing a ferry on Berwick Bay in Louisiana crossing to Brashear City (now Morgan City).

six thousand volunteers had been equipped by the state and were on their way to join General Zachary Taylor in southern Texas, but these troops had enlisted for only three months and they were soon recalled by the federal government. This action made many Louisianians angry, and it was characterized by the *Picayune* as "the supercilious insolence of an incompetent Secretary of War." Later many citizens organized or joined military units and fought in Mexico. One newspaper editor simply closed his printing shop and put the following sign on the door: "I voted

for Texas. I have gone to help do the fighting."

Parish, City, and Town Governmental Problems. During this period parish, city, and town officials faced many of the ordinary problems of local government. The parish judge was the chief executive officer of the parish and he had civil, criminal, and police jurisdiction. The Police Jury was the parish legislative body and also had some executive functions. The cities and towns had a mayor, a recorder, a council of aldermen, a clerk, a treasurer and other minor officials. The

160

city court and justices of the peace handled small crimes. In 1836 New Orleans was divided into three municipalities, but in 1852 they were consolidated into one city again.

Taxes were low during this period. The total tax levy for West Feliciana Parish in 1850, for example, was only $7,000, and five years later the parish spent only a little over $11,000, which included the burial of paupers, the care of the poor, and the expenses of the new courthouse.

Some of the parish and town regulations seem out of place today or at least a bit odd. In 1828 no one was allowed to have more than three dogs in Marksville. In 1843 anyone in Sabine Parish who was "aggrieved" by a wild or ungovernable horse, cow, or hog, could make a complaint to the nearest justice of the peace. Three years later the Police Jury declared a bounty of two dollars for every wolf killed. In 1848 the Methodist and Baptist churches were rented for use as a courthouse and as a jury room. In 1851 in West Feliciana Parish it became unlawful to race horses on the public roads. In 1852 the Avoyelles Parish Police Jury prohibited citizens from leaving "dead animals in the bayou in front of one's residence more than 24 hours."

During those years, however, the people of Louisiana believed that the government which governed least was the best government. The Legislature, the Police Juries, and the city councils passed only those laws and regulations they believed necessary to the well-being and happiness of the citizens.

17. ECONOMIC LIFE IN LOUISIANA, 1815–1861

Rapid Growth of Population. A rush of settlers came into Louisiana between the War of 1812 and the Civil War in 1861. The majority came from the older southern states, but many arrived from the Middle Atlantic and New England sections. Foreigners landed at New Orleans, some of whom settled permanently in the Pelican State. The Germans and Irish were the most important immigrant groups, but there were also smaller numbers of people from other countries. By 1850 approximately one-fourth of Louisiana's total population was foreign born. Thousands of Negro slaves were brought in from the older states and a few were smuggled from Africa or the West Indies. Sizable numbers of free Negroes from other states came to Louisiana until 1840, but after this the number entering decreased to comparatively few.

In 1812, Louisiana's total population had been slightly over 80,000; in 1820 it totaled over 200,000; by 1840 it had grown to over 250,000; and by 1860 it had topped 700,000. Throughout the period to the 1850's the Negro population outnumbered the white, the number of slaves growing from nearly 40,000 in 1812 to over 330,000 in 1860. The number of free Negroes increased from about 8,000 in 1812 to nearly 19,000 in 1860.

The majority of the free Negro group were mulattoes and they outnumbered the pure Negroes by about four to one. Most of them lived in the southern part of the state, though there were many along the Mississippi, Red, and other rivers and bayous. The majority of them were common laborers, but many were skilled in various trades or were farmers, planters, or businessmen.

In 1860 nearly 21,000 white and free Negro Louisianians owned slaves, but over half of this number possessed 5 slaves or less. Nearly 4,500 slave-owners had from 6 to 10 slaves and slightly over 2,600 owned from 11 to 20 slaves.

Almost 1,800 people owned from 21 to 50 slaves and slightly over 700 owned from 51 to 100 slaves. Only 274 people owned from 101 to 200 slaves and only 36 owned from 201 to 300. Six planters owned between 300 and 500 slaves and four planters owned between 500 and 1,000 slaves.

Many free Negroes owned a few slaves and some owned large plantations. Cyprian Ricard bought an Iberville Parish estate with 91 slaves for $225,000. Martin Donatto (also spelled Donato) of Iberville Parish died in 1845 and his estate included 4,500 arpents of land, 89 slaves, and personal property valued at nearly $50,000. In 1859 the Ricaud family estate in Natchitoches Parish included 4,000 acres of plantation land and some 350 slaves.

But only a small number of these free Negroes, some of whom had been well educated in Europe, ever voted, and none of them was ever permitted to hold public office.

Growth of Cities and Towns. The population of New Orleans grew steadily, and from a city of about 18,000 in 1812, it grew to over 100,000 in 1840, and to nearly 170,000 in 1860. There were obvious reasons for the growth of New Orleans. It was the largest trading and business center of the Lower Mississippi Valley and was the most important seaport on the entire Gulf Coast. A cosmopolitan city inhabited by people of all nationalities, it was also a "modern" city for that time; for by the 1830's it had large

162

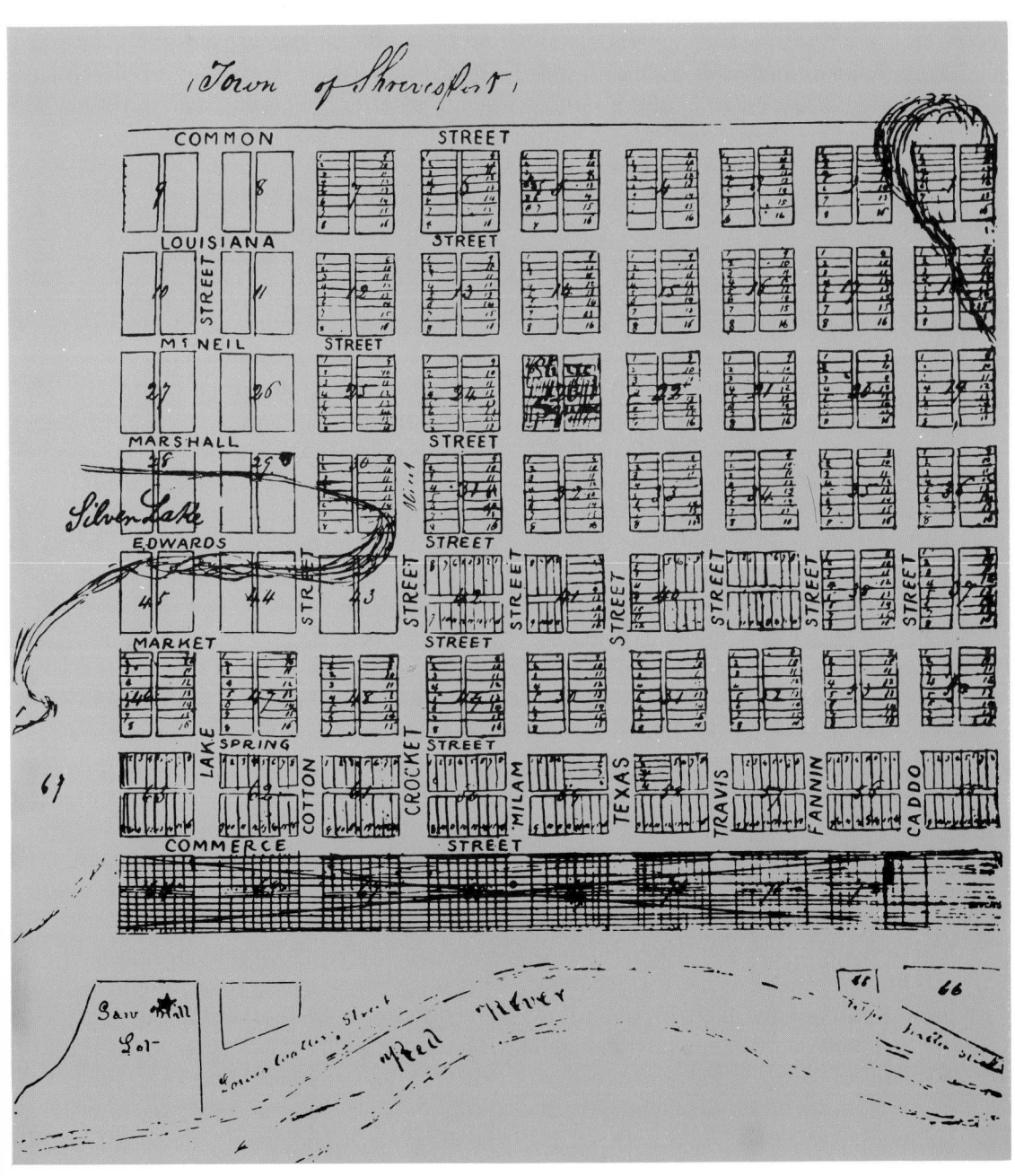

Map 22—Shreveport, 1848. This is
the first recorded map of the town.

hotels, city water and gaslighting systems, and many paved streets and other improvements. It also had recreational facilities, for there were theaters where operas and plays were presented, and numerous cafes, restaurants, ballrooms, and other attractions.

Most of the major Louisiana towns were located on rivers or bayous which could be navigated by steamboats, and of the few towns not located on these streams, most were parish seats. Only Baton Rouge and Algiers, outside of Lafayette, Jefferson, and Carrollton which were suburbs of New Orleans, had more than 5,000 population in 1860. The Shreve Town Company, headed by Henry Miller Shreve and a group of associates, was organized in 1836, and the new northwestern Louisiana river port was officially incorporated as Shreveport three years later. By 1860 the population was nearly 2,200. The smaller towns included Plaquemine with over 1,600; Donaldsonville, Alexandria, and Homer with nearly 1,500; Thibodaux with nearly 1,400; and Minden with nearly 1,200. All of the other towns had less than 1,000 inhabitants.

Thus, it can be seen that in 1860 most Louisianians lived in the rural areas. These people were planters and farmers, lumbermen, herdsmen, fishermen, or hunters and trappers. Until about 1830 the great majority lived in southeast Louisiana, but after this time northern and western Louisiana began to fill up rapidly.

Agriculture. White and free Negro farmers and planters lived over the entire state, their lands ranging from small frontier-like farms with only a few acres of general food crops to large plantations which produced sugarcane, cotton, or tobacco. Most of the agricultural holdings were, however, small or large farms rather than plantations. The large plantations were located chiefly along the Mississippi or lower Red River and along the streams and bayous of southeast Louisiana.

Land values varied greatly. During the early 1850's hill lands near Natchitoches could be purchased for two dollars to six dollars an acre. Along the Red River the price of good cotton or sugarcane land was between fifteen and thirty-five dollars an acre. Along the Lower Mississippi River, Bayou Lafourche, and Bayou Teche, land prices were even higher.

Most of the ordinary farmers lived in plain, but adequate houses, behind which were located barns, granaries, sheds, other outbuildings, and perhaps a slave cabin or two. They produced food crops, raised cattle, hogs, and poultry, and grew cotton or tobacco for money crops. They lived comfortable but work-filled lives. The pioneer farmers had only a few acres in cultivation, herded their livestock over the open or timbered land, lived in poor and sometimes ramshackle houses, produced few money crops, and lived hard lives.

In contrast, the planters were gen-

A sugar plantation on Bayou Teche.

erally fair businessmen with ample capital, sometimes living in luxury. The Tchoupitoulas Plantation, about twelve miles up the Mississippi from New Orleans, serves as a good example of the large plantation. The Soniat family had a large, two-story brick mansion, in front and on both sides of which were gardens of trees, plants, and flowers. On one side of the house was a *garçonnière* for visiting young men or travelers, and on the other side was the *pigeonnier* where doves and pigeons were raised. Behind was the kitchen, the storehouse, the slave hospital, stables, and other outbuildings. Farther to the rear was the sugarhouse and below it the overseer's house, beyond which were two long rows of brick slave cabins.

Only a man of considerable wealth could acquire, outfit, and stock a large plantation, particularly one which produced sugar. In 1830 it was reported that a 1,250-acre, 50-slave, sugar plantation in St. Martin Parish required about $90,000 capital.

Sugar production steadily increased throughout the period, for sugarcane cultivation spread up the Mississippi north of the mouth of the Red River and up that river to the Natchitoches country. After 1830 "ribbon" cane, which was a very hardy variety, replaced the older "Creole" cane. Steam-driven mills were introduced, and numerous improvements in the manufacturing process were made, one of the most important of which was the patenting of several types of multiple evaporators and vacuum pans by free Negro Norbert Rillieux. Sugar production grew from 75,000 hogsheads in 1833 to 449,000 hogsheads in 1853, which was the largest amount produced before 1860.

Cotton was grown over the entire state, the least amounts being produced in the low country of South Louisiana. Until 1837 prices were high, and after a five-year depression, good prices returned and there was a constant expansion of the cotton-producing areas into North Louisiana.

Tobacco was raised in large amounts north of the Red River. Frequently planters raised both tobacco and cotton, with the two crops cultivated and harvested at alternating periods. "Perique" tobacco, a strong tobacco used for flavoring, was grown only in St. James Parish.

Corn was grown over the entire state for human as well as livestock consumption. Oats were grown in central and North Louisiana and rice in the southeastern section. Hay, truck crops, fruits, and berries were grown on most of the general farms.

Livestock raising was most important in southwest Louisiana. Here there were large ranches, very much like those of the West, where herdsmen watched over large numbers of horses, cattle, and hogs. Much of this country was open prairie, dotted here and there with patches of trees along the watercourses. One traveler who viewed it in 1816 wrote: "It is no extravagant declaration to call this one of the meadows of America." This area produced cattle, hides, tallow, beef and pork, and some cheese.

Most of the agriculturists of antebellum Louisiana were plain "dirt" farmers, only a few of them being acquainted with "scientific" agricultural methods. But as time passed many of them subscribed to agricultural publications and organized local fairs. The Baton Rouge Agricultural Society was founded in 1827, while the Louisiana State Agricultural Society came into existence in 1833 and began to plan the establishment of a "model farm." After this farmers and planters began to buy more and better machinery, to rotate their crops in some sections, and generally to improve their methods of production. By 1860, Louisiana had one of the largest agricultural incomes in the Union.

Manufacturing. Manufacturing was of secondary interest to antebellum Louisianians. Only about 7,500 persons were employed in manufacturing industries in 1840, whereas over 79,-000 were employed in agriculture. No cotton or woolen manufacturing was reported in 1850 and only a little ten years later. By the end of the 1850's fewer than a dozen iron-casting establishments were reported, and these employed less than 500 persons In 1850 the total value of all manufacturing, mining, and mechanical products was slightly over $7,000,000, and this sum had not materially increased by 1860.

There was a considerable amount of small-scale home manufacturing. During the early years, for example, most of the cottonseed was separated by hand, and this was still being done on the smaller farms in 1860. The cotton was then carded, thread spun, cloth made, and dyed with certain plants or walnut hulls, after which the garments were sewn by hand. Other home industry included the making of hats, shoes, furniture, tools, and simple farm implements, such as rakes and hoes.

Clothing was made at home from material woven on simple looms.

Banks and Banking. Louisianians needed strong banks for the financing of their agricultural and commercial economy. The planters and farmers needed long-term loans to purchase land and slaves and short-term loans to pay expenses during the few months prior to the sale of their crops. The merchants and other businessmen needed funds to finance their businesses adequately.

Louisiana banking from 1812 to 1860 may be roughly divided into four periods. The period from 1812 to the late 1820's was generally a period of sound banking. Then came a period which has been called an era of madness, for the banks overexpanded. The panic of 1837 broke, and in the last ten months of that year over 2,500 foreclosure suits were filed in Orleans Parish alone. Hundreds of farmers and

The Great Raft on Red River before it was cleared by Henry Miller Shreve.

planters lost their farms and plantations. Deposits in banks decreased from nearly $12,000,000 in 1836 to about $3,000,000 in 1841.

In 1842 and 1843 the state Legislature passed new banking laws which placed all financial houses under state control. Business began to revive and by 1860 Louisiana was again a very prosperous state, its citizens having nearly $20,000,000 on deposit in the banks. Experts agreed that Louisiana's banks were the safest in the country and one writer said that they were simply "overflowing with gold."

Transportation. The numerous waterways offered the easiest means of transportation to antebellum Louisianians. During the early years of the period the rivers and bayous were filled with cargo pirogues, arks, broad horns, keelboats, and numerous other varieties of flatboats which were propelled by oars. The steamboat era began in 1812 when the *New Orleans* arrived in New Orleans from Pittsburgh, and, although she soon sank from a boiler explosion, earned $20,000 above her cost carrying passengers and goods to and from Natchez. By 1830 there

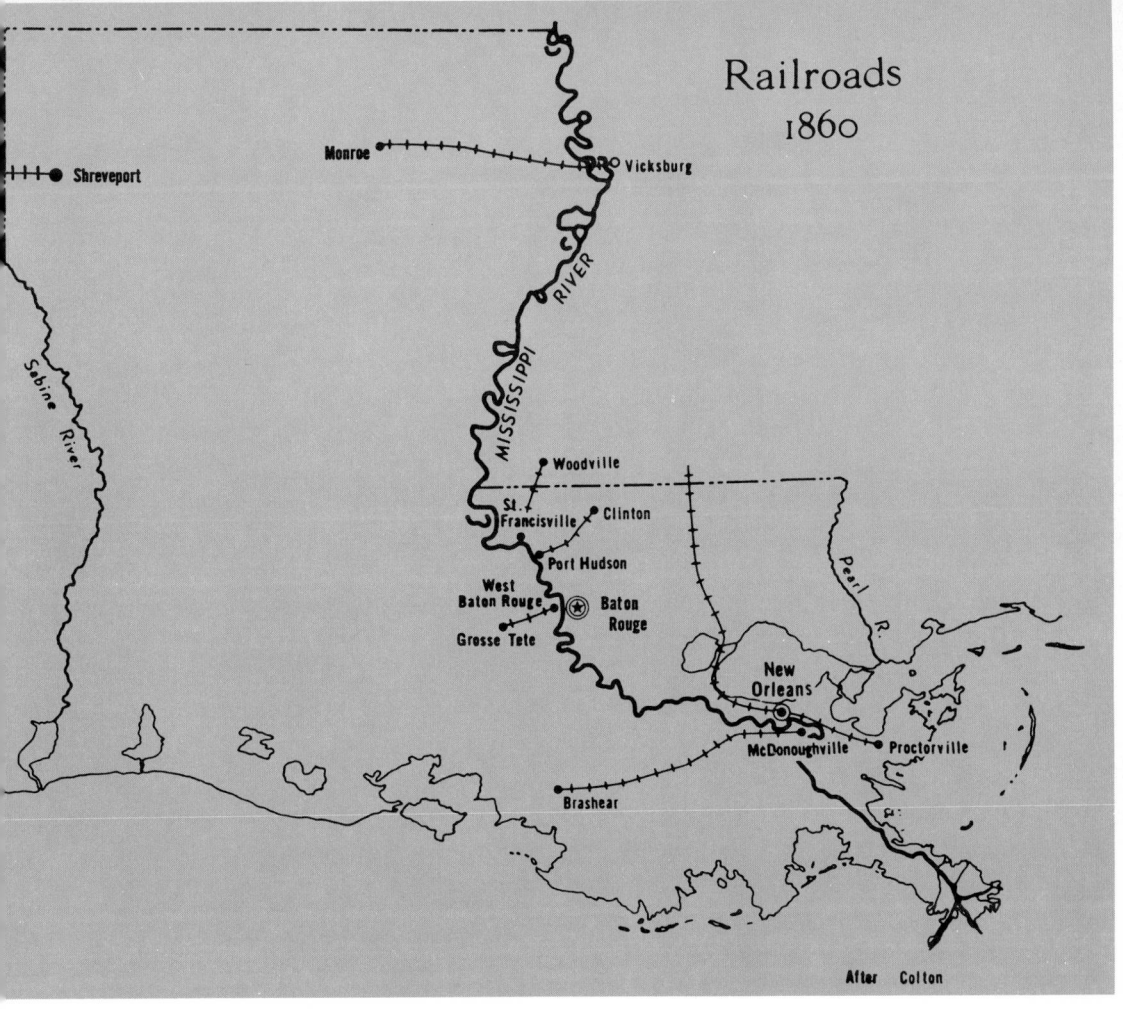

Railroads
1860

Shreveport

Monroe

Vicksburg

MISSISSIPPI RIVER

Sabine River

Woodville

St. Francisville • Clinton

Port Hudson

West Baton Rouge
Grosse Tete

★ Baton Rouge

New Orleans

Pearl R.

McDonoughville • Proctorville

Brashear

After Colton

Map 23—Louisiana railroads, 1860

were numerous steamboats on the Mississippi and the number of flatboats had begun to decline. Three years later Henry Miller Shreve began the task of clearing the Red River above Alexandria of the trees, snags, and drift—generally called the "Great Raft"—which blocked navigation, finally completing the task in 1840.

During the 1840's and 1850's large or small steamboats carried cargoes and passengers throughout the state. The larger boats became "floating palaces" with private staterooms, luxurious furnishings, and even gaslights. In the 1840's a British traveler, Sir Charles Lyell, thought the dinner on board the *Magnolia* "only too sumptuous." The meal began "with turtle soup, and two kinds of fish; then followed a variety of dishes, admirably cooked, and then a course of

169

cocoa-nut pies, jellies, preserved bananas, oranges, grapes, and ice-creams, concluding with coffee."

But travel was not so pleasant on board some of the boats which coursed the smaller rivers and bayous. In 1840 one traveler complained that the Red River steamboat *Concord* "should be named Discord, for the firemen abused the mate, the cook fought the steward, the mosquitoes waged war on the passengers, and the passengers are not yet done cursing mate, firemen, steward, mosquitoes—in fine, the boat and all connected with her. A more miserable, dirty, slow moving, improvided, chicken thievish craft never walked the waters . . . it excites my spleen to think of her."

Louisiana's first railroads were built in the 1830's and connected New Orleans with its suburbs. The Pontchartrain Railroad was the first (the first steam locomotive arrived in 1832), followed by the Mexican Gulf Railroad, and the New Orleans and Carrollton Railroad. Then short railroads were built to shipping points along the Mississippi River, such as the West Feliciana Railroad from Woodville, Mississippi, to Bayou Sara, and the Clinton and Port Hudson Railroad. By 1860 there were nine railroads in the state with a total of 334 miles of track.

Only a few canals were dug, for the numerous bayous and streams provided hundreds of miles of waterways. In 1860 the state had only four canals, with a total length of thirty-six miles. An interesting form of transportation which developed in New Orleans in the 1840's was one which used mules to pull passenger barges along one of the city's canals.

Louisiana had no state highways during this period, for road construction was left to the parishes. Most of the poorly graded dirt roads crookedly followed the line of least resistance around hills, trees, and other obstructions. There were a few "plank" roads, so-called because they were floored with heavy boards. Bridges were few in number and were found only across the smaller streams, the larger bayous and rivers being crossed by ferry.

Trade and Commerce. Nearly all products were carried by the various types of boats over the state's great water system. Hogsheads of sugar arrived at New Orleans from southern Louisiana plantations, tobacco from the northern sections and from St. James Parish, cotton from up the Red River, the Ouachita, or from the Mississippi above Natchez. Cattle, sheep, hogs, hides, and other products came from the western and southwestern sections. Manufactured goods, sundries and staples which the people needed were shipped to all points of the state.

The Mississippi was the great highway of interstate commerce. Goods from the entire Middle West came down the river either for consumption in Louisiana, reshipment to other

Courtyard of the first great New Orleans hotel. Built by Samuel Moore in 1799; demolished in 1907. Typical of southern European and Latin American hotels of that era.

states, or export to foreign countries. Trading boats stopped at the landings with manufactured goods from the East. Boats from the Ohio River country sometimes flew the "Wabash" coat of arms, which was a "flag-staff with a mammoth Irish potato, a big ear of corn, a golden-hued apple, and a side of bacon pendant, and at the topmost peak a bottle of whiskey."

In 1858 one boat, the *Philadelphia*, arrived at New Orleans with 2,000 barrels of flour, 1,990 sacks of corn, 1,100 sheep, 1,000 chickens, 400 barrels of pork, 400 turkeys, 180 hogs, and several hundred bales of hemp and cotton.

After the Louisiana Purchase, President Jefferson wrote that New Orleans was destined to be a "mighty mart of the merchandise brought from more than a thousand rivers." His prophecy soon came true for the "city walls were torn down, the forts demolished, the moat was filled and made into boulevards: Canal, Rampart, and Esplanade."

When a British traveler, Charles Mackay, came down the Mississippi in 1858, he wrote:

On the seventh day morning we entered
*   New Orleans,*
The joyous 'Crescent City'—a Queen

171

A log cabin at old German colony near Minden

among the Queens—
*And saw her pleasant harbor alive with
tapering spars—
With 'union-jacks' from England, and
flaunting 'stripes and stars,'
And all her swarming levee, for miles
above the shore,
Buzzing, humming, surging, with Trade's
incessant roar.*

New Orleans became a great commercial city. Before 1830 the Gulf and Atlantic ships sailed whenever they got a cargo, but after that date they began to sail on regular schedules.

Mail delivery was generally slow and irregular, but service gradually improved. Letters and newspapers were carried by boats, by stagecoaches, or by mail riders on horseback. Until 1848, when the envelope came into use, letters were simply folded and sealed with wax. The adhesive stamp made its appearance in 1847, and stamped envelopes became common after 1852. By 1855 it was possible to register letters.

Labor. Negro slaves furnished most of the plantation labor in antebellum Louisiana. While there was some slave labor in the towns and cities, with the exception of house servants most of the workers were white. Many free Negroes worked at skilled trades as carpenters, barbers, bricklayers, or blacksmiths.

Although conditions varied from plantation to plantation, slaves generally lived in poorly constructed cabins and had inadequate food and clothing. They worked from sunrise to sunset but on most plantations had Saturday afternoons off. They were sometimes permitted to own property and by working weekends and holidays accumulated a few belongings. Some were able to buy freedom.

Whites and free blacks who were laborers also worked from sun to sun and were poorly fed and clothed and inadequately housed. Only a small number were able to rise above poverty.

Numerous German, Irish, and other immigrants settled in Louisiana during this period. They dug the canals, built railroads, and did other kinds of unskilled work. Some of them became carpenters, blacksmiths, or other skilled or semi-skilled workers. They were generally paid by the day, though some contracted by the week, month, or even by the year. All were poorly paid and by 1860 averaged little more than one dollar per day.

But the greatest weakness of the labor system was that it permitted men to hold other men in bondage. Slaves were bought and sold just like other kinds of property. Their lives were completely controlled. The system always fostered injustice and degradation of the human spirit.

18. ANTEBELLUM SOCIAL AND CULTURAL LIFE

From Pioneer Cabins to Plantation Mansions. Louisiana's antebellum houses ranged from the rude cabins of poor white pioneers and free or slave blacks to the mansions of rich planters. In between these two extremes were the ordinary frame houses occupied by most of the people.

The pioneer settler who moved to the northern and northwestern sections of the state during this period usually built a rude log cabin where he lived until he could afford a house of rough-sawed lumber. Generally of British ancestry, he laid the logs parallel to the ground, in contrast to the French colonial pioneer who had placed them vertically. The slab doors and windows were hung with leather straps for hinges. The cabin had an earthen floor and contained only crudely made beds, tables, chairs, and a chest or two. Cooking was done at the fireplace.

Farther south, the simple homes of the French and Spanish Creoles were little changed from those of the colonial period. The typical "Acadian" house, as it is sometimes called today, had a front porch or gallery and a high, steep roof enclosing attic bedrooms, the stairway to which was on the outside, at one end of the porch. The timbers and boards were hand hewn, mortised, and wooden pegged. Fireplaces were either outside or inside the building, which sometimes was whitewashed. The furniture was plain

173

Acadians in Louisiana lived in homes like this reconstruction in the Longfellow-Evangeline State Park, St. Martinville.

and simple. A picket fence, called a *barrière de pieux,* enclosed a small yard.

In contrast to these homes were plantation mansions, built according to French or English architectural styles and with kitchens set apart from the main building. A few of them were huge palaces. "Chatsworth" had fifty rooms and "Belle Grove" had seventy-five. Most were plainly

furnished, but some were filled with fine furnishings brought from Europe.

Their names suggest Creole sensibility and American energy. There were "Versailles," "Chateau de Clery," "Fontainebleau," and "Austerlitz"; "Ivanhoe," "Rob Roy," "Kenilworth," and "Nottaway"; "Old Hickory," "Uncle Sam," and "Rattle and Snap." One of them, at New Iberia, now consid-

Rosedown, plantation home near St. Francisville.

ered one of the finest examples of plantation-home architecture in America, was called "The Shadows." Many of these are still standing and efforts are being made to preserve them.

Unusual features were sometimes found in these homes. In some South Louisiana mansions huge "punkah" fans were hung from the dining-room ceilings. After 1835 a few were equipped with gaslights. "Shady Grove," which was completed in 1857, had a bathroom, while "Walnut Grove" had running from the dining

175

room to the kitchen a miniature railroad which was used to bring in the piping-hot food.

Clothing. Until late in the period nearly all of the clothing of the common people was homemade of cotton, wool, or a mixture of linen and wool called linsey-woolsey. The women wore simple dresses of homespun cloth, sunbonnets reinforced with split-cane ribs, and crudely made shoes. The men wore pants of cottonade cloth, sewed with alternating blue and white thread; shirts and jumpers; heavy shoes; and straw, split-cane, or reed hats. Children, as in the colonial period, were dressed like their parents.

Wealthy planters or townspeople followed Paris or London fashions and employed tailors, dressmakers, seamstresses, and milliners. They used imported materials and seldom bought readymade garments. The men wore tight-fitting pants, waistcoats, high and pointed shoes, and high hats. The women were dressed in full skirts with hoops, tight bodices, fragile shoes, and well-trimmed hats. Their accessories included ribbons, parasols, and much jewelry. During the 1850's one writer described an old French gentleman. He wore a nankeen blouse, a loose-fitting frock coat, a yellow vest with bright buttons, gray trousers, light and fancy shoes, and gaiters. His hat "had a brim so narrow that two flies could not walk arm-in-arm around it," while the gray crown "rose upward into the air above him like a rusty stove-pipe."

Food. The climate and natural features of Louisiana gave the people a wider variety of food than most Americans. There were all types of meats and plentiful game and wild fowl. Fresh- and salt-water fish, oysters, shrimp, crabs, and turtles were obtainable for table use. Numerous varieties of vegetables, fruits, and berries were cultivated, as were corn, rice, and wheat. Common staples were brought from the northern states, while fancier goods were imported from Europe. Water came from cisterns or from the rivers and bayous and was purified with alum. Ice for cooling drinks and for ice cream was brought during the late winter from the north until the 1850's, when it began to be manufactured.

In North and northwestern Louisiana, dishes were generally plain and without much seasoning as they were in most of the United States. The common people ate various cornmeal breads, fried beef or pork, a few staple vegetables, and drank thin coffee. In South Louisiana everyone ate a wider variety of Spanish and French Creole dishes, quantities of fish and seafood, and drank thick, black coffee. One lady who visited South Louisiana in the 1830's wrote to a friend: "The oranges, the delicious wines and liquors, the coffee, the innumerable delicate dishes, you would be an epicure in spite of yourself."

In the larger towns and in New Orleans peddlers sold all kinds of edibles, and their picturesque chants advertised the specialties of each seller:

A New Orleans street peddler.

Cantal—ope—ah!
Fresh and fine,
Just offa de vine,
Only a dime!

or,

Oyster Man! Oyster Man!
Get your fresh oysters from the Oyster Man!

Bring out your pitcher, bring out your can,
Get your nice fresh oysters from the Oyster Man!

Sometimes the peddler added a bit of humor to his chant:

Ice cream, lemonade,
Made with brown sugar and a rotten egg!

Medicine and Social Welfare. Medicine made slow progress during those years, for there were few medical schools and most doctors had been trained by being apprenticed to older physicians. Few of them had received college medical training. While the larger towns and cities had enough doctors to care for the sick, there was a general scarcity in the rural areas, where the people depended upon home remedies and patent medicines to cure their ills.

Epidemics of yellow fever and cholera were a scourge to native Louisianians, and dealt even harder with those who had only recently arrived in the state. New Orleans was usually the hardest hit, but epidemics frequently covered the entire state. The epidemic diseases attacked quickly. One traveler on a steamboat saw a man "seized, dead within an hour, revived by being put in his coffin, dead again by noon, and finally cast overboard without a prayer."

The worst yellow fever epidemic occurred in 1853. At one time that year physicians reported that there were over 40,000 cases in the city. A writer

An old pamphlet contains this sketch of children carrying home coffins for members of their family who died in the New Orleans yellow fever epidemic of 1853.

has described New Orleans during one of these epidemics: "Funeral processions crowded every street. . . . The hum of trade was silent. The levee was a desert. The streets, wont to shine with fashion and beauty, were silent."

Many of the doctors were quacks.

One of them advertised that he could cure over twenty diseases by the use of "direct magnetism." There was much superstition—"night air" was bad for the health, wearing boots made of yellow paper covered with tallow, snuff, and mustard would cure the fever, ap-

178

plying leeches to the nape of the neck would cure a headache.

The state made some efforts to protect the public health and to provide for unfortunates. A State Board of Health functioned briefly during the 1820's and was reorganized in the 1850's. The state gave some assistance to the Howard Association, a New Orleans group which cared for the sick, and to various medical societies. Until the 1840's parish police juries cared for the deaf, dumb, blind, and insane, after which time the state provided institutions for these unfortunates. Orphans were usually cared for by private or religious asylums.

Amusements and Sports. Louisianians enjoyed all forms of amusements and sports; there were celebrations and rallies, processions and barbecues, firework displays and holiday parades, balls, parties, and charivaris. The people attended circuses, animal shows, and performances of freaks, acrobats, and sleight-of-hand artists. They heard lectures on scientific and general subjects—hypnotism, animals and birds, spiritualism, ventriloquism, laughing gas, and many others. They played billiards, cards, chess, checkers, and other indoor games. Weddings and family anniversaries were gay occasions.

Dancing was enjoyed by all classes of society. In the rural sections dances were held at private homes, to which people came on horseback or in buggies, the girls carrying their party shoes in little bags. The well-to-do had more formal balls. Slaves and poor free Negroes danced the calinda, the bamboula, the *carabine*, or the *pile chactas*. Masked balls were very popular, particularly in New Orleans.

By the end of the antebellum period the Mardi Gras season, from Twelfth Night to Shrove Tuesday, had developed into a time of fun and frivolity in South Louisiana and in New Orleans, culminating in maskings, parades, and balls on Mardi Gras day and night. The custom of celebrating Mardi Gras originated in southern Europe, was brought to Louisiana by the French, and later continued by the Spanish. During those colonial days, however, it was simple and only involved masking and walking along the streets on Shrove Tuesday. Masking was forbidden by the Spanish during the 1790's, was revived after the Louisiana Purchase, but was again forbidden by the Americans in 1806. Masked balls were permitted after 1823, and by 1827 masked marchers were thronging the streets of New Orleans and other towns.

The first formal Mardi Gras parade was held in 1838, and according to the New Orleans *Daily Picayune* featured "several carriages superbly ornamented—bands of music, horses richly caparisoned—personations of knights, cavaliers, heroes, demigods," and other figures, all mounted. The following year numerous balls were held during the weeks following Twelfth Night. The Mistick Krew of Comus was organized in 1857 and had John Milton's

Racing has always been popular in New Orleans. This is a sketch of the Metairie track made before the Civil War.

Paradise Lost as the subject of its parade.

Sports were always popular, and many planters bred and raced horses. There were several important race tracks in the state by 1860, the St. Francisville track and the Metairie track at New Orleans probably being the most notable. Perhaps the most famous race was run at the Metairie track in 1854, when the Louisiana horse Lecompte was beaten by the out-of-state horse Lexington in a match race.

Both bull- and bearbaiting were popular during the early years, but by the 1820's had generally disappeared. Boxing, cockfighting, foot racing, boat racing, ring tournaments, hunting, and fishing were all popular sports throughout the period.

One of the most unusual sports was shooting at the *papegai*. A crude animal or bird was made of wood, and each man paid for the chance to shoot at it and win a prize.

Education. Elementary education may be divided into two periods during the antebellum years. The first, or so-called Period of Beneficiarism, began in 1803 and ended in 1845. Public education was under the direction of the Secretary of State. During this period the state gave limited support to private, neighborhood, and religious schools, but state funds were intended to aid only these children whose parents could not afford to send them to other schools. Louisiana Catholics favored religious rather than public schools, and it was some years before Protestants and liberal Catholics could secure the establishment of a public school system. In 1817 there were fewer than 400 pupils enrolled in all the public elementary schools of Louisiana, but by 1840 the number had grown to more than 5,000.

The Period of Public Education began with the Constitution of 1845, which created the office of State Superintendent. Alexander Dimitry, who has been called the "Father of Louisiana Elementary Education," held this office from 1847 to 1851, during which period he organized and put into operation a state-wide public school system. By 1860 there were several hundred elementary schools in the state.

In rural areas schoolhouses were built of logs with holes left for windows. They had earthen floors, and seats made of split logs with wooden pegs for legs. Sometimes schools were conducted in the small Protestant churches of the Florida Parishes or the northern and western sections, being named after either creeks or biblical characters. The school term usually varied from six weeks to two months.

Throughout the period, however, most of the schools were operated and taught by private schoolmasters who advertised their schools in the newspapers. In one advertisement, it was announced that classes would be held from five to nine o'clock in the morning and from four to seven in the afternoon. The owner-teacher of the school guaranteed to teach the elements of reading, writing, and arithmetic in two to three months. He would correct the "most vicious hand-writing" in six to eight lessons, unless the student was "unprovided with intelligence."

Secondary education was handled by academies, most of which were short lived. They accepted boarding and day students, nearly all taught boys rather than girls, and very few of them accepted both sexes. By 1860 there were over 150 of these academies scattered over Louisiana with a total of nearly 450 teachers and nearly 12,000 students.

Few of the colleges were of modern college grade, and most of them would compare favorably with the better high schools of the present time. They were generally for men only and offered few scientific or professional courses.

The colleges may be divided into three groups. The first group was supported by the state and included the College of Orleans (1805-26), the College of Louisiana (1825-45) at Jackson, and the University of Louisiana which was founded in 1845 at New Orleans. The second group received limited

Louisiana State Seminary of Learning
and Military Academy, Pineville, 1860

state support, the most important of them being the College of Franklin (1831-45) at Opelousas and the College of Jefferson, which was organized in 1831 at Convent. The third group consisted of those colleges operated by the various religious denominations. The most important of these were: College of St. Charles, Catholic, founded in 1837 at Grand Coteau; the Centenary College of Louisiana, Methodist, founded in 1845 at Jackson; and Mount Lebanon University, Baptist, founded in 1852 at Mount Lebanon in North Louisiana.

The Constitution of 1845 also provided for the establishment of a state university, and the institution was chartered ten years later. The Louisiana State Seminary of Learning and Military Academy, the present-day Louisiana State University, was opened at Pineville in January, 1860.

Religion. When the state was admitted into the Union in 1812 most Louisianians were Catholics. In general the Catholics occupied South Louisiana, while the Protestants were more numerous in other sections of the state.

Baptists, Methodists, and Episcopalians migrated to Louisiana in large numbers during the territorial period, and by 1812 their churches were well established. Presbyterians, Lutherans, Disciples of Christ, Unitarians, and Universalists followed, and in communities where there were not enough members of any one denomination, the people joined together and organized "Union" or "Community" churches. Among the most noted Protestant ministers of the antebellum period were Dr. Benjamin M. Palmer, Dr. Theodore Clapp, and Bishop Leonidas Polk.

Louisiana boasted 572 churches in

1860; the Methodists had 199, the Baptists 161, the Catholics 99, the Presbyterians 42, and the Episcopalians 33. The Catholic churches were larger and more costly than the Protestant ones and were valued at nearly $1,750,-000. The Methodist churches ranked second with a valuation of about $337,-000.

Journalism. Many newspapers and a few magazines were published in antebellum Louisiana. During the period, New Orleans had over fifty newspapers and well over one hundred were printed in the smaller cities and towns. The newspapers tended to be short lived, were weeklies rather than dailies, and usually received some financial help from public printing or from political groups. They all copied news items from each other and from the newspapers of other states and foreign countries.

During the early years local political and general news received little space, but after the 1830's news of a local nature began to receive increasingly more consideration. Most of the news space was devoted to state news, agricultural material, communications from other papers, and tales and poetry copied from English or American magazines. Medical, legal, and local advertisements frequently occupied more than half of the total space. Most newspapers were printed on cheap paper in folios of four pages, and subscriptions ranged from $1.50 to $2.00 a year. Many southern Louisiana newspapers were published in both French and English, and in New Orleans several were published in Spanish and German.

The leading newspapers of New Orleans were the *Picayune, Delta, Crescent, Bee, Courier, True Delta, True American, Daily Topic,* and *Bulletin.* Other notable newspapers were the Baton Rouge *Advocate,* the Alexandria *Red River Republican* and the *Red River Whig,* the Opelousas *Courier,* the Vidalia *Concordia Intelligencer,* the Shreveport *Caddo Gazette,* and the Franklin *Planters' Banner.*

The most noted editors included George W. Kendall of the *Picayune,* John Gibson of the *True American,* and Alexander C. Bullitt of the *Bee.* Many of the smaller city and town editors were influential leaders in their communities.

A majority of the periodicals were published in New Orleans. *De Bow's Review* was filled with economic and agricultural information, the *Southern Quarterly Review* contained articles, fiction and poetry, and *La Propagateur Catholique (The Catholic Propagator)* printed articles of a religious nature. With the appearance in 1843 of *L'Album Littéraire,* whose guiding genius was Armand Lanusse, came the world's first recorded literary magazine published by Negroes. It presented stories, articles, poems, and folklore.

The library movement had started during the territorial period when the New Orleans Library Society was founded. By 1860 the state could boast

The French Opera House

over fifty libraries containing a total of over 100,000 volumes. The most noted of these libraries were the State Library, and the B. F. French Library and the Fisk Free Library, both of which were in New Orleans. Many towns had small subscription libraries. Some of the plantation families, such as the Butlers of "The Cottage" in West Feliciana Parish, had extensive collections of books, maps, and magazines. In New Orleans, booksellers sold volumes in English, French, Spanish, and other languages, while in smaller towns the general stores usually had a few books for sale.

The Theater, Music, and Literature. Although plays had been presented in Louisiana during the Spanish colonial period, it was not until after 1803 that theaters were built in New Orleans. In 1808 was built the St. Philip Theater, where plays were presented in both French and English. The Orleans Theater was completed in 1809, burned in 1813, and was rebuilt later, following another fire. Theatrical performances began about 6:30 P.M., lasting until nearly midnight, and the program would frequently include an opera, a serious drama, a farce or comedy, with several song, dance, and skit specialties in between. Throughout the period New Orleans was one of the leading theatrical towns in the United States.

Many of the smaller towns had theaters, one of the earliest of which was at St. Francisville, having been built sometime prior to 1812. By 1850 many towns had a theater and a theatrical group which presented plays, sometimes importing professional actors of national reputation.

The prominent theatrical managers of New Orleans included Noah Lud-

low, James H. Caldwell, Sol Smith, and John Davis. These men brought noted actors to New Orleans and to the larger cities of the state. Among them were Junius Brutus Booth and his son Edwin Booth, Charlotte Cushman, Lola Montez, Charles Keane and his wife Ellen Tree, Charles Macready, Fanny Ellsler, and many others. P. T. Barnum, who later became such a noted showman, had little success in Louisiana during his early years. After playing in New Orleans for a week in 1838, the company went to the Atakapas country. As Barnum later described the venture: "At Opelousas we exchanged the steamer for sugar and molasses; our company was disbanded, and I started for home."

New Orleans was the first American city permanently to establish opera. Beginning in 1808 it had a series of noted opera houses, ending in 1859 with the building of the New Orleans Opera House, affectionately called the "French Opera." New York did not open its first opera house until the 1830's. Many noted operas had their first American presentations in New Orleans. The opera was important socially as well as musically, and many planters and their families, together with their servants, went to New Orleans and remained for the entire opera season.

Concerts were also very popular, and Louisianians heard Jenny Lind, Anna Bishop, Ole Bull, and other vocal and instrumental artists.

The most noted native composer of the period was Louis Gottschalk. After

185

completing piano studies in Paris he toured Europe as a concert artist before returning to the United States. Among his best known compositions were "La Bamboula" and "Danse Nègre."

The blacks had their work songs and spirituals. They also played musical instruments, sometimes of their own making. One such band had only three musicians, with a group of singers; one tapped a cowhide-covered barrel with his hands, another beat upon the sides of a barrel with sticks, and a third scraped a stick over the teeth of a large jawbone. This percussion section was a forerunner of modern jazz music.

The educated free Negroes of antebellum New Orleans made music history in 1838 by organizing one of the first symphony orchestras in the United States. Edmond Dede, a black and one of several noted composers and conductors in New Orleans, migrated to France and became the conductor of a symphony orchestra in Bordeaux.

In the 1850's Louisiana's most serious writing was done in French, although English was rapidly being accepted. History was popular, as were poetry and drama. The two most important historians were François Xavier Martin and Charles Gayarré. Probably the best poetry was written by free Negroes. In 1845, eighty-two poems written by seventeen free black poets, including Victor Sejour (who had moved to Paris and become one of the most noted dramatists of his time), Camille Thierry, Joanni Questry, Armand Lanusse, and Pierre Dalcour were collected and published. *Les Canelles* (*The Hawthorns*) was possibly the world's first published collection of black poetry.

Thus it was in the years before the Civil War the free Negro group in New Orleans, largely through its own efforts, raised black culture to its highest level of achievement anywhere in the world, during this period.

19. THE ELECTION OF 1860 AND THE SECESSION OF LOUISIANA

Background. Twenty years before the election of 1860, New Orleans businessman Paul Tulane visited France

with his father. They viewed the economic desolation of Bordeaux, whose trade had been ruined by the abolition of slavery in the French West Indies. Tulane's father told him that slavery in the United States would one day be destroyed "and New Orleans will be ruined," not realizing that within two decades his prophecy would come true. The election of 1860 led to the secession of the southern states and civil war, and the following seventeen years were the most tragic in all Louisiana history.

The slavery issue had long troubled the United States. During the colonial period the people of the North had held slaves, but slave labor was not profitable there and the northern states had gradually abolished the institution. By 1820 they had begun to agitate for the abolition of slavery in the South, and by the 1830's this movement had politically divided the country.

It was hoped that the Compromise of 1850 would settle the problem, but during the 1850's a series of events further excited the people of both the North and South. *Uncle Tom's Cabin,* an antislavery book, appeared in 1852 and by mid-1853 had sold over a million copies in the North. The Republican Party was organized in 1854, principally to oppose the extension of slavery in the territories. Shortly afterwards came a bloody struggle between northern and southern settlers for the control of Kansas. The Dred Scott Decision of the United States Supreme Court irritated the North in 1857, and two years later John Brown's raid on Harpers Ferry, Virginia, inflamed the South.

In his last message to the Legislature in January, 1860, Governor Wickliffe recommended that Louisiana stand with the other southern states in protecting "our Constitutional rights." A week later, on January 23, Thomas O. Moore, the new Governor, spoke of the loyalty of Louisiana to the Union but insisted that every state "must be permitted to determine her own social institutions." It was his hope that harmony and peace would "be restored to our people without a sacrifice of interest or loss of honor."

The Election of 1860. The Democrats were the strongest political group in Louisiana. The old Whig Party was dead, and its former members could not join Abraham Lincoln and the Republicans, who were opposed to slavery. The Democratic Party split at the national convention, and the Louisiana delegates walked out with the other southerners, formed a southern wing of the party, and nominated John C. Breckinridge of Kentucky for President. Many Louisianians, however, were not satisfied with Breckinridge and instead supported John Bell, who was the candidate of a new party called the Constitutional Union Party. Only a small number of Louisianians supported Stephen A. Douglas of Illinois, the candidate of the northern wing of the Democratic Party.

The presidential campaign of 1860 was a lively one in Louisiana. There were meetings, barbecues, newspaper editorials, parades, fireworks, the firing of cannon, banners, music, and flags. Clubs were organized, the "Young Bell Ringers," the "Young Men's Douglas Clubs," the "Minute Men of '60," and numerous others. Lincoln was described as "the dirtiest and meanest Abolitionist alive," Bell was a "quaint, homely, sleepy old gentleman," and Douglas an "Abolition traitor" who wanted to rule or ruin the South. At a Breckinridge rally in New Orleans "20,000 voices uprose in earnest plaudits in approval of his manly sentiments."

Judah P. Benjamin spoke for most Louisianians when he said: "I have no stomach for a fight in which I am to have the choice between the man who denies me all my rights, openly and fairly [Lincoln], and a man who admits my rights but intends to filch them [Douglas]."

On election day, Louisiana gave Breckinridge 22,681 votes, Bell 20,204 votes, and Douglas 7,625. It is not recorded that Lincoln received a single vote. The Breckinridge majorities were principally in the central and northern sections, while Bell and Douglas received their majorities in the plantation sections of the southeast and in the industrial and commercial center of New Orleans.

Lincoln had, however, been elected President. As his course of action was not clear, public opinion was sharply divided in Louisiana, some hoping for a compromise solution to the critical problems. One group believed that the South should wait until after Lincoln's inauguration and see what he would do before taking any action; another argued that the time for the secession of the southern states had arrived; yet another group counseled a convention of all the southern states. A few people proclaimed that "we are doomed if we proclaim not our political independence."

Governor Moore called a special session of the Legislature, to meet on December 10, 1860, whose deliberations were marked by general harmony. The Governor recommended an election of members to a convention which would "determine the relations of Louisiana to the Federal government," for the problem rose "high above ordinary political considerations. It involves our present honor and our future existence as a free and independent people." A bill was passed calling for an election on January 7 of delegates to a state convention to meet on January 23 at Baton Rouge.

Most Louisianians approved of Governor Moore's action. The New Orleans *True Delta* stated that "Governor Moore is not what may be called a 'fast man' in politics; but if he is slower than some others, he is just as sure to come right in the end."

Public Opinion During Early Winter of 1860-61. The winter of 1860-61 in New Orleans promised to be gayer than usual. The crops had been good and prices were satisfactory. The hotels were filled with planters and businessmen and their families from all sec-

Louisiana Parishes 1860

Map 24—Louisiana parishes, 1860

tions of the state; the opera house and the theaters were crowded and excitement was in the air. Everyone talked politics, on the street, at public places, even at church. On November 29 Bishop B. M. Palmer preached a sermon using a text taken from Psalms 94:20: "Shall the throne of iniquity have fellowship with thee, which frameth mischief by a law?" He argued that the South should stand against the North, even to the extent of war, and that the South had a trust to defend, perhaps with the sword. "Not till the last man has fallen behind the last rampart, shall it drop from our hands; and then only in surrender to the God who gave it." Within a few days over thirty thousand copies of the sermon had been printed and sold. Many people no longer spoke of cooperation with the North. Instead, they talked of secession, *and then* cooperation with the United States.

But public opinion throughout the state was divided. One citizen challenged Palmer in the *True Delta*: "You would destroy the constitution and the union—this glorious and peerless fabric which has so long and so safely sheltered us, and what, sir, would you rear in its stead?" At a mass meeting at Franklin it was resolved to oppose the "unconditional secession of Louisiana," while those attending a St. James Parish meeting believed that the northern states should be expelled from the Union. At a New Orleans meeting "The Southern Marseillaise" was sung: "Sons of the South, awake to glory!"

Most newspapers favored secession, though some argued that the movement should not be hurried. Of the important newspapers the New Orleans *True Delta* and the Baton Rouge *Weekly Gazette and Comet* led the fight against secession. The New Orleans *Propagateur Catholique* counseled moderation. The Alexandria *Constitutional* joked about secession: "If Louisiana secedes from the Union . . . we shall be compelled to advocate the secession of the parish of Rapides from the State. . . . We have a large territory and a numerous population and are perfectly able to take care of ourselves."

Perhaps one New Orleans newspaper best summed up the public's attitude when it stated: "We are secessionists because we honestly believe that it is the only possible way in which we can enjoy the rights and privileges which the Union, as originally designed, was intended to bestow

upon all the States, according to the just measure of perfect equality."

As the election of January 7 approached, the people divided into two groups. The "Immediate Secessionists" believed that Louisiana should secede at once, while the "Cooperationists" thought that Louisiana should cooperate with the other southern states, and wait and see what Lincoln would do when he became President.

The Secession Convention. In the election of January 7, 1861, twenty-nine parishes were for secession, while nineteen parishes were for cooperation with the Federal government. To the Convention went eighty secessionists, forty-four cooperationists, and six men who were undecided.

The Convention met at Baton Rouge on January 23. Former Governor Mouton was elected president of the meeting and a committee of fifteen members was selected to report on the matter of secession.

Governor Moore reported that during the week after the election he had seized Forts Jackson and St. Philip below New Orleans, the United States Arsenal at Baton Rouge, a Federal revenue cutter, and some other government property.

On January 24, Chairman John Perkins, Jr., of Madison Parish, presented the report of the committee. The report was in the form of an ordinance, "An Ordinance to dissolve the union between the State of Loui-

The Ordinance of Secession of Louisiana.

siana and other States, united with her under the compact entitled 'The Constitution of the United States of America.' " The next day the Convention heard speeches of commissioners to Louisiana from Alabama and South Carolina asking for the cooperation of Louisiana in the forming of a Southern Confederacy. A communication from Louisiana's United States Senators John Slidell and Judah P. Benjamin asking for secession was also read.

Several members of the Convention opposed the Ordinance of Secession when it came up for debate, led by James G. Talliaferro from Catahoula Parish. Joseph A. Rozier of Orleans Parish and James O. Fuqua of East Baton Rouge Parish offered substitute ordinances, which were voted down. A motion to submit the matter to the people likewise failed.

The arguments were completed on January 26. The Ordinance of Secession was adopted by a vote of 113 to

Louisiana Secession Convention, Old State Capitol

17. When the vote was announced Mouton proclaimed: "I now declare the connection between the State of Louisiana, and the Federal Union dissolved; and that she is a free, sovereign and independent Power."

Later, when the Ordinance of Secession was signed, it received an overwhelming vote of 121 to 9.

Public Reaction to the Ordinance of Secession. Most of the newspapers received the news with enthusiasm. The *Picayune* said: "The deed has been done.... The Union is dead.... To the lone star of the State we transfer the duty, affection and allegiance we owed to the congregation of light which spangled the banner of the old Confederacy.... The South says to every child of hers, 'Son, give me all your heart.'" The New Orleans *Crescent* reported: "With a calm dignity and firm purpose, Louisiana resumes her delegated powers, and escapes from a Union in which she could no longer remain with honor to herself or to her sister States of the South."

Some of the newspapers, however, took an opposite position or counseled moderation. The *True Delta*, for example, flatly stated that "everything in this city appears to be in rapid progress towards a war establishment."

Other newspapers expressed sincere regret at leaving the Union. The Shreveport *South-Western* stated with emotion: "We this day, as orderly citizens, lower the 'stars and stripes' from our masthead! It is with heartfelt emotions, better imagined than portrayed, that we fold the saucy looking 'star spangled banner' that we have always loved, and place the precious memento under our pillow."

Most people were enthusiastic. In New Orleans, guns thundered at the foot of Canal Street, state flags were flung to the breeze, and at night public buildings and private homes were brilliantly lighted. The *Picayune* reported that the people were ready to "defend the sovereignty of Louisiana, come what might, and in the face of every obstacle."

The Republic of Louisiana. For almost two months, from January 26 until March 21 when it joined the Confederate States of America, Louisiana was an independent nation. Governor Moore acted as president, the Legislature acted as Congress, and the state courts served in the place of Federal courts.

For nearly three weeks the old state flag was the national flag of Louisiana. Then on February 11 the Convention adopted a new flag. It had thirteen stripes, six of white, four of blue, and three of red. In the upper left-hand corner was a red field with a five-pointed yellow star. The flag represented the thirteen stripes of the original Union, the tricolor of France, and the red and yellow colors of Spain. The first flag was made by H. Cassidy, a tent- and sailmaker of New Orleans, and it flew over the New Orleans City Hall until the city was captured in April, 1862.

By the middle of February, Governor Moore had appropriated all the property of the United States in Louisiana. Forts Pike and Macomb had been occupied by the state militia; the United States Mint and Custom House in New Orleans had been secured, along with over $600,000 which was in the Mint.

The state Legislature and the Secession Convention continued to meet, with the Legislature passing laws and the Convention adopting ordinances which had the same effect as laws. The work of the Convention was the more important, but it performed functions which should have been handled by the Legislature. It held four meetings in Baton Rouge and then moved to New Orleans. It named delegates to the Convention of the Southern States at Montgomery, Alabama; it transferred the powers of the national government to the government of the state and handled problems of finance, court, and postal affairs; it opened the Mississippi River to all friendly nations. Finally, on March 21 it ratified the Constitution of the Confederate States of America, which had been organized at the Montgomery meeting of the southern states, and transferred funds to the new national government of the South.

Meanwhile, the Legislature invited the people of southern Indiana and Illinois to join the Confederacy as a state. It appropriated $1,500,000 for the defense of Louisiana, provided for the organization of military units, and outfitted warships at the Algiers shipyard.

The Legislature and the Convention adjourned on March 26. During those two months Louisiana had been successively a state of the American Union, an independent nation, and a member of the Confederate States of America.

The people of the state generally supported the action of the two bodies. The *True Delta,* however, blasted the work of the Convention. "The Lyceum hall wigwam, jocosely called a state convention, ingloriously fizzled out yesterday. By the usual appliances of the rag-and-lampblack aristocracy, they succeeded in getting all they required of the wigwam convention." It predicted a dreadful and bloody future for Louisiana.

Louisiana Mobilizes for War. During these months Louisiana was busy mobilizing her military strength. The Governor appointed a Military Board and by February 14 the board had issued weapons to nearly 1,800 eager young members of volunteer companies. These volunteers took an oath to "bear true allegiance to the state of Louisiana, and serve it honestly and faithfully . . . and obey the orders of the governor and such officers as may be appointed over me."

The organization of military companies continued over the entire state. A British traveler wrote that Confederate flags were flying everywhere, military companies were constantly parading, and that New Orleans looked like a military camp. The "Louisiana Marseillaise" was sung everywhere. New Orleans Irishmen implored New Orleans Spaniards to join the colors: "For the love of the Virgin and your own soul's sake, Fernandey, get up and cum along wid us to fight the Yankees." All but one of the cadets at the State Seminary at Pineville marched off to enlist in the Confederate army. "Get ready for the fight," urged the *Crescent,* "and meet it to the death when it comes."

The War Begins. On April 12, 1861, Confederate batteries opened fire on Fort Sumter, at the entrance to the Charleston, South Carolina, harbor. The fort surrendered and on April 15, President Lincoln called for 75,000 volunteers to force the South back into the Union. Four days later the first of these troops passed through Baltimore and in a fight with the citizens killed and wounded a number of them. The next morning the *Crescent* screamed with the headline, "NORTHERN TROOPS MOVING SOUTHWARD."

The next night young Maryland-born James R. Randall, a teacher at Poydras College in Pointe Coupee Parish, seized his pen and wrote the words to one of the most noted songs of the Confederacy:

The despot's heel is on thy shore, Maryland!
His torch is at thy temple door, Maryland!

.   .   .   .   .   .

Thou wilt not yield the vandal toll;
Thou wilt not crook to his control;
Better the fire upon thee roll,
Better the shot, the blade, the bowl,
Than crucifixion of the soul.
Maryland! My Maryland!

In New Orleans, on May 27, 1861, young Kate Stone, not yet twenty-one, sat down and wrote in her diary: "A nation fighting for its own homes and liberty cannot be overwhelmed. Our Cause is just and must prevail."

The conventions and the campaigns and the speechmaking were over. It was time for the work of war.

Map 25—Lower Mississippi River area, 1850's

MAP OF THE

MISSISSIPPI RIV.

from
PRINCETON
to the
GULF OF MEXICO.

Alexandria
riverfront
during the
Civil War

PART SIX
Civil War and
Military Occupation,
1861–1877

20. LOUISIANA AND THE WAR
FOR SOUTHERN INDEPENDENCE

A Name for the War. Many names have been given to the war which was fought between the United States of America and the Confederate States of America from the spring of 1861 to the late spring of 1865. When the official records of the war were published by the United States government some years after the war had ended it was called the War of the Rebellion. Southerners have generally called it the War Between the States. A New England historian, Edward Channing, titled it the War for Southern Independence and this title, in the writer's opinion, is the best and the most accurate. Most people today simply call it the Civil War, for this is a short and handy title. Whatever its name, it was the bloodiest war in American history.

1861. This was the year of preparation. Military supplies of all types were assembled in Louisiana government warehouses. Small industrial plants were established for making those

197

goods which normally were imported from outside the state. Boats were sent along the rivers and bayous to collect scrap iron to be sent to iron foundries in New Orleans for manufacturing war supplies. Uniforms, hats, shoes, tents, and other goods were produced. The planting of food crops was encouraged. It was a year of feverish activity.

Governor Moore called for volunteers, and the towns and villages were soon witnessing drills and parades. One visitor to New Orleans wrote that "the streets are full of Turcos, Zouaves, Chasseurs; walls are covered with placards of volunteer companies." The Louisiana soldiers gave picturesque names to their companies—the Knights of the Border, the Catahoula Guerrillas, the Caddo Lake Boys, the Mounted Wild Cats, the Yankee Pelters, and of course the Louisiana Tigers. Over sixty thousand troops were enlisted in the state during the war and about one-third of this number during the first nine months of 1861. Many of the companies, however, marched off to war without adequate supplies or proper equipment.

The government fitted out gunboats for river patrol work and strengthened the defenses of Fort Jackson and Fort St. Philip below New Orleans. The Legislature, meeting in November of 1861, passed several emergency laws; the state spent over $1,500,000 during the year on military equipment and supplies; and by December New Orleans boasted that "Chalmette's glories

will be repeated," should the enemy attack the city.

1862. Governor Moore was fearful of an attack on New Orleans, and early in 1862 he made plans for improving the city defenses. Under General Mansfield Lovell entrenchments were prepared, additional cannon were mounted, and adjacent bayous were obstructed. Rafts held together by heavy chains were strung across the Mississippi between Forts Jackson and St. Philip.

In mid-April the attacking Federal fleet commanded by Flag Officer David G. Farragut appeared off the mouth of the Mississippi, accompanied by a large military force under the command of General Benjamin F. Butler. The bombardment of the forts began on April 18, and early on the morning of April 24 the fleet succeeded in running past them. As General Lovell had only about three thousand militia troops, he ordered them to withdraw from New Orleans to Camp Moore, just north of Amite.

One Confederate soldier described the scene in New Orleans on the night of April 24: "It was in the wildest confusion. Anxious men and women thronged the streets. . . . The burning of cotton in various parts of the city added a grim feature to the scene."

New Orleans was officially occupied on April 28, and on May 1 General Butler took formal possession of the city. Not long after the fall of New Orleans, the Federal fleet moved up

The Opelousas courthouse was the temporary state capitol in 1862.

the river, took possession of Baton Rouge, and on May 28 a military force arrived at the capital. In early August of that year a Confederate army attacked Baton Rouge but failed to capture the city, which, however, was evacuated by the Federals late in the same month. Butler had previously ordered that the town be burned, but at the last moment he relented and countermanded the order. However, a Federal officer wrote: "This place has been nearly completely sacked by the soldiery. . . . Even officers' tents are filled with furniture from deserted houses."

In October a strong Federal force commanded by General Godfrey Weitzel marched down Bayou Lafourche and defeated the Confederates at Labadieville. Weitzel then continued on to the Bayou Teche country to attack General Alfred Mouton, son of former Governor Mouton, near Franklin. In the middle of December General Nathaniel P. Banks superseded Gen-

199

The burning of the State Capitol.

eral Butler in command of the Federal army in Louisiana, and on December 17 reoccupied Baton Rouge, which he called "the first rebel position on the river."

Eleven days later the State Capitol burned and most of the state's official records were destroyed.

By the end of the year, all that stood between Federal control of the Lower Mississippi were the Confederate strongholds at Port Hudson, on the river north of Baton Rouge, and Vicksburg, Mississippi, further upstream.

1863. Early in 1863, General U. S. Grant invaded northeast Louisiana as part of his movement against Vicksburg and although there was little fighting in this area, much property was destroyed. In March a Federal detachment occupied a considerable portion of the Florida Parishes but was forced to return to New Orleans a short time later.

The following month General Banks advanced up Bayou Teche, captured Opelousas, and in early May occupied Alexandria; Confederate opposition came from two small armies

Union encampment at Baton Rouge in
1862.

commanded by General Mouton and General Richard Taylor, the son of former President Zachary Taylor. Though this campaign was of little military importance, during the course of it the Federal army destroyed or carried off considerable property from the countryside. Banks reported that he had *confiscated* over 20,000 horses, mules, and cattle, over 5,000 bales of cotton and "many hogsheads of sugar." One northern soldier wrote that "the army is doing nothing else but gathering cotton." Later in May, Banks crossed the Mississippi at Bayou Sara, moving south to lay siege to Port Hudson, and within a few weeks the Con-

federates had recaptured Alexandria, Opelousas, and the towns along the Teche.

The Port Hudson stronghold was defended by slightly over 5,000 Confederate troops, while the Federal army in the area has been estimated at from three times to six times that number. The siege lasted forty-five days, including twenty-one days of hard fighting. The Confederates ran out of food supplies, and one soldier reported that a boiled rat was a "better dish than I had expected." On July 4, Vicksburg surrendered to General Grant and five days later Port Hudson fell. All the Confederate forts along

201

Union artillery firing on Confederate positions at Port Hudson, 1863.

the Mississippi had now been captured and President Lincoln could say that "the Father of Waters rolls unvexed to the sea."

1864. Federal military plans called for the complete occupation of Louisiana in 1864. This was to be accomplished by sending a large military and naval expedition up the Red River to capture Shreveport, after which the Federal army would be able to invade Texas. At the same time the central Louisiana area would yield large amounts of cotton, livestock, and other supplies.

In early March, Admiral David

Porter of the United States Navy assembled a strong fleet of gunboats at the mouth of the Red River, where he was quietly joined by an army of about 10,000 men which had come down the Mississippi from the vicinity of Vicksburg. As this combined force began to move up the Red River, about 20,000 Federals moved northward from Franklin. Fort DeRussy, about thirty miles below Alexandria, was captured on March 14, and two days later Alexandria fell.

The united Federal armies, under General Banks, then moved up the south bank of the Red River, followed by the river fleet. The Confederate

202

army of under 9,000 men, commanded by General Richard Taylor, retreated, fighting rear-guard actions to slow up the enemy. It retreated through Natchitoches but stopped about three miles southeast of Mansfield, where the bloody Battle of Mansfield was fought on April 8. It was a costly Con-

One of the big guns manned by Confederate troops on the bluffs at Port Hudson.

FRED BENTON, JR.

A mortarboat used by Admiral David
D. Porter in the bombardments of Port
Hudson and Forts Jackson and St.
Philip.

A Confederate charge up the slope at
the battle of Pleasant Hill.

federate victory, for General Mouton was killed. General Taylor reported that "the charge made by Mouton across the open was magnificent" and that "seven standard-bearers fell one after another with the flag of the Crescent Regiment." The defeated Federals retreated about twenty miles that night to Pleasant Hill. The next afternoon there was another battle, which was won by neither side, although the Federal army immediately afterward retreated toward Alexandria.

The retreating Federal army left such destruction in its wake that the area became known as "the burnt district." As one Louisiana woman described it: "Houses, gins, mills, barns, and fences were burned; negroes all carried off; horses, cattle, hogs, every living thing, driven away or killed." Before the Union troops retreated from Alexandria they set fire to the city, despite the orders of General Banks. Other Federal officers were not so considerate—General A. J. Smith was reported to have said, as he looked back at the burning city, "Boys, this *looks like war!*" The angry Confederates closed in on the Federal army below Alexandria, and the Federal retreat became a rout until the protection of the powerful Mississippi River gunboats was secured.

1865. There were no important battles or campaigns in Louisiana during 1865. The Federal armies controlled the whole of the southeastern part of the state and the Confederate forces were not strong enough to attack them.

By the beginning of 1865 the South was exhausted and even the army of General Robert E. Lee in Virginia could not be supplied. Louisiana's Confederate Governor Henry Watkins Allen had hopes of continuing the war, but the people had become dispirited. Soldiers began to desert and go home, one soldier reporting that from six to twelve of his comrades were deserting every night. The war was almost over.

General Lee surrendered at Appomattox, Virginia, on April 9 and General Joseph E. Johnston in North Carolina a few days later. On May 17 Major David F. Boyd wrote from Alexandria: "All is confusion and demoralization here, nothing like order or discipline remains. . . . We must look the matter square in the face and shape our actions (personally and officially) accordingly."

On May 26, General Simon B. Buckner, acting for General Kirby Smith who had gone to Houston, surrendered the Confederate armies west of the Mississippi. General Smith signed the official documents on June 2. On that same day Governor Allen left Shreveport and headed toward exile in Mexico.

The fighting had ended. The South had lost its war for independence.

Billy Yanks and Johnny Rebs. Both Federal and southern soldiers generally accepted army life without much complaint. The northern soldier, being much better equipped, complained less than his southern opponent about clothing, food, and other supplies. As the war progressed, the Confederate supply system gradually failed and her soldiers had to acquire clothing as best they could and learned to eat practically anything.

Northern soldiers complained about Louisiana rains, snakes, lice, and particularly mosquitoes. One soldier wrote: "I don't suppose there is a spot on earth where there are so many snakes to the acre as right here." From Port Hudson, another soldier complained: "Every hollow became a puddle before the fellows sleeping in it could get out. . . . We are soaking wet before we know. . . . We stand around and growl for awhile and then settle down and are soon asleep again." Body lice did not cause too much trouble for "we just boil our clothes and that's the end of them. Their feeding time is when we are still for awhile, but at the first move they all let go and grab fast to our clothing." All the soldiers hated mosquitoes: "If I had a brigade of men as determined as these Brashear City mosquitoes, I believe I could sweep the Rebellion off its feet in a month's time."

The citizen soldiers of both sides adapted themselves to war and the constant threat of death as best they could. One Confederate wrote that "some of the boys seemed a little frightened under their first fire; as to myself, . . . I did not feel brave at

all." A northerner scrawled in his diary that the cannon balls "keep coming, and we dodge less and less. If they keep at it long enough I suppose we shall get used to it, as we have to a great many other things." Another Yank complained that "the Rebs seem to be getting madder all the time," while a third grumbled, "those cusses jest shot my pipe square out of my trousers' pocket. Look at that hole, now! . . . I wish I was in Massachusetts."

Northern and southern soldiers believed strongly in the cause for which they fought. Young Robert Patrick of Clinton thus expressed his feelings at the grave of a dead enemy: "You were not satisfied to remain at home, and let us alone; you must come to the South to murder our citizens, burn our houses, desolate our homes and lay waste to our country. . . . You for one have met your just reward, which is a grant of land from the Confederates, of three feet by six, in an obscure spot, where your friends, if you have any, will never be able to find your body, for there is nothing to mark the spot except a small hillock of red clay, which a few hard rains will wash away and it will disappear forever."

However, most soldiers, North and South, fought bravely, accepted hardships, remained loyal, and were a credit to their armies.

Government During the War.
Thomas O. Moore served as Governor

The Confederate attack on a Union wagon train at Mansfield

"With Fate Against Them," from a painting by Gilbert Gaul, picturing the embattled Confederacy

until January 25, 1864, when he was succeeded by Henry Watkins Allen. Both governors were conscientious men who did the best they could for a war-torn state.

As the Federal armies advanced, the state capital had to be moved. It was at Baton Rouge when the war began, but with the occupation of that city in May, 1862, it was moved to Opelousas. There it remained until January, 1863, when it was moved again, this time to Shreveport. The Caddo Parish Courthouse was used as a capitol, while the Governor's office was in an old frame building on the north side of Texas Street.

The state government faced many wartime problems. The Legislature passed laws which, because of the presence of the Federal army, were impossible to enforce. The raising of armies and the furnishing of supplies were problems of outstanding importance. Supply depots were established, and numerous small factories were built, including packing houses, cotton-cloth factories, and medical laboratories. The raising of war funds and the collection of taxes were difficult. Many governmental and legal records were captured or destroyed.

Local police juries and town officials also had many responsibilities. They paid bounties to men who enlisted, equipped the soldiers, furnished relief to needy families, repaired roads, bridges, and ferries, and tried to maintain order in the towns and parishes.

Not all Louisianians were loyal to

Confederate Governor of Louisiana, Henry Watkins Allen.

the state. Outlaws hid in the hills and swamps, while bands of armed men called "Jay-Hawkers" evaded military service, plundered the countryside, burned houses and other buildings, and killed civilians. Patrols, Home Guards, and Rangers were organized to defend the people of Louisiana who lived within the Confederate lines. The great majority of Negroes remained loyal to their masters or to the state until the invasion of the northern armies.

Louisiana state and local government began to disintegrate during the spring of 1865. Governor Allen did what he could to keep the processes of government in action, but to no avail. Soldiers and civilians broke into warehouses and carried off supplies; law enforcement ceased. Finally, the Governor issued his last message to the people of Louisiana. He advised them to accept defeat, to refrain from acts of violence, to go to work and rebuild the state. He said: "If possible forget the past. Look forward to the future. Act with candor and discretion, and you will live to bless him who in parting gives you this last advice."

Allen was one of many Confederate officials, both civil and military, who left for foreign countries.

Life in the Federal Occupied Areas. Many sections of the state were occupied by Federal armies during the war, some of these areas being occupied continuously, while others were held for short periods only. Generally speaking, the southeastern section of the state was occupied after the fall of New Orleans in April, 1862.

General Butler took formal possession of New Orleans on May 1, 1862. He was a former Massachusetts Democratic political leader, a stout man, with a fair complexion and bright but squinting eyes. He was generally popular with his soldiers, largely because they enjoyed making fun of his high-pitched voice and his somewhat grotesque actions. One of them wrote that "he tumbles all to pieces with distress. His body jerks forward; his elbows flap up and down like wings; he seems

to trot several feet ahead of his horse; he arrives at the scene of confusion with a face of anguish."

One of General Butler's first acts was to order the execution of forty-one-year-old William B. Mumford, who had pulled down an American flag flying from the United States Mint two days before the formal occupation of the city. To the people of the South, Mumford was a hero and a martyr, and Butler was his murderer.

Butler issued strict orders regulating the actions of the people of the city, and when the women refused to obey the regulations or to act with discretion toward the Union soldiers, he issued his infamous Order No. 28 against them. Southerners believed that this order gave the Federal troops permission to insult the women of New Orleans. There was severe criticism from southern and foreign leaders alike. Butler tried to enlist Louisiana Negroes, then drafted them. At war's end four regiments, a total of 25,000 blacks, had been enrolled in the Federal army. Only in Kentucky and Tennessee were there comparable Negro enlistments. He ordered the people of New Orleans to take an oath of allegiance or register as "enemies of the United States."

These acts inflamed the people of New Orleans, all of Louisiana, and the entire South, and made Butler the most hated man in all Louisiana history. But Butler did much for which the people of New Orleans should have thanked him. He fixed prices so

209

that profiteers could not operate, installed a system of public works which cleaned up the city, and gave free food and clothing to the destitute. He closed the gambling houses and stopped the sale of intoxicating liquors. Finally, he brought teachers from the North and reorganized the school system.

But on September 24, 1862, Butler ordered the Confiscation Law to be put into effect. This law stated that the property of all citizens who had not registered their allegiance to the United States was to be subject to confiscation. By late October nearly seventy thousand persons had registered, and those who had not done so suffered greatly. While the common soldiers were held in tight rein, Butler's officers began to acquire property of all types under the guise of confiscation. In all probability Butler himself did not acquire property in this manner, but his brother, A. J. Butler, was reputed to have made a fortune for the family by various forms of unlawful practice. The word "Butlerize," meaning "to steal," came into common use.

General Butler was replaced in December, 1862, by General Nathaniel P. Banks. One New Orleanian reported Butler's departure from the city: "There was not one hurrah, not one sympathizing cry went up for him from the vast crowd which went to see him off—a silent rebuke. I wonder if he felt it!"

General Banks eased regulations but

the confiscation of property in areas occupied by the Federal armies continued until the end of the war. Most Louisianians, in New Orleans and throughout the rest of the state, never became reconciled to Federal occupation. On one occasion someone remarked to General Banks that New Orleans was a Union city. Banks replied: "A Union city? I could carry every Union man in it on a hand-car."

Life of the People During Wartime. Life was difficult for the people at home during the war. The state and local governments were unstable and often powerless to enforce the laws; sugar, cotton, and other crops could not be sold; banks did not have money to lend and merchants could not afford to give credit; ordinary manufactured goods could not be found. Crop production fell off, and some families left the state and went to Texas in order to make a living. Much of the labor had to be performed by women and children, since the men were in the army.

Nearly all goods sold for high prices, which many people could not afford, and Confederate money consistently depreciated in value. By 1864 butter sold for $5.00 per pound; eggs, $5.00 a dozen; and beans, $2.50 a quart. Watermelons were sometimes priced as high as $5.00 each, but from Alexandria in August, 1864, one soldier wrote that melons were plentiful "and in consequence I was never meloncholly."

210

People used many substitutes. Old-fashioned home remedies took the place of ordinary medicines, cloth was woven at home and then hand-sewn into clothing, socks were knitted, straw hats were woven, and shoes were made from odd bits of leather and cloth, and sometimes soled with paper and wood. He lived well who could secure or afford the bare necessities of life.

Much property was destroyed wherever the armies moved. The Federal forces systematically looted the countryside, thus preventing supplies from being sent to the Confederate soldiers and compelling them to live off the country through which they marched. Many Federal officers deliberately ordered the burning of property. Years afterward, General James Tuttle admitted that he had been a "house-burner" and that he was the "General Tuttle whose troops, on the march from Milliken's Bend to Grand Gulf, burned so many fine houses on Lake St. Joseph."

Federal soldiers also carried slaves off to New Orleans, enrolled them in newly organized Negro companies, or encouraged them to quit work and have a "perfect jubilee." A neighbor wrote Governor Moore, regarding his plantation, that every morning he could "see the beeves being driven up from the woods to the quarters," and that the contents of the plantation house were distributed among the slaves. But many slaves were completely loyal to their master and cared

General Benjamin Franklin Butler, "the most hated man in all Louisiana history."

for and protected his family while he was away fighting in the Confederate army.

Most Louisianians accepted the hardships of war and loss of property without complaint and were proud of their fathers, brothers, and sons who served in the armies of the Southern Confederacy.

Buildings were burned in Baton Rouge during the Federal occupation.

General Kirby Smith at Shreveport, May 23, 1865

21. THE PERIOD OF MILITARY OCCUPATION, 1862-1877

Explanation. This period falls into two separate divisions. The first was the war period, which began in April, 1862, when New Orleans fell, and lasted until the surrender of General Kirby Smith in June, 1865. New Orleans was held by the Federal army until the end of the war, while other sections of the state were occupied and controlled by Federal military forces for periods of varying length. The second period began with the end of the war and lasted until the spring of 1877, when President Rutherford B. Hayes withdrew the United States army units from Louisiana.

In American history the era from 1865 to 1877 is generally referred to as Reconstruction. This name, however, is hardly apt. "Reconstruction" means "rebuilding," and there was little of that done by the Federal government in the South during those years. More accurately, it was a period of military occupation, for troops remained in the South for a number of years after the war had ended. They stayed in Louisiana from June, 1865, to April, 1877. During these years the army commanders directed or controlled Louisiana's political, economic, and social life.

General Summary of the Period. The soldiers of Louisiana returned home in 1865 to a war-ravaged state. They faced four major problems: the restoration of state and local self-government, the rebuilding of agriculture, the development of industry to supply basic home needs, and the definition of the place in society of the newly freed Negro. Louisianians would have liked to be left alone to solve their own problems but this, of course, was not to be.

Many northerners wanted revenge on the South. One northern historian has written that "Northern revenge in the guise of the preservation of the dearly won Union was worse for the South than the war." At Alexandria, General George Custer's wife expressed the wish that "Abraham Lincoln could have been spared to bring his justice and gentle humanity" to solve the problems.

213

Oscar Dunn

The most important problem was the relationship between the former slaveowners and their former slaves. The whites, unaccustomed to the change, still treated the Negroes as slaves. With freedom a reality, many of the former slaves, large numbers of whom had never been taught to read or write, expected more than their new status gave them. It would have required wise statesmen to solve these problems, but there appeared to be few of this category in Louisiana.

It was a time of almost constant disorder. Soldiers of the occupying army insulted and humiliated both blacks and whites. Former slaves left the plantations and roamed the land. Radical political leaders kept in power by the Federal army looted the state and committed other excesses.

The Radical politicians who controlled state government during the years from 1865 to 1877 might be divided into three groups. "Carpetbaggers" were persons from outside

Louisiana who had packed their belongings in a carpetbag and come to the state to win political power and make personal fortunes. "Scalawags" were Louisianians who joined the Radical group for reasons of personal profit. Former slaves and poor free Negroes formed the third group.

Many of the United States army officers stationed in the various towns sincerely attempted to prevent disorder. They counseled moderation, urged former slaves to return to farms and plantations, and tried to prevent lawlessness. They advised the Negroes —who were the first black voters in a white-dominated nation anywhere in the world—to accept their duties of citizenship.

Several blacks rose to positions of political importance. Oscar J. Dunn served as Lieutenant Governor for over three years, until his death in the fall of 1871. P. B. S. Pinchback was Acting Governor for about five weeks prior to the inauguration of Kellogg in January, 1873.

Hundreds of Negroes became minor officials or were given offices in town, parish, or state government. Many of these men were not able to read or write. A black historian has written that while many of the Negroes were "illiterate and unprepared for such a transformation in the majority of cases," here and there among them were well-qualified men.

The Negro Radicals, however, should not be blamed too harshly for the part they played during this tragic period. The majority of them were only a short time removed from slavery, had little if any education and no experience in politics or government, and were used as tools by unscrupulous white men. The New York *World* admitted that a "White Man's Party" had been forced upon Louisiana through the organization of a "Black Man's Party," which Radical white leaders had used to rule the state.

The Governorships of Shepley and Hahn. President Lincoln believed that a state could not lawfully leave the Union. As soon as New Orleans was occupied, plans were made to establish a civil government and General George F. Shepley was appointed Military Governor of the state on June 11, 1862. He was, however, under the authority of General Benjamin F. Butler.

Shepley restored partial civil government in those areas which were under Federal control. He ordered a congressional election to be held in December in the first and second districts, and Michael Hahn and Benjamin F. Flanders, both of whom were citizens of the state, were elected. They were finally admitted to their seats in the House of Representatives, serving until March, 1863. No other Louisiana Representatives or Senators were admitted to Congress until after the end of the war.

Two political parties were organized, the Conservative Party and the Free State Party, which was favored by the national government. In August, 1863, Lincoln asked General Shepley to aid the citizens of the southeast portion of the state, which was controlled by the Federal armies, in the reorganization of their government. An election was held in February, 1864, and Michael Hahn was elected Federal Governor of that section of Louisiana. Hahn was a Bavarian who had been reared in Louisiana and had taken the oath of allegiance to the United States after the surrender of New Orleans.

Federal Governor Hahn was inaugurated in March, 1864. A few days later an election was held for members to a constitutional convention which met in New Orleans in early April. The Constitution of 1864 abolished slavery, permitted limited Negro suffrage, broadened the powers of the Legislature, and extended public education. Otherwise there were few fundamental changes from the Constitution of 1852. Federal Governor Hahn resigned in March, 1865, after his election to the United States Senate.

Generally, the governorships of Shepley and Hahn were marked by good government and a sincere desire to help the people of Louisiana.

During this period, of course, Thomas O. Moore and Henry Watkins Allen were the governors of Confederate Louisiana. The regular election had been held in November, 1863, and Allen had been elected Governor, taking office in January, 1864.

215

The Louisiana Returning Board, taking the oath

A mass meeting of New Orleans citizens around the Clay statue on Canal Street in 1874

Until the end of the war, therefore, Louisiana had two state governments, the Confederate government and the government supported by the Federal army in the occupied areas.

Governors Wells, Flanders, and Baker. Lieutenant Governor J. Madison Wells of Rapides Parish became Federal Governor of the occupied section of the state upon the resignation of Governor Hahn. The war ended soon after, and the paroled Confederate soldiers, many of whom recovered their citizenship by taking President Andrew Johnson's amnesty oath, returned home. The civil government of Louisiana was recognized, and at the November election Wells was elected for a regular term. It was not long, however, before he was accused of exceeding his authority as Governor and thereby lost the respect of many white citizens. On June 3, 1867, General Philip Sheridan, the army commander in Louisiana, removed him from office, probably because he had not followed closely enough the Radical congressional legislation which had been passed in March, 1867.

Benjamin F. Flanders was appointed to succeed Governor Wells, but resigned after serving only about six months. In January, 1868, General Winfield S. Hancock, who had succeeded General Philip Sheridan, appointed Joshua Baker as Governor. The Constitution of 1868, which was chiefly designed to give blacks political and social rights, was ratified in March. It was the first such Louisiana document to contain a formal bill of rights. It was, for the most part, a Radical constitution.

A state election was held at the same time that the Constitution of 1868 was ratified, and Henry Clay Warmoth was elected Governor, with Negro Oscar Dunn as Lieutenant Governor. Warmoth was to take office on July 13, 1868, but on June 27, General U. S. Grant removed Governor Baker and appointed Warmoth to serve until he was inaugurated for his regular term.

Henry Clay Warmoth as Governor. The worst evils of the entire period began with the administration of Governor Warmoth. Louisiana historian Alcée Fortier stated that Warmoth "may have had good intentions . . . but his administration proved to be as disastrous to Louisiana as the scourge of the epidemic and the torrents of the Mississippi." Factional politics plagued the state, each faction stealing as much money as possible. The Governor secured the passage of the Metropolitan Police Bill which organized a police force for Orleans, Jefferson, and St. Bernard parishes under his personal control, and he became practically a dictator through his control of the Legislature and through his police powers. He secured the election of a Legislature in which nearly 50 per cent of the House of Representatives and nearly 20 per cent of the Senate were blacks, some of

217

Shreveport in the 1870's. From a contemporary drawing.

them ex-slaves who could neither read nor write. This Legislature ratified the Fourteenth Amendment to the Constitution of the United States giving Negroes citizenship, and the Fifteenth Amendment giving them the right to vote.

These actions brought a storm of protest. The Knights of the White Camellia and other secret organizations spread fear among blacks and whites, scalawags and carpetbaggers, and broke up Radical Negro-white political meetings.

The Radicals organized the Union League, and it was not long before Louisiana was virtually in a state of civil war, with race riots and other disorders occurring in many sections.

In the election of 1872, William Pitt Kellogg was the candidate of the Radical faction, while the Democrats and Liberal Republicans supported John McEnery. Although the election returns proved the election of McEnery, the Radical Returning Board declared that all the Radical candidates had been elected. However, Warmoth and his faction quarreled, and on December 9, 1872, he was impeached by the House of Representatives and suspended from office. He was succeeded by P. B. S. Pinchback, a Negro who had been elected President of the Senate after the death of Lieutenant Governor Dunn (which made him acting Lieutenant Governor and next in line for the governorship).

Little of importance occurred during the one-month governorship of Pinchback. Warmoth denied the legality of the Legislature's action in impeaching him and refused to appear to answer the impeachment charges. Thus matters remained until the inauguration of Kellogg on January 14, 1873.

The Governorship of William Pitt Kellogg. If Warmoth's governorship had been stormy, Kellogg's days in office were tempestuous. It was a period of constant lawlessness and political turmoil.

There were bloody riots in Colfax, New Orleans, Coushatta, and other cities. The people refused to pay taxes and organized the People's League for resisting their collection. Kellogg added to the Governor's power by persuading the Legislature to organize the Metropolitan Police into a Metropolitan Brigade on a state-wide basis, subject to the call of the Governor. About this time the White League was organized in Opelousas to oppose the Radical white and Negro domination of the state. A unit of the Brigade was soon sent to St. Martinville where Alcibiade De Blanc, a former Justice of the State Supreme Court, organized a unit of the White League and defeated the Brigade.

Reaction set in, and Negroes in several sections of the state deserted the Radicals and joined the Liberal Democrats and Republicans. Radical officials were forced to resign in some parishes. President Grant realized that the military occupation of Louisiana must end or a new Civil War would begin, but he left the decision to withdraw the troops to his successor.

The Election of 1876. The campaign of 1876 began with the organization of political clubs throughout the state. The Radicals organized the Packard Guard, the Councils of Freedom, the Antoine Defenders or the Invincibles. The Liberal groups, in turn, organized the Nicholls-Wiltz Club, the Tilden-Hendricks Club, the Conservative Colored Club, and numerous others. The Radicals nominated Stephen B. Packard for Governor, while the Liberals nominated Francis T. Nicholls, a Louisiana war hero.

The campaign was a bitter one and was the final fight for the restoration of Home Rule. Both the Republican presidential candidate, Rutherford B. Hayes, and the Democratic candidate for the presidency, Samuel J. Tilden, were known to be well-disposed towards the South. The New Orleans *Republican,* a Radical newspaper, threatened Negroes who had joined the Liberals:

> *He that from the polls shall stay,*
> *May live to vote some other day.*

The Liberals came back in their newspapers with such jingles as:

> *Then come, boys, come,*
> *Make haste to crowd the polls,*
> *The tide of reform,*
> *It rises and it rolls.*
> *The thieves and the rogues*
> *Will have to hunt their holes.*

The Radical Returning Board, which counted the election ballots, threw out thousands of Liberal votes and declared Packard elected. On inauguration day, January 8, 1877, the Liberals marched to St. Patrick's Hall in New Orleans and swore in Nicholls as Governor; at the same time Radicals inaugurated Packard at the St. Louis Hotel, which was then the State Capitol.

The Nicholls Legislature immediately went to work. Departments of the state government and parish and city governments recognized his authority; he appointed a new Supreme Court which began holding sessions; taxes poured into his government's treasury. Packard's followers began to desert him. President Grant refused to permit the troops to interfere.

On March 24, Nicholls proclaimed that his state government was complete in all its branches, and a few days later newly elected President Rutherford B. Hayes dispatched a commission to Louisiana to secure information regarding the election. On April 20, the President directed that the troops be removed from the State House as soon as possible. This took place on April 24, following which the Nicholls government took possession. The period of military occupation had ended. Home Rule had finally returned to Louisiana. The *Picayune* exultantly said that the day of the Radical had ended: "His sun has gone down in the gloom of an infamy which will never have a returning dawn in Louisiana."

Finances and Corruption During the Period. The total cost of this corrupt period will never be accurately determined, for much of the corruption was well covered and many of the most damaging records were deliberately destroyed. The state bonded debt rose to over $50,000,000, while taxes increased over 500 per cent. Parishes and towns alike suffered severely.

In 1861 the valuation of all property in Natchitoches Parish, for example, was slightly over $8,000,000. By 1869 it had dropped to under $3,000,000, and by 1873, to only about $1,275,000. In 1873, when the parish income exceeded $82,000, it had only one 3-teacher black school in operation. Many black and white Radicals made fortunes. A Federal investigating committee in 1873 reported the following figures regarding Governor Warmoth: "He has been governor four years, at an annual salary of $8,000, and he testified that he made far more than $100,000 the first year, and he is now estimated to be worth from $500,000 to $1,000,000." Others may not have done as well as the Governor, but there is little doubt that they did not fare badly.

By 1874 property valued at $3,250 was taxed a total of $258.01. The same year the parish had a school fund of $15,000 to $20,000, yet had only one three-teacher Negro school operating. Raford Blunt, an illiterate Negro state senator, was one of the teachers and was also a member of the parish school board.

22. EVERYDAY LIFE DURING THE MILITARY OCCUPATION

Economic Conditions at the End of the War. Shortly after the end of the Civil War, aged Dr. Sol A. Smith of Alexandria wrote to General Kirby Smith that Louisiana was quiet and that the people were displaying great heroism and fortitude in accepting the destruction caused by the war. He said that Louisiana, like the other states of the South, "lies mangled, rent and palpitating in supreme agony of a ruined and trodden down people." His own plantation, which before the war had been valued at about $200,000, was now worth about $10,000 and had a $14,000 mortgage. Because of the Negro-labor situation, he did not believe that his plantation could be successfully operated and had decided to move to New Orleans and practice medicine. Returning soldiers were working at all types of jobs to make a bare living.

Many other persons have described Louisiana during those summer days of 1865, and one observer, Stephen Powers, wrote that the saddest thing about the war was its ending. The victorious soldier of the North returned to his home, which had been untouched by the bloody conflict, to "ovations, to pensions, to a happy home." The southerner, on the other hand, returned "to humiliation, to unspeakable poverty and despair."

Another writer described the areas of destruction: the Mississippi River section, the Red River Valley south of Natchitoches, the whole of southeast Louisiana, and concluded that "the state had been quite well destroyed." The Shreveport *Times* described the water front along Red River, as "a barren waste, over which now and then could be seen probably a sleepy mule with an empty dray." Mark Twain wrote that the "whitewash is gone from the negro cabins now; and many, possibly most, of the big mansions, once so shining white, have worn out their paint and have a decayed, neglected look. It is the blight of the war."

A small number of the returning soldiers and civil leaders did not return immediately to their homes, believing that the government meant to prosecute them for their actions during the war. Some went to Mexico and Central America, others to Brazil, the West Indies, or to Europe. Former Governor Henry Watkins Allen wrote from Mexico that every boat was bringing families from every section of the South.

However, Louisianians faced the future with calm courage. One ex-soldier wrote that "we must build a new life, a new South, and not die in the memory of the old." He said that Louisiana was still "our country," and that Louisianians must "not pull apart and refuse our share of work." Armand Lanusse, who before the war had been a prominent free Negro poet-editor, wrote to a friend that it was up to the young to rebuild the state's broken economic life.

Negroes During the Period. Before the war Louisiana Negroes were divided into two groups, the free Negroes and the slaves. The majority of the free Negroes were educated to some extent and possessed property, and many of those who lived in New Orleans were cultured and had traveled in the North and in Europe. The slaves, on the other hand, were uneducated and possessed little if any property.

During the occupation period many of the former free Negroes enjoyed economic prosperity and political prestige. They organized businesses which were patronized by the occupying military forces and established newspapers, such as the New Orleans *Republican,* *La Tribune de la Nouvelle-Orleans* published by Dr. Louis Roudanez (the first black daily newspaper in this country) and in Opelousas the *St. Landry Progress.* But the old antebellum wealthy, cultured free Negro group, under whose leadership the New Orleans Negro had reached a higher level of culture than had any Negro group anywhere in the entire world, gradually passed from the scene. Closely allied economically with white slave-holding planters and businessmen, they fell victim to the Civil War and the war's radical aftermath.

Of all the population groups, it was the former slave who suffered most during the period. At the end of the war wild rumors flooded the state that he would be given land, farm animals, and equipment, and even that the government would completely support him. Unscrupulous politicians promised him "riches, free markets, continual basking in the sun, places in the Legislative Halls, possession of white people's houses, and a great deal more." Misdemeanors and even criminal acts were generally protected during early months of freedom.

After the first glorious days of freedom had passed, the rural Negroes realized that the government was not going to support them. A Federal officer advised: "Return to the plantations owned by your former masters. Those who once held you in slavery are not your enemies, they are your best friends. . . . The government will not give you any land or stock. . . . You can get nothing except by working for it."

Many of the rural Negroes had remained loyal to their masters during the war and afterwards worked for wages or a share of the crop. On Brokenburn Plantation in northeastern Louisiana, for example, one ex-slave was given land rent free, and eventually became a successful farmer. Former Governor Henry Watkins Allen, soon to die in exile, wrote from Mexico to his former slave Vallery: "You must be temperate, and prudent, and industrious, and save your money. If I am ever a rich man again, I will help you. . . ." Many former slaves returned to farms and plantations where they greatly contributed to the economic rebuilding of the state. Although some were fairly paid for their labor, many others were gradually reduced to a position approaching agricultural peonage, a situation which lasted until after World War II.

Slow Economic Progress. Agriculture made slow progress during the period. Markets had been destroyed; lands had depreciated in value; livestock had been killed or driven off; implements and tools had been stolen or had worn out. Large areas had not been planted

223

A New Orleans street railroad car,
about 1870.

for some years and had grown up in
brush, while many farmers and planters were bankrupt and could not
secure working capital or credit. There
were bad crop years, and insects and
other pests attacked growing plants. In
1870 and 1872 there were serious
floods. It was several decades before
agricultural production equaled that
of 1860.

Transportation facilities also recovered slowly. During the war roads
had been neglected, railroads had been
worn out or abandoned, and steamboats had been destroyed by Federal
gunboats. By 1870, however, some of

the roads had been repaired, the railroads were partially in operation, and
steamboats were again carrying products and goods along the rivers and
bayous.

The banks suffered greatly during
both the war and the period of occupation. In 1861, Louisiana had had
thirteen banks representing a total
capital of nearly $25,000,000. In 1865
there were only ten banks, whose joint
capital had dropped to slightly over
$7,650,000. Ten years later only five
banks were left, with a total investment of slightly over $3,700,000.

Prices for goods and supplies re-

New Orleans during the period of military occupation

mained high throughout the period. The average Louisianian could afford few if any luxuries, and many could not afford all of the necessities of life. Home manufacturing of furniture, clothing, tools, and other items in general use was common throughout the country.

Little assistance was received from the Federal government in restoring the economic well-being of the state. The Radical state government polit-ical leaders did little, for their principal objective was to line their own pockets. Some assistance was given by Federal officers in the various towns and parishes, but their efforts were limited by governmental red tape and lack of funds.

Education. Public education had languished during the war but in 1865, State Superintendent Robert M. Lusher started a program of recovery

225

which continued until 1868. In that year Lusher was ousted and a carpetbagger named T. W. Conway was placed in the position to enforce the educational provisions of the new Constitution of 1868.

Little was accomplished, for the Radical political leaders stole most of the funds which should have gone to education. The newspapers of that time labeled Conway as an "ignorant, drunken, incompetent politician," and he was finally succeeded by William G. Brown, a Negro. Shortly afterwards P. B. S. Pinchback was appointed Director of the New Orleans school system.

Education reports during the period reveal that only a small percentage of the children were actually in school. In 1870, for example, Conway reported that Plaquemines Parish had 4,000 educables with only 100 enrolled, while Livingston Parish had 2,000 educables with only 34 enrolled. Even New Orleans had only 19,000 students out of a total of 90,000 boys and girls under the age of twenty-one. Seven years later, out of a total of over 265,000 white children in the entire state, only 54,390 were in school. The percentage of Negro children not attending was considerably higher. Many of both races failed to secure even a fourth-grade education.

At the first Louisiana Teachers Convention, held in New Orleans in 1872, delegate W. Jasper Blackburn from Claiborne Parish threw the convention into an uproar when he made charges against the Radicals. He said that the public schools were "utterly worthless, serving no purpose whatever except to provide salaries for the higher-ups." Blackburn could have said much more. The state public school fund in 1870 totaled over $500,000, but in New Orleans alone over $370,000 was expended on only 350 teachers. By 1871 the sale of public school lands had yielded nearly $2,200,000, most of which was stolen by politicians. Thefts by school boards, superintendents, and principals became common occurrences. In 1875 in Concordia Parish, the secretary of the school board was charged with the theft of $34,000.

Realizing the educational plight of the South, London businessman George Peabody, who had lived for a time in the United States, established a large fund to assist southern education. From 1867 to 1877 the white schools of Louisiana were kept alive mainly by this fund and by individual contributions.

Several Negro colleges or universities were established, the most important of which were Straight University, New Orleans University, and Leland University. Despite private and state assistance, these institutions remained small, but they accomplished much in the way of Negro education.

After being open for a short period during the war, the Louisiana State Seminary of Learning and Military Academy was reopened in October, 1865, under the leadership of Major David F. Boyd and four instructors.

A Creole audience at the New Orleans French Opera House.

The seminary building burned four years later, and the institution was moved to the Louisiana State School for the Deaf, Dumb, and Blind at Baton Rouge. The school consistently refused to admit Negroes and after 1872 barely remained alive because of the lack of state appropriations. It was reorganized in the fall of 1877 with the new name of Louisiana State University and Agricultural and Mechanical College.

Religion. Religious institutions languished during the period because of the lack of money to pay ministers and repair churches and because of the poor conditions of travel. But there was much religious activity: both Protestant ministers and Catholic priests tried to bring whites and Negroes closer together. They also performed heroic work for the relief of people of both races and all creeds. When Father Louis Gergaud, for example, died of yellow fever in 1873, everyone in Monroe remembered how he had labored during the epidemic; and the entire population, regardless of their religious beliefs, attended the funeral.

Revivals or "protracted meetings" were popular among the Protestants, particularly in northern and western Louisiana, during the summer and early fall seasons. In New Orleans, Dr. B. M. Palmer preached with renewed vigor, thundering out his matchless eloquence to crowded congregations. Numerous Negro Catholics left the Church in South Louisiana after listening to the missionary preachings of Protestant ministers.

But the general moral life of the people was at a low ebb during the entire period. New Orleans was a "wide-open" city where every kind of vice existed, and conditions were almost as bad in other towns and cities.

Social Life. During the years following 1865 all forms of amusement flourished in New Orleans, where corrupt politicians and practices made easy money available. In winter there were operas, plays, concerts, variety troupes, circuses, horse races, and balls. In summer the people enjoyed water sports, athletic events, and numerous other attractions. After 1869 roller-skating was introduced and the New Orleans Lawn Tennis Club, one of the first tennis clubs in the United States, was founded in 1876.

In the other sections of the state people provided their own amusements, for they had little money. There were "calico balls," "starvation parties," and dances where everyone dressed plainly and jointly furnished modest refreshments. There were church "socials," picnics, fishing and hunting parties, and amateur dramatics.

End of the Period. When the period of military occupation finally ended, the people of Louisiana had suffered the presence of troops and of Radical political control longer than had the people of any other state in the South. The memory of the corrupt government, the economic distress, and the many social problems gradually faded as Home Rule returned and economic, cultural, and social conditions improved.

Map 26—Louisiana during the
Civil War

The inauguration of
Ruffin G. Pleasant
as Governor of
Louisiana, 1916

PART SEVEN
Conservatism and slow Progress, 1877–1920

23. FOUR DECADES OF POLITICAL CONSERVATISM

Conservative Politics and Politicians. The period from 1877 to 1920 was one of political conservatism. Louisianians had witnessed too many excesses during the period of military occupation and Radical rule to take chances with liberal ideas or liberal legislation.

Although the Republican Party was active in political campaigns until 1900, it never seriously rivaled the Democratic Party, to which Louisiana, like other southern states, had developed a strong allegiance. This one-party system gave rise to factions within that party, and the political campaigns of the time were usually struggles between two or more Democratic factions. However, no single group was able to dominate state politics for very long at a time.

Louisiana is ordinarily divided for political purposes into three sections: North Louisiana, South Louisiana, and the parish of Orleans. Until 1900, North and South Louisiana generally united against New Orleans to elect governors and to control legislatures. After the turn of the century, groups from the two sections joined with New Orleans in order to win elections. Both candidates and factions called themselves "conservatives" or "liberals," but it made little difference. "Safe" governors were the rule, governors who were in the broader sense conservative in their political beliefs. The result was that comparatively little political and legislative progress was made during this period.

Major Political Issues. Between 1877 and 1900 several major political issues caused the people concern and led to hard-fought campaigns. By 1900, however, when most of these issues had been settled, voters lost much of their former enthusiasm for politics.

The most important single issue during those years was the position of the three groups which had committed so many excesses during the occupation. The carpetbaggers and scalawags lost their political offices first. But for thirty years after 1868, the blacks held on, led by the old pre–Civil War free Negro group of New Orleans.

During that time more than thirty Negroes were elected to the state Senate and nearly a hundred to the House of Representatives, in addition to those who were elected or appointed to state, parish, or local offices. Louisiana led the South in black political leadership.

But during the late 1880's and 1890's that leadership began to decline as the older generation passed from the political scene and whites

began to fear the possibility of a union of working-class white and Negro groups. The segregation of the two races in public places began about 1890, and the "separate but equal" principle was declared constitutional in 1896. The last Negroes were elected to the Louisiana Legislature in 1896 (until Ernest Morial, a black attorney, was elected to the House of Representatives from Orleans Parish in 1968). The Constitution of 1898 ended the right of suffrage for the great majority of blacks and for many illiterate whites as well. The doors of Negro suffrage would not open for another half-century.

State lotteries were the cause of considerable political agitation. Lotteries had long been used in Louisiana by societies and by religious and educational institutions to raise money. The largest of the lotteries was organized as the Louisiana Lottery Company in 1868. It was not long, however, before antilottery societies began forming. The fight against lotteries, and particularly against the Louisiana Lottery Company, continued until 1892, when the Legislature passed an antilottery bill. The company then moved to Honduras and continued to sell tickets in Louisiana until an act was passed in 1894 which prohibited the sale of tickets and ended the lottery business throughout the state.

State Government. During the period from 1877 to 1920 nine men served as the state's chief executive. All of them

A Louisiana Lottery wheel.

were Democrats and were conservative in their general political beliefs.

There was little dishonesty in government; nearly all political leaders were men of high purpose, many of whom were war veterans and very popular with the people. Francis T. Nicholls was probably the most beloved. He had lost a leg and an arm during the war and this gave opportunity for some interesting stories about him. Once, when he spoke on Bayou Lafourche, an old Confederate veteran, who was also minus an arm and a leg, came up to him and said: "General, all what's left of me is going to vote for what's left of you."

Governor Nicholls, whose term was shortened by the Constitution of 1879, served until 1880, when he was succeeded by Louis A. Wiltz. Wiltz died the following year and was succeeded by the Lieutenant Governor, Samuel D. McEnery. McEnery was elected in his own right in 1884 and was followed by Nicholls, who served a second term. Murphy J. Foster served two consecutive terms, from 1892 until 1900, but many people did not approve of a Governor succeeding himself and they prohibited this practice in the Constitution of 1898.

After 1900 the governors were William W. Heard, Newton C. Blanchard, J. Y. Sanders, Luther E. Hall, and Ruffin G. Pleasant, and they completed the economic reconstruction of the state. As more money was available by that time, additional funds could be appropriated for education, roads, ferries, bridges, and other improvements.

New State Constitutions. The constitutions of 1864 and 1868, having been drafted by Radical governments, were generally unsatisfactory to the people of Louisiana. A constitutional convention, therefore, was called in 1879. The new constitution of that year was the first in Louisiana to ask for the guidance of Almighty God, "the author of all good government." It took away many of the former powers of the Legislature and gave them to the Governor. It was a long document of over 260 articles, and it served the state well until near the end of the century.

By 1896 the vote of the Negro and the illiterate white working class had grown so large that many political leaders felt they might combine and gain control of the state, and that there might then be a return to Radical government. A constitutional convention was therefore called and the Constitution of 1898 was drafted restricting voters to three groups; those who were literate, property owners and their sons, and the voters of 1867 and their descendants. These restrictions cut the number of Negro voters about 95 per cent and white voters by nearly 24 per cent. The Constitution also forbade the Governor and the State Treasurer to succeed themselves, improved the court system, and gave additional powers to parish and local governments. It was even longer than the Constitution of 1879, having 326 articles.

By 1913 yet another constitution was needed. This one, which contained the same number of articles as that of 1898, completely revised the old constitution, and for some time the state government was in a state of confusion. On the whole, it was not a satisfactory document and was rewritten in 1921.

Parish and Local Government. After the withdrawal of the occupation troops in 1877, parish and local governments quickly reverted to control by the native whites. Of first importance was the repair of parish, city, and town buildings which had been allowed to fall into near ruin. Many records, particularly land records, had been destroyed during either the war or the period of Radical government and those that remained were in disorder. These records had to be organized to enable the various offices to function properly. Taxes had to be lowered although there were many jobs to be done, so local governments economized as much as possible.

Parishes, cities, and towns made slow but steady progress. In 1888, for example, the Concordia Parish Police Jury reported that the parish was out of debt. The president of the Police Jury congratulated the Jury: "The rate of taxation is now lower, the roads are in better condition, . . . and more cash is now in the treasury than at any time since the Civil War." By 1907, Concordia Parish had enough money to begin building new and more modern roads.

Some parishes relocated their parish seats as towns grew larger. Delta was the parish seat of Madison Parish until 1885, although by this time Tallulah was its largest town. After much argument and agitation, the records were suddenly moved to Tallulah one night in a boxcar, and the next morning Tallulah, "by right of possession," was declared by the Police Jury to be the new parish seat. A new courthouse was completed there two years later.

Some regulations made by police juries and local officials during this period sound a little out of place today. In 1887 the Donaldsonville town council adopted resolutions complaining loudly of the "reckless, furious and noisy manner in which plantation carts, etc.," were being driven through the streets. In 1895 the Police Jury of Ascension Parish adopted an ordinance "requiring three or four-mule carts and wagons to zig-zag on the public roads." There were only dirt roads at the time and deep ruts were cut by the wheels of the carts and wagons unless they zigzagged along the roads.

The Police Jury of Avoyelles Parish made many improvements between 1897 and 1918. In 1897, the sum of $300 was appropriated for a new well at Marksville, the well to have a windmill with a thirteen-foot wheel atop a forty-foot tower. In 1901 the Avoyelles Telephone Company was given the right to build lines from Bunkie to Marksville, Simmesport, Bordelonville, Plaucheville, Moreauville, and in-between points. In 1906 the parish voted $250 to defray expenses of fighting yellow fever and built a new six-foot-wide brick walk around the courthouse square. A new jail was constructed in 1908, and the same year

Street scene in Baton Rouge in the early 1900's.

a watering trough for horses was built in front of the courthouse square and spittoons were furnished to the offices and rooms of the courthouse.

In 1910 new regulations were passed regarding automobiles. The speed of cars was limited to fifteen miles per hour on straight roads, eight miles per hour on roads with curves, and only four miles an hour while crossing a bridge or passing a buggy, a rider of a horse, a wagon, or in front of a church. Automobiles, when signaled, must stop until a buggy or other horse-drawn vehicle had passed. An eight-inch-square number had to be attached to the rear of every automobile, white on a black car and black on a white car, and each automobile had to

be registered with the sheriff, who collected a license fee of $10.

In 1915 owners of dogs were required to purchase dog licenses. By 1918 automobiles were permitted to drive as fast as twenty miles an hour on country roads and twelve miles an hour in towns, but signals must be given when passing other vehicles and headlights must be equipped with "dimmers." Fines for violations of these regulations were set at $10 to $25.

Residents of Plaquemine received a real scare when it was discovered that the 1782 title to the original plantation on which the town was built was defective, but in 1897 the United States Congress passed a special act confirming all land titles in Plaquemine.

During the period the city of New Orleans was ill-paved, ill-policed, and spent little money on public improvements. Much of the time the city government was controlled by a ring of money-hungry politicians, and it was not until the time of World War I that the city began to emerge into a modern, up-to-date metropolis.

Law and Order. The disorder of the period of military occupation slowly subsided in all parts of the state except New Orleans after the restoration of Home Rule in 1877. In New Orleans, however, the change from Radical government brought little improvement despite the efforts of citizens' groups "to suppress crime, to compel the authorities to perform their duties, to watch the city government," and particularly to assist in securing the punishment of dishonest city officials.

Gangs of so-called "tuffs" or "knockers" roamed the city and openly violated the law.

After 1877 many Italians settled in New Orleans and some of them belonger to a secret society called the Mafia, whose members committed all kinds of crimes. In October, 1890, Chief of Police David C. Hennessey, who had begun to prosecute all classes of criminals, was shot to death by the Mafia. Nineteen Italians were arrested for the crime, and when a jury freed six and failed to convict the remainder, a mob formed, raided the city prison, and killed eleven of the men. The lynching caused international complications, three of the murdered men being Italian citizens, and the United States government finally paid nearly $25,000 to the families of the slain men.

There were relatively few crimes of a serious nature in the rural sections or in the small towns of the state.

Social Legislation. Little legislation was passed for the care of the blind, insane, deaf and dumb, or for the aged or poor who could not earn a living. The state maintained schools for the deaf, dumb, and blind, but the Legislature appropriated only small amounts of money with which to operate them. Most of these unfortunates were cared for by the various parish governments.

The insane were usually placed in jail if their families could not take care of them. Private citizens or religious organizations were paid to take care of other unfortunates. After 1880, poor farms were established by many parishes to care for those who could not support themselves.

Many of the sick people of the state were sent to Charity Hospital in New Orleans. The hospital had suffered much during the Civil War and afterward, but after 1880 conditions improved. Modern ambulances were purchased in 1884, electricity was installed in 1890, and new buildings were constructed between 1898 and 1910. By

237

Louisiana Volunteers entering Havana,
Cuba, 1898.

1914 the total annual expenses of the hospital amounted to over $300,000, part of which was paid by the City of New Orleans and part by the state. That same year the hospital treated over 17,000 patients.

Leprosy, now usually called "Hansen's Disease," had existed in Louisiana since colonial times. During the Spanish period those suffering from the disease had been treated at a hos-

pital built by Governor Miro on a ridge of land between the Mississippi River and Bayou St. John near New Orleans. Some years later the number of diseased declined and the hospital was abandoned. In 1892 the Legislature passed an act which provided a modern hospital, and two years later the Leprosarium was established at Carville, on the river south of Baton Rouge. This hospital was taken over

238

A group of soldiers at Camp Beauregard, Louisiana, inspect one of the planes kept there during World War I.

by the Federal government in 1921.

The Spanish-American War and World War I. The United States fought two wars during this period and Louisiana did her part in both conflicts. The old bitterness which followed the Civil War had almost disappeared, and Louisianians were loyal American citizens again.

In 1898 the United States declared war against Spain in order to help the Cubans win their war for independence. The First Louisiana Infantry Regiment and three batteries of Louisiana artillery did not leave the United States, but the Second Infantry Regiment served in Cuba for several months.

During World War I in 1917 and 1918, Louisiana responded with strong patriotism. Louisianians were eager to assist France, for many of them were the descendants of French Creoles. One lady, who lived in New Orleans, reported that the Crescent City "was thrown into a state of wild excitement." As the troops completed their training and departed, thousands of people assembled at railway stations; the bands played the "Marseillaise" and patriotic American songs. Later there were many heartbroken families whose sons and husbands had died in France.

Thousands of men joined the military services; several military camps were established in the state; and various local organizations raised money and furnished needed war supplies. The Jennings Cavalry became a part of the noted Rainbow Division. Marine Major General John A. LeJeune of Pointe Coupee Parish later became Commander of the Marine Corps.

Failure of Democracy. The political tragedy of the period was the failure of Louisiana Democracy. Blacks and a few European immigrants were politically active until the 1890's. But at that time the blacks lost their right to participate in the political, economic, and social stream of Louisiana life. The "separate but equal" legislation and the Constitution of 1898 virtually closed the door to their participation in local and state affairs.

24. SLOW ECONOMIC PROGRESS, 1877–1920

General Observations. Louisiana made slow but steady economic progress between 1877 and 1920. The major task was recovery of the ground that had been lost between 1860 and 1877, and in some economic fields this was not achieved until after 1900. The discovery and exploitation of new raw materials speeded up progress.

Most towns grew slowly, with the exception of New Orleans, which made rapid growth as a trade--distribution and commercial center. By 1912 it was written that "the swamp-land all around New Orleans is rapidly being reclaimed. Pretty, quaint little houses and bungalows, brilliantly painted, are being built, and the outskirts of the town offer a gay and exotic appearance."

The cities and towns outside New Orleans had not yet awakened to the

Front Street in Alexandria in 1891. The street has since been covered by the modern levee.

activity of the twentieth century and were just beginning to install such modern conveniences as city lighting and water systems, paved streets, and good drainage facilities. In 1890, Louisiana historian Alcée Fortier visited St. Martinville, describing it afterwards as a quaint "old Creole town" where there was not much activity in business, but "order and decency prevailed everywhere and the people were uniformly affable and polite." The town had but one hotel, which had a wide gallery and massive brick columns, where "everything is as in antebellum days; no register awaits the names of the guests, and the owner seems to have implicit confidence in the honesty of his boarders."

New towns were being established in the northern and western sections. Ruston, for example, was founded in 1884 when the Shreveport, Vicksburg and Pacific Railroad pushed westward across the northern part of the state. The new town was named for R. E.

Russ, who owned the land on which it was built. Prospective merchants drew lots for the locations for their establishments, and the first business was the "eating-house" of Joe Schwab, "who possessed a mockingbird that whistled popular tunes and a wife with a generous disposition but a quick temper." Crowley was founded in 1887 and named for a Southern Pacific Railroad employee named Patrick Crowley. Plans for the town were drawn, streets were laid out, drainage ditches were dug, and the first sale of lots totaled over $25,000. Crowley became the parish seat of newly formed Acadia Parish the same year, and the year following, a brick courthouse was completed. By the end of the period in 1920, the cities with a population of more than 5,000 included:

New Orleans	387,219
Shreveport	43,874
Baton Rouge	21,782
Alexandria	17,510
Lake Charles	13,088
Monroe	12,675
Crowley	6,108
Minden	6,105
Morgan City	5,429
Houma	5,160

Agriculture. During the late 1870's the editor of the Chicago *Tribune* visited the state. He wrote that if Louisiana could be moved to Illinois "it would create a commotion that would throw the discovery of gold in California in the shade" and that the land would bring "three to five hundred dollars per acre." A few years later, at a statewide fair in Shreveport, a speaker made a strong plea for exploiting the "wonderful resources" of the state. These men and others like them helped to awaken Louisianians to the economic opportunities to be found in agriculture.

It was not until after 1900 that agriculture and general agricultural production recovered the ground which had been lost during the period from 1860 to 1877. In 1860 the value of farm lands had been approximately $248,000,000; in 1890 their value was only $110,500,000. Farm equipment had declined from over $18,000,000 to about $7,000,000 and the value of livestock from $24,500,000 to $18,000,000.

The increasing use of scientific agricultural methods gained momentum as the years passed. The World's Industrial and Cotton Centennial Exposition, which was held in New Orleans in late 1884 and early 1885, greatly stimulated the farmers. The first agricultural experiment station was established at Kenner about the same time and others were soon in operation, all under the directorship of Dr. W. C. Stubbs. Demonstrations were given in the terracing of land to prevent erosion, in the use of new farm machinery, and in the treatment of animal and plant disease, but many farmers were slow in adopting the new discoveries and methods. One man refused to admit that farming could be taught by a "college professor," saying: "Why I've worn out two farms; you can't tell me how I ought to farm." Dr. Seaman A. Knapp came to Louisiana

Wagonloads of rice at Abbeville, Louisiana, in the early 1900's.

in 1885, and for nearly twenty years taught farmers how to provide their own laboratories, teach themselves new methods, and through this new knowledge to make more profits. When he died in 1911 at the age of seventy-seven, the entire nation paid tribute to his genius and to his achievements.

Up to about 1905 the home, blue-ribbon, or Noble varieties of sugarcane were most cultivated, but they became subject to various diseases, and the D-74 and D-95 varieties were then introduced from Cuba. These varieties were soon attacked by root rot, the

mosaic disease, and insect pests of several types. About 1920, D. W. Pipes, Jr., and Elliott Jones of Houma introduced POJ seed canes from Java. Still later other varieties were introduced from Florida and from India.

In 1914, 4-H clubs came into existence, and the next year witnessed the introduction of home-canning clubs and the organization of the Agricultural Extension Service by the State University. Agricultural meetings and conferences, where papers were read and discussions were held on various subjects of interest to farmers, increased in number.

243

James B. Eads, the builder of the Mississippi River jetties system

Industry and the Exploitation of Natural Resources. After 1900 the state entered a new industrial era. Not only were additional natural resources of great commercial value discovered in many sections of the state, including natural gas, sulphur, oil and new beds of salt, but the older known resources, such as fur-bearing animals, fish and seafoods, and lumber, also entered a new period of development. Industries began settling in Louisiana because of the location of her raw materials and, in addition, because of the mild climate, abundant water resources, low-priced fuel, good labor supply, and new transportation facilities.

Oil was discovered in 1901 in two places, near Jennings and White Cas-

tle, but did not become really important until five years later, when it was also discovered near Shreveport. The commercial mining of sulphur began in Calcasieu Parish in 1895, and until 1914 this field produced about 75 per cent of the nation's supply. Meanwhile, other deposits had been discovered in South Louisiana. Gas was found near Monroe in 1916 and soon the North Louisiana oil and gas fields were booming. Large-scale lumbering operations began in western Louisiana during the 1890's and in the Bogalusa area shortly after 1900.

Spanish moss, another natural resource, began to be extensively used in the manufacture of mattresses and upholstered furniture. The national fur industry was supplied with Louisiana opossum, mink, skunk, raccoon, and muskrat pelts. The state's more than 7,000 square miles of tidewaters supplied abundant amounts of shrimp and oysters, and fresh-water and salt-water fisheries furnished many varieties of fish, as well as turtles, frogs, and crawfish.

By 1920 the leading natural-resource industries were petroleum refining, lumbering, sugar refining, paper manufacturing, and rice cleaning and polishing. General manufacturing plants produced lumber products, boots and shoes, brick, cigars and cigarettes, barrels, soda, packaged foods, fertilizers, and hundreds of other products. While Louisiana was still a rural, agricultural state, she was rapidly developing a balanced economy.

Drilling operations in progress at Louisiana's first oil well, near Jennings in 1901.

In the early days of Louisiana's lumber industry, teams of oxen hauled logs to the narrow gauge track laid in the pine woods. The logs were then placed on a train which carried them to the sawmill.

Transportation. When the period began, water transportation was the most important method of travel and all of the larger Louisiana rivers and bayous were highways of trade and commerce. By the end of the century, railroads had been built throughout the state, and the smaller lines had been consolidated into the major systems. Roads were greatly improved during the years after 1900.

Regularly scheduled steamboats ran from New Orleans, Baton Rouge, Alexandria, Shreveport, and other Louisiana towns to Natchez, Vicksburg, Memphis, St. Louis, Louisville, Pittsburgh, and other upriver cities. Smaller and unscheduled boats threaded the smaller and shallower waterways of the state. These river boats carried the farmer's products to market and brought him farm tools, supplies for his family, and the luxury goods which he desired.

Steamboats still had to meet the usual river problems of snags, shallow water, crevasses, boiler explosions, scarcity of wood for fuel at given points, and trouble with the roustabout crews. The larger oceangoing ships sometimes were unable to get over the bars at the mouth of the Mississippi, but this was remedied in 1879 when James B. Eads completed his jetty system which deepened the mouth of the river. The Red River had been cleared of its obstructions much earlier by Henry M. Shreve, but those in the smaller streams and bayous still caused steamboat captains considerable worry. Bayou Plaquemine had become unnavigable in the 1880's, but work to correct this was started in 1895, and the bayou was cleared and a new lock at Plaquemine completed in 1909. Boats could then pass from the Mississippi into Bayou Plaquemine and continue by way of Grand River to the Atchafalaya.

The larger steamboats had become

The steamboat "America"

Interior of the main lounge of the
steamboat "J. M. White."

In the 1880's this woodburning engine pulled a two-car train between Schriever and Thibodaux.

"floating palaces" by the 1880's. Steam hoists replaced manpower, coal replaced wood for fuel, and electric lights took the place of kerosene lamps and wood torches. The cabins were fitted with elaborate furnishings, the dining-room chefs prepared banquets, and the passengers lived in complete comfort.

The old boat songs, however, were still sung and they amused many a passenger.

We'll give her a little more rosin,
And open her blower wide,
To show them the way to Natchez,
Runnin' against the tide.

Oh, a little more rosin,
A little more pitch and pine!
Throw in a can of glycerine
And a barrel of turpentine.

The old steamboat days came to an end shortly after 1900 when the railroad networks were completed. Boats began to decline in number on the Mississippi, the Red, and other rivers, but men long remembered them for their whistles, each of which had an individual sound. Albert L. Grace wrote fondly of the "melodious" whistle of the *Edward J. Gay*, which was sunk in 1889. He wrote that the *Jesse K. Bell* had the "loudest whistle," and

Railroads
1900

Map 27—Louisiana railroads, 1900

that the *Paris C. Brown* had "the freakiest of all river whistles; it was of the 'wild cat' variety, up and down, tending to startle one out of two nights' sleep." Another writer sadly admitted that "stately steamboats with mellow whistles have no place in the modern hurly-burly of reeking gas fumes, nerve-shattering shrieks of freight locomotives and buzz-saw drones of airplane motors."

In 1861 there were only a little over 300 miles of railroad track in the entire state and the longest line

was only 88 miles in length. The many miles of track abandoned during the war were reclaimed and a few new lines built between 1865 and 1877. The New Orleans, Mobile and Chattanooga Railroad reached Donaldsonville and began to run trains to New Orleans in 1871. The Donaldsonville *Chief* of October 14 proudly announced that the train arrived at noon each day and departed on its return trip at one o'clock and that city papers not six hours old could now be purchased. The trains had some disad-

Lake Charles

vantages, however: "A man might find a lucrative business in traveling up and down the railroad and picking up the hats that blow from the heads of the passengers. . . . We are of the opinion that there have been enough hats scattered along the road since it has been opened to fill a small size hat store."

Other railroads were organized or reorganized: the New Orleans, Opelousas and Great Western; the New Orleans and Pacific; the St. Louis, Avoyelles and Southwestern; the Vicksburg, Shreveport and Pacific; and several others. Baton Rouge was reached in 1881, and it was proclaimed that "trains will run through from New Orleans to Baton Rouge, and return every day." So many New Orleans people wished to visit the capital of the state that the railroad organized excursion trains. In 1883 the first through-train service was started between New Orleans and California. The Shreveport, Vicksburg and Pacific pushed westward to Shreveport in 1884.

Most people still traveled to small towns and parish seats over ungraded dirt roads, which were dusty in both summer and winter when the weather was dry and filled with ruts and mud-holes when it was wet. There was no system of state highways, individual parishes having to build and maintain the roads within their boundaries.

During the early years of the period, caravans of wagons traveled over the state, hauling goods into the country areas from the river towns. The wagoneers usually stopped at night at "wagon yards" where stalls and feed were provided for their horses, and the men slept either in their wagons or in near-by rooming houses. One of the last wagon yards in Louisiana was operated at West Monroe.

Louisiana's most unusual road during this period was the so-called "Shed Road" of Bossier Parish. This road ran from the hills southward to within

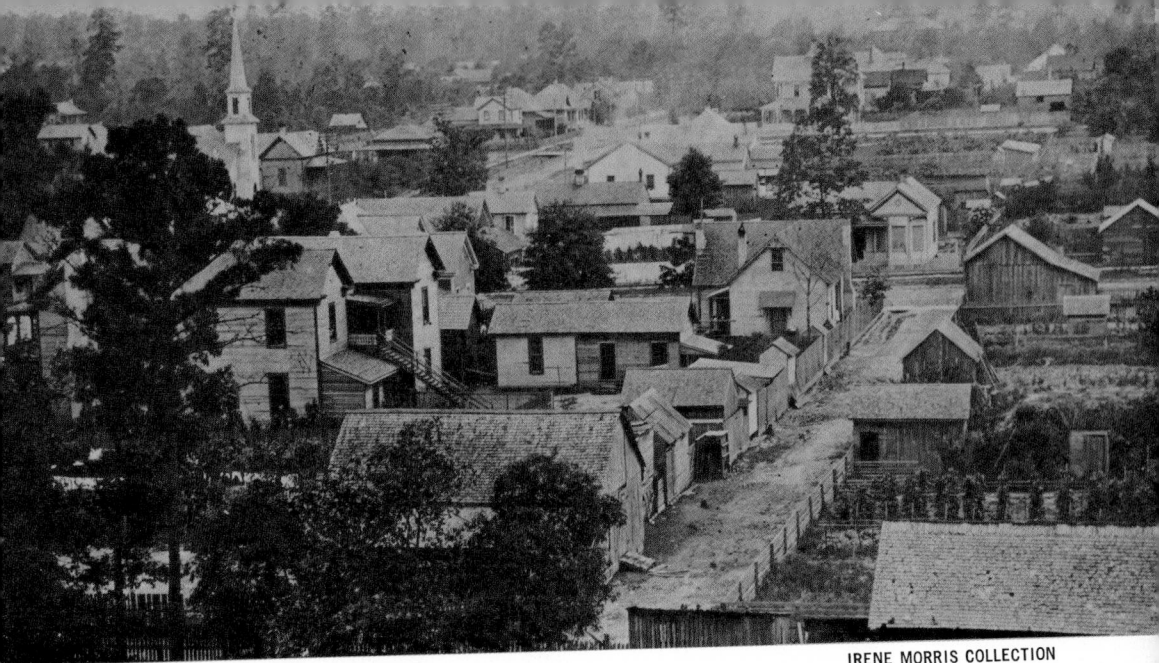

Kentwood, Louisiana, 1908.

about two miles of Bossier City. The brownish-red soil of the Red River Valley was without bottom when it rained, so the planters and farmers tried to make a satisfactory "corduroy" road of logs laid crosswise but failed, for the reason that the mud would not hold the logs firmly in place. Finally Judge John W. Watkins of Minden secured a special charter from Congress to build an entirely different type of road; a nine-mile shed was constructed, with ditches on either side, and the road was built under the shed. A four-yoke ox team and wagon was charged a toll of $1.50; a four-mule team and wagon, $1.00; and a person afoot, five cents. The road was profitably operated for a number of years.

Distributing Everyday Commodities. Goods in everyday use were distributed to the people of Louisiana in several ways. In New Orleans and the larger towns were both general stores which sold all types of merchandise and stores which specialized in one particular commodity, such as shoes, men's or women's clothing, or hardware. In the smaller towns and villages the general store was usually the only one found. Though the stores in the large towns were much as they are today, the small-town general stores have largely disappeared. They carried everything that was needed by the farmers, planters, and townspeople— clothing, shoes, foodstuffs of all sorts, tools, farming machinery, harness,

An old bridge near Columbia

patent drugs, notions, saddles, hats, bolts of cloth, spices, and many other goods.

The floating store, or trading boat, was another distributive agent. The owner put his stock of goods on a boat and traveled along the rivers and bayous selling his goods to both townsfolk and farmers. The trading boat resembled an ordinary ferryboat, except that its large cabin was filled with groceries, hardware, and other goods.

The peddler operated in much the same way, except that he carried his goods on his back or in a covered wagon or hack and camped by the roadside at night or stopped with customer friends. He traded for his food supplies, supplementing his meat supply by hunting or fishing. While the majority of peddlers carried general

stocks, some of them specialized in a particular commodity.

However, the trading boats and peddlers began to disappear after 1900 and few were still operating by 1920. A few stalls are still found in New Orleans, but only during fruit and vegetable seasons can one hear occasionally the cry of the old street peddler.

Banks and Banking. Finances in Louisiana were at a low ebb when the state was returned to Home Rule in 1877. The state debt was enormous and taxes were high. Agriculture was in a bad condition and farmers had little money. Business generally was poor. The result was that in 1879 there was a business and financial panic. Banks closed throughout the state and three large banks in New Orleans could pay

253

their depositors only 15 to 50 per cent of their deposits.

In 1882 the Legislature passed a new banking act. This act permitted the organization of banks with only a small amount of capital, $10,000 in towns with a minimum population of 2,000 and $100,000 in cities of over 25,000 persons. This act did not completely relieve the financial situation, and until late in the period many small communities were without banks. Marksville, for example, did not have a permanent bank until 1897.

However, the situation steadily improved. While in 1881 there were only seventeen banks in Louisiana with total resources of about $23,500,-000, by 1899 the number had increased to over seventy-five banks with resources of nearly $55,000,000. In 1898 the new constitution created the office of Bank Examiner, and in 1916 a legislative act ordered him to report to the Legislature every two years. This greatly aided banking conditions.

Throughout this period many people did not trust the banks to keep their money, burying it instead in the yard or under the fireplace, or hiding it in other places. One man bored a deep hole in the leg of a chair, inserted his money, and put a stopper in the hole.

As the state was heavily in debt in 1877, public officials economized in every way possible in an effort to pay off the indebtedness. It was not until 1914 that the State Treasurer could

report that practically all of the debt had been funded.

Labor. After 1877 there was much competition between white laborers and the newly free Negroes and it was not long before the leaders of both races began to establish labor organizations. Some of these unions lasted only a short time, while others performed good service for a number of years. By 1880 there were twenty unions in New Orleans alone. The years 1880 and 1887 witnessed many strikes, but it was not until the fall of 1892 that a general strike of major importance occurred in New Orleans. Although labor continued to organize and strike for higher wages and better working conditions after 1900, comparatively little real progress was made until the modern period.

In 1879 many Negroes left Louisiana to settle in such northern states as Illinois, Ohio, and Kansas. Henry Adams, a Louisiana Negro, was one of the most important leaders of the movement, and he claimed to have led nearly one hundred thousand Negroes from several southern states into Kansas alone. Within a few years, however, many of the Negroes became dissatisfied in the North and returned home.

One of the most important labor developments was the tremendous increase of women workers. By the 1880's approximately one-fifth of the women of Louisiana were gainfully employed. Slightly less than one-half of them were engaged in professional or personal services, while most of the others were working in agriculture. However, there were also numerous teachers, nurses, boardinghouse keepers, waitresses, restaurant keepers, factory workers, and even a few barbers and professional musicians. These women workers greatly aided the general economy of the state.

25. EDUCATIONAL AND CULTURAL PROGRESS

Educational Progress. Education progressed slowly at all levels during the years following the end of the Civil War. The Federal army-enforced integration of state public schools was not accepted by most whites and was not favored by some blacks. White private schools were organized. By the 1890's, "separate but equal" legislation had separated the races in all state educational institutions. Public conveyances, hotels, cafes, places of entertainment were no longer open without racial distinction.

The Constitution of 1879, moreover, was not sufficiently liberal and authorized only small appropriations. In 1887, Professor Henry E. Chambers of New Orleans made a stirring speech to a convention of school leaders, urging the provision of adequate, permanent school funds and the training of qualified teachers, principals, and parish superintendents. The next year a new State Board of Education was established, with authority to regulate education throughout Louisiana.

In 1898 the educational provisions of the new state constitution made possible the beginning of more rapid progress in public education. Examination and certification of teachers began shortly afterwards. The movement for school libraries started in 1905 and was followed the next year by the Library Act directing parish school boards to furnish funds for school libraries. In 1907 the State Department of Education established special departments, including the High School Division, the Elementary Division, the Agricultural Division, and the Home Economics Division. Seven years later the practice started

255

of basing teachers' certificates on the number of college credits earned. The State Department of Education was reorganized by the Johnson Act of 1916, which also made other educational improvements.

The Louisiana State Educational Association was organized at Minden in 1884, being reorganized under a new name, the Louisiana State Teachers' Association, during the 1890's. The association held annual meetings in different cities and discussed educational topics and problems. The publication of educational magazines began in 1879 when Robert M. Lusher and W. O. Rogers founded the *Journal of Education*. During the entire period, school institutes were held in the various parishes and annual educational assemblies called chautauquas met at Ruston.

While in 1880 only slightly over 50,000 children were enrolled in Louisiana's schools, by 1903 the number had risen to nearly 210,000, and by 1920 to nearly 355,000. During those years the state gradually increased its educational budget, from $450,000 in 1885, over $840,000 in 1889, nearly $6,000,000 in 1912, to over $16,000,000 in 1920.

James B. Aswell, who successfully initiated and publicized an improved educational program, became State Superintendent in 1904, but resigned shortly after his re-election in 1908. T. H. Harris, during a thirty-two-year period as State Superintendent (1908-1940), constantly expanded, reorganized and modernized the services of a progressive state educational system.

Elementary and Secondary Schools. Public schools made more rapid progress in New Orleans and in the northern and western parts of the state than in South Louisiana, for many South Louisianians still favored private or church schools. Plaquemine, for example, did not have a public school until 1887, when a two-room schoolhouse was built, and its first high school was not erected until 1911. Monroe, on the other hand, had public schools prior to 1880 and began high-school work in 1885. The "Separate but Equal" schools for Negroes, however, never materialized. Buildings, equipment, books and educational materials, well-trained teachers—all were far below the standards of white schools. Equality was not approached until after the middle of the twentieth century.

V. L. Roy, a former school superintendent, recalled the schools of the 1880's and 1890's. The first school he attended had a dirt floor and "we sat at tables and ordinary store counters on hard wooden benches. There were no blackboards, maps, globes, or charts. The only desks were those some of the boys had made themselves for their own use." The best teachers were paid $50 a month and the annual school term ran from two to five months. In many cases a vacant store served as the schoolhouse.

As late as 1896 a teacher at Cotton-

256

There were many one-room schools like this one (in Avoyelles Parish) throughout Louisiana during the nineteenth century.

port complained that he was compelled "to rent an old dilapidated building in a field," for which he had to pay "the sum of $5.00 per month." He reported that "with two exceptions, the parents of the children refused to send wood," and that during winter weather he "was compelled to teach in the cold."

The Legislature passed a compulsory school attendance law in 1877 requiring all children between the ages of six and eighteen years of age to attend school, but the law was never enforced. After 1914 all children between seven and fifteen were ordered to attend school for at least 140 days each year. By 1920, however, only

about 70 per cent of the children of school age were actually attending elementary school.

The first high schools were established during the 1880's, most of them including all students of the eighth through the eleventh grades. The courses offered included languages, grammar and composition, mathematics, history, literature, music, and the sciences. Recitations were generally for forty minutes and there were frequent examinations. Outside activities included literary societies, typewritten school papers, military training, and athletic contests in football, basketball, and baseball. Only about 10 per cent of those who started high school finished the course and less than 30 per cent of the graduates entered college.

After 1900, high schools were improved. Better buildings and equipment were provided, teachers were better trained, and school libraries were enlarged. Numbers of small schools were consolidated into larger ones and supervisors were appointed to help improve the quality of instruction.

In addition to public elementary and high schools there were many private or religious academies and institutes scattered throughout the state. These schools generally accepted boarding pupils who lived at the schools, as well as day students. The Cadeville Normal School and Commercial Institute, about seven miles south of Calhoun in Ouachita Parish, for example, was opened in the mid-1880's. Here students could "get board, including fuel, lights, washing, etc., at the boarding hall at $8 a month." The school advertised that the students were "free from all the evils and distracting influences that corrupt their morals." No "loafers, roughs or dudes" were admitted.

Colleges and Universities. There had been many colleges in Louisiana before 1860, but between that year and 1877 these schools had had difficulty in even staying alive. After 1877, however, the colleges began a period of growth.

In 1886 the Louisiana State University was moved to the old United States military barracks at Baton Rouge. It was relocated on its present campus during the 1920's. The modern Louisiana State University system has campuses in New Orleans, Shreveport, Alexandria, and Eunice, in addition to medical and health centers, agricultural experiment stations, extension centers, and other divisions.

Several teacher training colleges, which have in recent years developed into universities, were organized during the years after 1880. These institutions include Northwestern State University at Natchitoches, Louisiana Tech at Ruston, and the University of Southwestern Louisiana at Lafayette. Southern University, the state university for Negroes, founded in 1880 in New Orleans, was moved to Scotlandville in 1914. A sister institution, Grambling University, at Grambling, was established in 1901.

Meanwhile several endowed or religious colleges and universities were founded, including Tulane University, Loyola University of the South, St. Mary's Dominican College, Dillard University (Negro), Xavier University (the only Catholic college for Negroes in the United States), New Orleans Baptist Theological Seminary, Louisiana College, Leland College (Negro), Sophie Newcomb College (now joined with Tulane), and Centenary College.

Libraries. In addition to the large library of Louisiana State University, there were sizable collections of books

LSU cadets at a class lecture.

at the various other state and private institutions. The Louisiana State Museum and the Howard Library, both in New Orleans, acquired large collections of books and manuscripts pertaining to the history of the state. In 1897 the Fisk Free Library in New Orleans was combined with the Lyceum Library, later becoming the New Orleans Public Library.

During the 1900's, however, Louisiana fell behind the rest of her sister states in providing for the preservation of the records of her past. Although the neighboring states of Arkansas and Mississippi established departments of history and archives, nothing comparable was done in Louisiana.

Newspapers and Magazines. Only a small number of newspapers and magazines continued publication during the Civil War and military occupation period, the majority being forced to stop publication because of lack of financial support. After 1877 the news-

Grace King

Kate Chopin

papers began to recover their former prestige. However, because of consolidation and competition, fewer papers were published in 1900 than in 1860. By 1900, however, the city, town, and parish newspapers were adequately reporting the news.

The most representative and best-edited magazine was *De Bow's Review*, which had been founded before the Civil War and which ended publication in 1880. In all, about a hundred magazines were published in the state, but none of them achieved a national circulation after the 1880's.

Literature. Literature flourished during the period. George W. Cable wrote novels and short stories about the Louisiana Creoles, many of which the Creoles believed did not picture them accurately. *Old Creole Days*, a collection of stories, is probably his most noted work. For over thirty years Grace King published histories, biographies, articles, short stories, and novels which gave a more flattering picture of the Creoles.

Though not a native Louisianian, Lafcadio Hearn wrote brilliantly on local subjects, and *Chita*, an account of the Last Island hurricane in 1856, is one of the finest books in all Louisiana literature. Kate Chopin wrote numerous stories and sketches which far surpassed others of their time for realism and frankness. Eliza Ripley re-created the old social life of New Orleans, and Father Adrien Rouquette, noted missionary to the Choctaw Indians of Bayou Lacombe, wrote poetry.

Charles Colton, one of the humorists of the period, sometimes wrote rhymes, and one of them, "A Kitchen Free-For-All," began:

The fork said the corkscrew was crooked;
  The remark made the flatiron sad;
The steel knife at once lost its temper,
  And called the tea-holder a cad.
The tablespoon stood on its mettle;
  The kettle exhibited bile;
The stove grew hot at the discussion,
  But the ice remained cool all the
    while.

Negro literature declined during this period. Many of the old cultured Negro groups of New Orleans lost their wealth or moved from the state, and most Negroes at this time were more interested in journalistic writing and in political advancement. Poet Victor-Ernest Rillieux was probably the most prolific writer of the period, for a flood of songs, satires, odes and other writings came from his pen, some of which were set to music. The last important work in French published by a Negro was Rodolphe L. Desdunes' *Nos Hommes et Notre Histoire (Our People and Our History)*, 1911, translated into English in 1973. It tells the interesting story of the blacks who contributed to Louisiana literature and other artistic fields.

Despite the fact that the state took no official interest in preserving its history, many Louisianians discovered and wrote about its past. Richard Taylor, William Miller Owen, Alfred Roman, Henry Clay Warmoth, Sarah A. Dorsey, William Preston Johnston, and others wrote books on the Civil War period. Charles Gayarré had published his four-volume *History of Louisiana* before 1860, but he revised the work during this period and published many historical articles. John Dimitry, Grace King, John R. Ficklen, and Albert Phelps wrote one-volume histories of the state. Alcée Fortier published a four-volume *History of Louisiana* in 1904 and afterwards wrote other books and numerous articles on

Louisiana history. In 1900, Henry Rightor published the first complete history of New Orleans.

Painting and Sculpture. The war-ravaged 1860's and the radical and disordered 1870's gave little encouragement to painting, sculpture, and the other allied arts. A revival of art, however, began during the late 1870's, and painting in particular has flourished until the present time.

Enoch Perry painted portraits. Fabrino Julio painted the noted picture the *Last Meeting of Lee and Jackson*, which now hangs in the Cabildo. George Sullivan and Achille Peretti painted after the style of the great masters. Samuel Walker became noted as a portrayer of Louisiana people. Erasme Humbrecht painted murals for the St. Louis Cathedral and other churches. Alexander Alaux painted a large panorama of *De Soto's Discovery of the Mississippi*. After 1914, Luis Graner became noted for his scenes of rural Louisiana.

Alexander J. Drysdale had a studio in the Board of Trade Building in New Orleans where he operated a one-man picture "factory," turning out paintings of Louisiana lowlands by the dozen, and selling them for small prices. It is said that he lined up his boards and canvases and painted all of the skies, followed by the grasses, the trees, and the water of lakes or bayous. His misty landscapes look as though they were seen during a light rainfall. Since his death his works have

261

become much in demand and now sell for high prices.

Comparatively few sculptors made noteworthy reputations during this period. Achille Parelli made head studies, Joseph Domenget and Romeo Celli lived and worked for many years in the New Orleans French Quarter, as did Florville Foy and Eugene and Daniel Warburg.

Several art associations or leagues which encouraged art and displayed various of its forms to the public were founded in the state, particularly in New Orleans. The Art Union, the Southern Artist's League, and the Arts and Exhibition Club were among those founded in the 1880's. The Art Association of New Orleans came into existence in 1905 and about the same time the Louisiana State Museum, located in the Cabildo, began to gather together the artistic work of the entire state. In 1911 the Delgado Museum was completed in New Orleans through the generosity of Isaac Delgado, a wealthy sugar broker. Meanwhile, the colleges and universities in the state began to offer art courses.

The Drama. New Orleans had been a noted theatrical city during the period before the Civil War, and other cities and towns in the state had witnessed performances of both permanent groups and traveling companies. The state rapidly revived its interest in the drama after the war ended.

During the 1860's and 1870's Negro actors performed at the Orleans Theater in plays by Negro writers, such as Victor Sejour, Adolphe Duhart, and others. Many of these performances were benefits to help the needy of the city. Soon the whites started to introduce visiting troupes of performers and to sponsor local groups. By the 1890's the Tulane and the Crescent theaters were among the city's best, where Julia Marlowe, George Arliss, Richard Mansfield, Sarah Bernhardt, Minnie Maddern Fiske, Otis Skinner, Walter Hampden, and many other noted actors of the day could be seen.

After the beginning of the new century the Baldwin, Lyric, Elysium, and other theaters were built. At Welch's Hippodrome, later called the Winter Garden, and at the Schubert, musical comedies, dramas, and vaudeville were presented. These popular theaters charged only ten cents for an ordinary evening's entertainment. The first amateur nights were at the Winter Garden, where, if acts did not satisfy the audience, the people yelled, "Get the hook," and the actors were pulled off the stage.

Shakespearean dramas were popular with whites and Negroes alike. Early in the 1900's a Negro theatrical troupe brought all-Negro-performed drama to the Pythian Hall, the Lyric, and the Palace.

Meantime, other towns in the state welcomed troupes of traveling players. The minstrel show had been popular as early as the 1820's, and after the war the entire state swarmed with professional and amateur minstrel perform-

Interior of the St. Charles Theater, New Orleans

ers. New Orleans was the center of this type of entertainment, and a success in the Crescent City meant a successful tour of the state.

Showboats still cruised the rivers and bayous, giving plays, minstrel shows, and other forms of entertainment.

Music. The people of Louisiana were always a musical people. They enjoyed attending concerts and the opera as well as singing and playing instruments at home. Before the war New Orleans had been one of the great opera centers of the nation, but after it there was a sharp decline in professional music performances throughout the state. Music theaters closed their doors, music societies disbanded, and

even the French Opera Company of New Orleans could support only scattered performances. This lasted until after 1900, when there was a revival of interest in music.

After 1880, German singing clubs were active in New Orleans, community singing became immensely popular in the northern and western sections of the state, and brass bands were organized in many towns and communities. Louisiana's composers added new vitality and new Louisiana folk themes to the world of music. The New Orleans Philharmonic Society was organized in 1906. Negro concert pianist and music teacher Camille L. Nickerson collected and scored Creole and Negro folksongs and featured them in lectures and recitals.

Slow Passing of the Old Ways. The years from 1877 to 1920 have been called by some writers and historians the period of "Old Louisiana." It was a leisurely time when no one was in too much of a hurry. Until the coming of the automobile, people seldom traveled, and when they did, it was generally for short distances, either in a buggy, hack, or wagon, or on horseback. They still retained most of their old customs and living habits.

Older Louisianians remembered the days before the War for Southern Independence, and many veterans wore suits of "Confederate Grey," with small buttons of the "Southern Cross of the Confederacy" on the lapels of their coats. Memories of the war and the years of military occupation lingered long in Louisiana and many persons did not become real Americans again until their sons and grandsons marched off to World War I.

Improvement of Everyday Living Conditions. The modern conveniences of living which are accepted without thinking today were unheard of at

the beginning of this period. During the 1880's William Edwards Clement, who lived on a plantation, learned to read by coal-oil lamps. His home had no plumbing: "The first bathroom, too, was quite a curiosity. Somehow I first looked upon that new innovation as 'sissy,' encouraging softness." Drinking water, which generally came from an unscreened cistern or shallow well, sometimes contained wiggle tails (mosquito larvae) and small snakes. As there were no door or window screens to keep out flies and mosquitoes, mosquito bars of fine gauze were placed over the beds. In the summer people cooled themselves with palmetto fans. In winter, the rooms were warmed by fireplaces, and on Saturday night "we did not turn on the hot and cold water. Instead we luxuriated in the embrace of a big tin bathtub, carried into the bedroom for that purpose—the portable kind, with a raised, roundish back and curved arm rests."

Improvements in everyday living came slowly after 1877 and new inventions provided more comfort, especially in cities and towns which installed city-wide utilities. Though rural life changed too, it was a very much more gradual development.

At the beginning of the period none of the Louisiana cities had underground sewage systems, the first such system being installed in New Orleans in 1880, and in most towns water was secured from individual cisterns or open wells. "Fire-wells," which were public wells from which water could be drawn in case of fires, were common in most towns. In 1886, for example, Napoleonville had six fire-wells and was about to dig a seventh, whereupon the Donaldsonville *Chief* announced: "Donaldsonville has none and ought to be ashamed of herself."

A large city like Carrollton, now a part of New Orleans, had over two dozen fire-wells. By the 1890's many towns were beginning to drill deep wells and establish city water systems.

Some of the larger cities had mule-drawn street railways. New Orleans had a city-wide network by 1861, and a mule-car line began operating at Shreveport in 1870. But most of the other lines in Louisiana were built about 1890. Baton Rouge, Lake Charles, and Alexandria all got street railways at about the same time.

Shreveport was the first city in Louisiana to use electric cars, operating by means of an overhead system of wires and trolleys. Three years later, in 1893, New Orleans and Baton

Shreveport in 1889. Texas Street, looking west from Commerce Street.

SHREVEPORT TIMES

Electric streetcars crowded the tracks on Canal Street in New Orleans during the late 1890's.

Rouge put electric "trolleys" into operation. But in New Orleans, mules did not disappear from street railway service until 1899.

The appearance of the electric streetcars created excitement as late as 1906, when Alexandria and Monroe put their systems into operation. When the first electric car at Alexandria made its ceremonial run, "people ran out of houses or leaned from win-

dows to wave the jouncing, swaying and humming little car along." Dogs tucked their tails and ran, and horses "leapt into gardens and backed through fences." Riders in some instances dismounted and held coats or jackets over their horses' heads.

Towns were still lighted by coal-oil street lamps which had to be lit every night by a lamplighter. In 1896 the Donaldsonville lamplighter cared for

Alexandria's mule-drawn streetcars were not replaced by electric trolleys until 1906.

more than fifty street lamps, and one of the newspapers once complained: "Through what is supposed to have been the carelessness of James Jones, the lamp on the corner of Mississippi street and Railroad avenue caught on fire last evening at about 9:30 o'clock. . . . There is a complaint that the lamplighter fails to properly trim the wicks." Two months later the same newspaper urged the installation of electric lights: "We are too big to remain in the dark any longer." Shortly after this it was announced that an electric company was soon to be organized. Crowley, Monroe, Opelousas, and other cities began to install electric lights, but many towns followed their coal-oil lights first with artificial gaslights, then with natural gaslights after 1916, and finally with electric lights.

Most towns still depended upon volunteer companies of firemen to fight fires. These companies took great pride in their organizations, each company becoming a sort of social club. The men wore bright uniforms, kept their fire engines shining brightly, and paraded their equipment at every opportunity. The Hope Hook and Ladder Company of Plaquemine was organized in 1882 and built a large hall, the upper floor to be used for dances, social gatherings, and theatricals, and the lower floor to house the company's fire truck. Until 1885 the bells of the Catholic church in Plaquemine were used to sound the alarm of fire; after this the fire companies installed bells at their headquarters.

Sidewalks went through four stages of development, starting with a low levee-like banquette, which was afterwards topped with wooden planks, usually laid lengthwise. The third stage was the brick sidewalk. Modern concrete sidewalks did not make their appearance in many towns until after 1920.

Before this period Louisiana had depended during the winter months upon shipments of northern ice which was packed away in icehouses in towns and on plantations to await the uses of summer. Frequently this supply was exhausted before the coming of cool weather in the fall. During the 1880's most Louisiana towns still received their ice supply from New Orleans in barrels packed with sawdust, but by the 1890's many of them had "ice factories."

Special delivery of mail in towns was started in 1885 and free rural delivery in the 1890's. In 1912 the first "Official United States Aero Mail Delivery" brought mail from New Orleans to Baton Rouge in one hour and thirty-two seconds.

Telephones made their appearance during the 1880's. William Edwards Clement has written: "I remember the erection of the first poles in front of our plantation and the stringing of the wires. All this was quite a curiosity, of course, and we greeted it with the doubt and contempt any such fool enterprise should properly merit. People like us, with swift horses always ready could send messages, or visit around at will. We were getting along fine, saw no use for crazy innovations such as telephones. It was just a fad and would soon die out." But the "talking telegraph" stayed and became a part of ordinary daily life.

Motion pictures did not make their appearance until the early 1900's. The first "movies" were short (and soundless) one-reelers.

Lingering Customs. The old time-honored customs of the people lingered on, however, despite improvements to everyday living.

Courtship was not as easy and simple as it is today. At least during the early years of this period, if a young man wished to call on a young lady he sent

Rural mail was delivered at a leisurely pace.

a friend to ask permission of her father. Couples were seldom left alone, but instead were "chaperoned." Many a young man spent the entire evening playing dominoes with the girl's father.

If he continued to call, papa asked him what his intentions were. This was to save the young lady's time,

which she could not afford to waste on a young man who "had a heart like an artichoke," meaning "a leaf for everyone," for she would be considered an "old maid" at the age of twenty-five.

Mondays and Tuesdays were considered the best days for weddings; Saturdays and Sundays were considered "common" days on which no one would consider being married, and Friday was "Hangman's Day," when criminals were executed.

A Catholic couple who lived in or within easy travel of New Orleans and who wanted a really fashionable wedding were married in the St. Louis Cathedral; otherwise the wedding was in the bride's church. Protestant weddings caused less fuss and bother; the groom simply went to the courthouse, got the license, and the wedding was performed, either at the church or at the home of the bride. But everyone got excited just the same. On one occasion at Delhi a young Irishman had considerable trouble. He rode sixteen miles to Rayville, got the license, and returned to his waiting bride-to-be. However, the license did not have the last name of the young lady on it, only her first name; so back he went to the parish seat. While he was gone the news leaked out, and he returned to find the whole town gathered to witness the wedding.

When someone died, all the clocks in the house were usually stopped, the mirrors were covered, and black crape was hung on the front door. Older people were usually buried in black coffins, while lavender or gray coffins were used for the middle-aged, and white for children. Everyone dressed in black mourning clothes, and in many homes the night before the funeral there was a "wake," at which the family provided food and drink for the neighbors, relatives, and friends who called or who "sat up" all night with the corpse.

A black hearse, drawn by horses draped with black and decorated with black plumes, was used for old and middle-aged people, while white horses and decorations were used for children. There were no funeral homes then. Everyone was buried from his own home. If his family was in poor or even moderate financial circumstances, the undertaker redecorated the parlor with carpets and coverings for the chairs and sofas and hung black or white curtains and drapes. Sometimes a band playing funeral music went with the procession to the graveyard, and some of the horses drawing the hearse were trained to keep step with the music.

The home, throughout the period, was the center of life. Not long ago an old man said: "Nowadays people are born in hospitals, get married in hotels, are buried from the undertaker's. All they use their homes for is a place to change clothes."

Old Superstitions. The people of that day were superstitious, and though not everyone believed all the current superstitions, many believed in at least some of them. Some thought the future state of the weather could be determined by certain signs: gulls flying excitedly in circles meant that bad weather was coming; fogs were on the way if the light of the moon and stars reflected clearly in water. On the Lower Mississippi heavy rains were thought to come from Morgan City, so the appearance of a cloud in the southwest caused steamboatmen to say:

"Morgan's gonna take the lid off the well."

There were superstitious cures for every kind of human ill: babies were sometimes given mud-dauber-nest tea to make them strong and healthy; aching joints were treated with an ointment made from mashed lightning bugs; sassafras tea taken in the spring was supposed to thin the blood which had become thick during the winter; weakly children slept on mattresses of moss gathered from cypresses, in order that the strength of the trees might flow into them. Boils were cured with mixtures of sugar and egg yolks or charcoal and lard, and some believed snake bites could be cured if the wound were immediately dipped in water, causing the snake to die instead of the person.

Bad luck or death was foretold by many signs. Sneezing at the table meant that someone would soon die. To have a haircut on Friday would certainly bring some sort of illness. To prevent losing money, a person burned onion peelings or carried a sprig of verbena in his pocketbook; and burned clothing was never patched or repaired, for to do so meant death in the family. Coffin lids were often left unnailed in order that the spirit could get out on Judgment Day. Though dreams warned of approaching bad luck, it could be warded off by carrying the ninth bone of a black cat's tail in a pocket or by tying butterfly wings to the right leg.

Some people of southern Louisiana believed in evil spirits, some of which inhabited the bodies of living persons and animals, especially wolves, snakes, or bats. There were *loups-garous* (werewolves) and zombis, and children were sometimes warned to be careful or "the *loups-garous* will get you." Here and there, especially in South Louisiana, were those who still practiced voodoo.

Amusements. Louisianians did not lack amusements at this time. In the country areas there were hay rides, watermelon and bee-tree cuttings, sugarcane peelings, family dinners and other gatherings, dances, singing parties, amateur theatricals and musicals, and many other forms of entertainment. In New Orleans there were balls and dances, plays, operas, concerts, picnics at Lake Pontchartrain, and numerous other activities. One old man recalled a few years ago how people used to take rides on the "horse-cars," dance at Hopper's Garden or at the Washington Artillery Hall, take walks along the levees to watch the ships, or ride "old Smoky Mary," the railroad train, out to Spanish Fort.

Circuses, animal shows, and trapeze and sleight-of-hand performers toured the state. Medicine shows, some of which were called "Kickapoo Indian Shows," presented Indian dances and tomahawk-throwing exhibitions before selling their cure-alls. Organ grinders walked along the streets of New Orleans and other towns, cranking their "hurdy-gurdies" for a few coins.

The people of the cities and larger

271

Church picnics and socials were extremely popular during the 1890's.

towns gave "balls" while country and village folks gave "dances," which in South Louisiana were called *fais-do-dos.* Country and village dances were usually held on Saturday night. On that morning the young men rode through the villages and countryside calling out that the dance that night would be at so-and-so's house. At sun-

down everyone climbed on horses or into buggies, carts, or wagons and went to the dance; the smaller children were put to bed and the dancing began. Supper was served at midnight. In South Louisiana the supper was usually fish gumbo or bisque, while in the northern or western sections of the state it was soup, fried fish, or fried

Lake Charles schoolteachers during
the 1890's

Stalebread Lacoume's Razzy Dazzy Spasm Band, 1899.

chicken. The dancing continued after supper until the musicians got up, went out into the yard, and fired several pistol shots into the air, yelling that the dance was over.

City and town balls were much more formal, particularly in New Orleans. Everyone dressed in elaborate fashion, the supper was served formally, and deportment and etiquette were carefully observed. It took a newspaper several days to present all the details of one ball given in Tallulah in 1884.

Negro dances were much as they had been during slavery days, when many of the plantations had slave dance halls. The calinda and the bamboula were still danced, though these violent, primitive dances were going out of fashion.

The custom of celebrating the Mardi Gras season had been discontinued during the Civil War years, but was revived in 1866, and by 1870 the various organizations were again giving balls and sponsoring parades. By 1900 the festivities had assumed their modern pattern, and while New Orleans was the center of interest and activity, there were also celebrations in numerous other towns and cities in southern Louisiana.

One of the most unusual amusements was the ring tournament, where mounted men rode along a course at breakneck speed and with the point of

274

a lance stabbed suspended rings. The riders dressed up as knights of old, and the champion named the queen of the grand ball which followed the tournament. Ring tournaments began before 1860 and lasted until about 1900, when they went out of fashion. They have recently been revived in a few communities in the southern part of the state.

There was much home and community singing, and song festivals were not unusual. Many of the old Creole, river, and water-front songs and Negro spirituals and work songs have become a part of the folklore of Louisiana.

"Spasm" bands developed in New Orleans during the 1880's, and by the 1890's there were dozens of them. The musicians used violins, kettles, cowbells, gourds filled with pebbles, harmonicas, banjoes, guitars, all sorts of drums, whistles, and anything else that would make a noise. About 1900, one of these bands began to advertise itself as the "Razzy Dazzy Jazzy Band." The music, with its syncopated beat, gradually became known as "Jazz" and by 1915 had been introduced to Chicago. Thereafter it spread over the nation and throughout the entire world.

Sports. Louisianians have always enjoyed sports. Boys learned to fish and hunt as soon as they were strong enough to shoulder a fishing pole or a gun. With so many streams and bayous no one was out of reach of a place to fish; even the Gulf of Mexico was not far away. Men hunted bear, bobcats, deer, small game, and all kinds of wild fowl. Wild-hog hunting became so popular in the swamp areas west of the Mississippi that the "hog dogs of Catahoula" were developed, one of the finest breeds of hunting dog in the world. Theodore Roosevelt hunted in the Catahoula country and wrote vividly of one of the guides. "Holt Collier," he wrote, " had all the dignity of an African chief, and for half a century he had been a bear hunter, having killed, or assisted in killing, over three thousand bears."

In 1890, Louisiana became one of the first states to legalize prize fighting, and New Orleans became a center for the sport. A "round" lasted until one of the fighters was knocked down. In 1893, Andy Bowen and Jack Burke fought a 110-round fight which lasted for 7 hours and 19 minutes. The fight ended in a draw.

After 1877 the "baseball fever" hit Louisiana and it was not long before every village and town had its team. Rules were different from those of today and huge scores were common; the Donaldsonville *Chief* reported in 1877 a game that was won by a "majority of nineteen runs."

Bicycles appeared in 1884, clumsy, large-wheeled affairs which often had a third smaller wheel on the side to help the rider balance himself. Automobiles began to make their appearance shortly after 1900, and in 1909, Ralph DePalma set a world's record at New Orleans with a speed of 60

A Sunday drive on a Louisiana country road.

miles per hour. In 1910 an "international aviation tournament" was held at New Orleans. One of the planes rose to over 7,000 feet and recorded a mile in 57 seconds. The featured event of this tournament was a race between an automobile and an airplane. The car defeated the plane, which was piloted by John Moisant, for whom present-day Moisant Airport was named.

Out of the Old, the New. Louisiana remained largely unchanged during the years from 1877 to 1920. Within the period, however, especially after the 1880's, more and more Americans from other states settled within her borders. They brought with them the seeds of change, for these aggressive and energetic people had different and new ideas and attitudes about living. Gradually the Old South and the Creole civilization began to fade. And although they may have felt regret at the passing of the leisurely ways, Louisianians generally agreed with Alcée Fortier when he wrote: "Let us not scorn . . . the Old South, for the New South . . . is but the continuation of the Old South: the New is possible only because the Old has existed."

Map 28—State of Louisiana, 1877

Many modern
industrial processes
require that plants
operate day
and night.

HUMBLE OIL AND REFINING COMPANY

PART EIGHT
Modern Louisiana
1920 to
the present

27. POLITICS AND POLITICIANS AFTER 1920

A Period of Change. The period in which Louisianians now live has been one of great change. The depression of the 1930's, the Second World War, the fantastic political, economic, and social progress made by the black citizens of the state since the 1950's have had great impact upon Modern Louisiana.

Few Louisianians in 1920 foresaw the transformation of a primarily rural, agricultural state to one that is becoming increasingly urban and in-dustrial. But even fewer foresaw the technological advances which the young people of Louisiana today take for granted—for instance, color television and jet travel.

These changes have of course had an effect upon every facet of Louisiana life.

Characteristics of the Period. In the period between the end of military occupation in 1877 and the election of John M. Parker as Governor in 1920,

John M. Parker

The Constitution of 1921. The Constitution of 1921 grew into the longest state constitution in the nation and by 1973 filled about nine hundred pages, including the index. The reason for this was the nearly five hundred amendments which had been added, 1921–1975, when the Constitution of 1974 went into effect. Despite its length, the old constitution served Louisiana well for over fifty years and made progress possible in the Pelican State.

Political Issues. The chief political issues since 1920 have been roads, education, social welfare, labor, taxes, the proper use of natural resources, and the relative power and authority of the Governor, the Legislature and local government officials. Political leaders and factions have disagreed about these issues and have fought bitter battles over them. At times the people have become very excited over campaign issues, while at other times they have seemed to take little interest and campaigns have been quiet. Louisiana has, on the whole, however, been a politically active state.

Governors Parker, Fuqua, and Simpson. John M. Parker of New Orleans, who had supported Theodore Roosevelt and his national "Bull Moose" Party, became Governor in 1920. It was an exciting term, for he was an enthusiastic and progressive political leader who worked actively for many projects to which there was opposition.

the major political issues had been economy in government, conservative legislation, and the maintenance of white leadership. Political campaigners had promised liberal reforms but after their election had accomplished little, and although some advances had been made, Louisiana, like the other southern states, had failed to progress as much as it should have.

After 1920 the people became intensely interested in political issues, joined political factions, and actively campaigned for their chosen candidates. Political candidates were beginning to promise more and more reforms, the majority of which were of the type which would improve the living standards or the welfare of the farmer and the working classes of society.

280

He urged the Constitutional Convention of 1921, the planning of a statewide highway system of hard-surfaced roads, the building of a new state university, new Civil Service and social legislation, and other needed reforms.

While there was public approval of some of the Governor's progressive proposals, others caused controversy. Only a part of his program succeeded, but much progress was made. Parker has been called a "trail-blazer," the "Father of Modern Louisiana." Not long ago a Louisiana statesman wrote that "the foundations he laid, and advocated, remain today. They are his monuments."

Parker was followed by Henry L. Fuqua, whose most colorful opponent in the 1924 election was a young North Louisiana lawyer named Huey Pierce Long. Fuqua died in office in 1926 and was succeeded by Lieutenant Governor Oramel H. Simpson.

It was during this administration that the move from Louisiana State University's old campus to the new was made. The Ku Klux Klan problem continued, so legislation was passed outlawing all sorts of hoods, masks, or robes, with the exception of those which were worn at Mardi Gras time or at masked balls or parties. A toll bridge east of New Orleans across a part of Lake Pontchartrain was authorized. In 1927 a terrible flood caused Louisiana, Arkansas, and Mississippi to league together to secure Federal aid for future flood prevention.

Huey Long in Control of Louisiana Government. In the campaign of 1928, Huey Long again ran for the governorship. This time, however, he had as allies many New Orleanians who had not supported him in 1924. Long was an ardent progressive. He promised a free bridge east of New Orleans so that the people would not have to travel over the toll bridge which was being built across Lake Pontchartrain. He promised free textbooks, better roads and other new bridges, improved schools, and more care for unfortunates who were poor, blind, deaf, aged, or sick. He promised natural gas for the city of New Orleans.

A son of rural Winn Parish, Long constantly toured the state, speaking and organizing the farmer and working classes against the wealthy and politically powerful groups which had formerly been in control of the state government. He spoke the language of the country people when in the country districts and the language of the city dwellers when in the cities and towns. His most noted speech was supposedly given at St. Martinville, at the Evangeline Oak, where he attacked the old governing groups:

Where are the schools that you have waited for your children to have that have never come? Where are the roads and the highways that you spent your money to build, that are no nearer now than ever before? Where are the institutions to care for the sick and the disabled? Evangeline wept bitter tears in her disappointment. But they lasted

281

Huey P. Long leading the Louisiana
State University band

Crowds attend Huey P. Long's funeral
at the capitol.

through only one lifetime. Your tears in this country, around this oak, have lasted for generations. Give me the chance to dry the tears of those who still weep here.

Long spoke in small communities where a speech by a candidate for Governor had never been heard. He called people by their first names, and developed an art of speechmaking which delighted the people by its humorous and plain language attacks on his opponents. Everyone laughed when he walked mincingly across the stage, explaining that he had finally saved enough money to buy a new pair of shoes and that his feet hurt. He won the election.

Examples of progress were numerous. Free school books and improved buildings, better roads, a great state university, a new Governor's Mansion, a new State Capitol, and more care for unfortunates soon became realities. Although the blacks made small educational gains, they made little real progress in breaking down the barriers of racial segregation, gaining the ballot, or holding public office.

In 1929 an attempt to impeach Long failed, and the next year he was elected to the United States Senate. He remained Governor, however, until January 25, 1932, when Alvin O. King, the president pro tempore of the State Senate, officially succeeded him.

During these years Long built up a political machine which controlled every phase of the state government and many of the parish governments. In so doing he made many enemies who opposed his policies, argued that he was moving too fast, were envious of his personal power, or deplored his sometimes strong-arm political methods. To these Louisianians he had become the "Dictator of Louisiana." To his followers he was a dynamic, liberal, progressive, much beloved political leader. Senator Long was assassinated in the State Capitol in September, 1935.

Meantime, in 1932 Oscar K. Allen, one of Long's first supporters, had been elected Governor. He continued Long's program until his own death in 1936. His term was completed by the

acting president of the Senate, James A. Noe, Lieutenant Governor John B. Fournet having been elected to the State Supreme Court.

The election of 1936 saw the beginning of the period in Louisiana politics in which we live today. In most elections there have been two political factions, one group composed of former followers of Huey Long, the other of those who had opposed him. These two groups have campaigned in each election since 1936; in many first primary elections, however, they have split into smaller groups, led by one candidate or another.

Governor Sam Jones

Governor Leche and the "Louisiana Scandals." Richard W. Leche, a member of the Long faction, was elected Governor in 1936 and served until his resignation in the summer of 1939. Earl K. Long, the Lieutenant Governor and Huey Long's brother, completed his term of office. Leche resigned because of the so-called "Louisiana Scandals," scandals which shocked the entire nation. A number of political leaders and their friends had been using their positions or connections to make money. Some of this moneymaking was within the law, but some of it was outright corruption and stealing. During the next few years several of these men, including former Governor Leche, were tried by the courts and given prison sentences.

The Period of Reform and War, 1940-1948. The gubernatorial campaign of 1940 was a stormy one. The anti-Long reform faction was represented by Sam H. Jones, a Lake Charles lawyer, while Earl Long was the candidate of the Long faction. Jones was elected in the second primary election by a 20,000-vote majority.

The Legislature passed most of the Jones reform program. More than a hundred state agencies were removed from the control of the Governor. A Civil Service system was adopted for state employees. Legislation was passed restricting payroll padding, deductions (from employees' salaries), dual jobholding, and other such practices.

The campaign of 1944 was less hotly contested than the one which preceded it, because the interest of Louisiana and the entire nation was centered on World War II. The anti-Long candidate, Jimmie H. Davis, sought harmony and goodwill as opposed to political factionalism. He conducted a colorful vote-getting campaign, touring the state with a "hill-billy" band, singing "You Are My Sunshine" and other popular songs at barbecues and political rallies. In the second primary he won over Lewis L. Morgan, the Long candidate, by nearly 35,000 votes.

Davis' governorship was marked by a rapidly rising state income and the retention of the Jones reforms in government. One of the most surprising events during his administration was the election of reform candidate deLesseps S. Morrison, a former anti-Long legislator, as mayor of New Orleans. Morrison defeated Mayor Robert S. Maestri, who was the old machine-politics candidate.

The Governorships of Long and Kennon, 1948-1956. Earl Long became the Long-faction candidate in 1948 and was again opposed by Sam Jones. Long touched the match to the campaign when he charged former governors Jones and Davis with "do-nothingism" and pledged what his opponents called "do-everythingism." Both candidates promised increased appropriations for almost every kind of public service. Long won the election by a majority of over 200,000

285

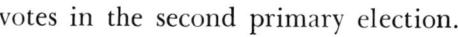

Robert F. Kennon

Earl K. Long

votes in the second primary election.

When Jones learned that Long had won the election, he said he hoped that "the new governor will rise above the past." But the Long faction had been out of power for eight years and its leaders wanted jobs for themselves and for their followers. The Civil Service legislation was repealed, and many people charged that the state had returned to the old Huey Long practices of "tax and spend and politicalize."

More money was needed to carry

out Earl Long's campaign pledges; taxes were therefore increased and bond issues were voted so that additional public welfare services could be provided. While the opposition charged that Long was "trying mighty hard to wear Huey's shoes," he carried out many programs of which the people in general approved. However, the heavy state government spending, and disagreements among the Long faction leaders led to trouble even before the election of 1952. The Governor's proposal to call a constitutional conven-

Jimmie H. Davis

John J. McKeithen

tion to draft a new constitution, which would not be submitted to the people for final ratification, caused some of the Longite leaders to leave the ranks.

Nine candidates entered the first primary in the election of 1952; Long candidate Carlos G. Spaht of Baton Rouge and anti-Long candidate Robert F. Kennon of Minden were the candidates in the second primary election. The members of the anti-Long faction settled their differences, and Kennon won by more than 175,000 votes.

Kennon's term of office brought many state governmental changes. Several departments were placed under the control of citizen boards. The Budget Office was reorganized. A constitutional amendment was ratified requiring a two-thirds majority for the passage of bills increasing taxes or levying new ones. Voting machines were required for all precincts. Civil Service was made a part of the constitution. A Legislative Council was established.

However, the anti-Long faction

A session of the Louisiana legislature.

made political mistakes, the national election of 1952 had caused leaders to disagree, and certain "lobby" groups were not satisfied with the appropriations which they had received.

Long and Davis Again Serve as Governor, 1956-1964. Five candidates ran for the governorship in the first primary election of 1956, and it was a

rousing, old-fashioned Louisiana Governor's race. The important issues were the settlement of the tidelands oil ownership controversy with the Federal government, repeal of the Right to Work Bill, increased old age assistance, advancement and improvement of the state educational and highways systems. All candidates promised no increase in taxes, and Earl Long

288

even hoped to reduce taxes, with some assistance from forthcoming tidelands income. Long was swept back into the governorship by a large majority in the first primary election.

Earl Long's last administration was a stormy time and reminded many citizens of the days of his brother Huey from 1928 to 1935. Earl forced the resignation of many members of the citizen boards. He forced bills through the Legislature removing the State Insurance Department and the custodianship of state voting machines from the Office of the Secretary of State.

Long's health had begun to fail shortly after he took office, and after hospitalization and weeks of inactivity during the summer of 1959, he resumed his duties as Governor. He was elected to the United States House of Representatives in 1960, but died in early September of the same year.

Former Governor Jimmie H. Davis and deLesseps S. Morrison became the two Democratic opponents in the second primary election of 1960. Davis won the nomination in a close election.

Davis was challenged by three opponents in the general election of 1960. He was elected by four-to-one.

Davis' accomplishments during the years 1960–1964 included organization of a State Sovereignty Commission to aid in protecting "the sovereignty of the state from encroachment by the Federal government," the building of

a new Governor's Mansion, new highway and bridge construction, and the creation of a Legislative Budget Committee and the Office of Legislative Auditor.

Governorship of John J. McKeithen, 1964–1972. Two of the ten Democratic candidates for Governor in the 1964 first-primary election received more than 150,000 votes: deLesseps S. Morrison and John J. McKeithen.

McKeithen won the runoff campaign and defeated Republican candidate Charlton Lyons of Shreveport in the general election.

A new amendment to the state Constitution during McKeithen's first administration made it possible for the Governor to succeed himself. In the first primary of the election of 1968 McKeithen defeated John R. Rarick. McKeithen was unopposed in the general election and was the first Louisiana Governor to succeed himself in the twentieth century.

During his eight years as Governor, McKeithen enlarged and amended the "Sell Louisiana and Louisiana Products" program. The Louisiana State Science Foundation was created to stimulate scientific, economic, and technological research. Government officials made increasing use of the Public Affairs Research Council, founded in 1950 and headed by Edward Steimel, in researching and aiding in the solution of governmental problems.

Edwin W. Edwards Becomes Governor, 1972. Edwin W. Edwards of Crowley and J. Bennett Johnston of Shreveport led the seventeen candidates for Governor in the Democratic first primary election of 1972. Gillis W. Long of Alexandria came in third, and former Governor Jimmie Davis of Baton Rouge, fourth. Edwards won the second primary by a close vote and then decisively defeated Republican candidate David C. Treen of New Orleans in the general election.

Perhaps the most significant result of the election was that eight blacks won seats in the State House of Representatives, thus raising Louisiana to ninth position in the nation in Negro legislative representation.

Governor Edwards had campaigned on a dynamic reform platform and in his address to the joint session of the Legislature on May 10, 1974, outlined his proposed reform legislation. He prefaced his proposals by saying that he was recommending "some sweeping reforms to make government more visible, more reflective of a society coming to grips with the latter part of the twentieth century."

The most important of the Governor's fourteen categories of reforms included the drafting of a new state Constitution, abolition or consolidation of over fifty state agencies, inauguration of a state-wide economy program, and the construction of a Gulf of Mexico Superport.

The Governor also listed some of the "major problems in Louisiana," including 100 percent assessments, tax equalization, and the need "to obtain maximum benefit from our natural resources at a minimum cost to Louisiana residents."

Perhaps the most significant of the Governor's changes in Louisiana government are the abolition or consolidation of numerous state agencies and adoption of the new and eleventh state Constitution by the people in the spring of 1974. The new Constitution went into effect on January 1, 1975.

Summary of the Period. No one would deny that the period since 1920 has been the "Progressive Age of Louisiana," for during these years Louisiana emerged and has continued to develop as a progressive state.

During these years the Long faction and the anti-Long faction have battled for leadership and control of state affairs, and the majority of state officials have held their offices for short periods. Secretary of State Wade O. Martin, Jr., first elected in 1944, is now the state official with the most years of public service.

The first serious attack upon racial barriers to political rights in modern times began in 1952 when Kermit Parker became the first Negro to run for Governor since the years following the Civil War. Sixteen years later Ernest Morial was elected to the Legislature, and in 1969 John Bobb, Jr., was elected mayor of Grand Coteau.

Governor Edwin W. Edwards

At the present time, blacks hold several hundred appointive and elective offices at municipal, parish, and state levels.

The advancement of the political and economic position of blacks in Louisiana has probably been the most significant development of the past two decades.

Louisiana's Senators and Congressmen have well represented their state in Washington, D.C. during past years. Senator Allen J. Ellender served from 1936 until his death in 1973. Representative F. Edward Hebert has ably served since 1941 and is now dean of the Louisiana delegation. Senator Russell B. Long, the eldest son of Huey P. Long, has been re-elected since 1948 and has won strong loyalty in his native state.

Timber barge on the Red River

28. ECONOMIC DEVELOPMENT SINCE 1920

General Observations. The economic life of Louisiana since 1920 can be divided into four distinct periods. The state made steady progress until 1929, when the entire country was hit by a major depression which severely affected Louisiana as it did the other states. The depression years ended with the United States' entry into World War II in 1941. During that period the state's entire economy was geared to meeting wartime emergencies. Since the end of the war, Louisiana has made rapid strides in all phases of economic life.

The population of the state and its cities has grown rapidly. In 1920 the population of Louisiana was approximately 1,800,000; by 1950 it had grown to nearly 2,700,000; and in 1970 it had reached 3,650,000. The projection is that by 1980 there will be 3,850,000 people living in the state.

During recent years Louisiana's people have begun to move from the rural areas to the towns and cities in greater numbers than ever before. Now more than 65 per cent of the people of the state live in urban centers. New Orleans is still the largest city, with a population of about 750,000, while Shreveport and Baton Rouge are running a close race for second place with over 175,000 each. The adjoining metropolitan areas which they embrace of course make them somewhat larger. Lake Charles ranks fourth with over 75,000; Lafayette is in fifth place

New Orleans

with over 65,000. Many of the villages of 1920 are now sizable towns, and many of the towns have grown into cities.

It has been estimated that by 1980 New Orleans will have a population of nearly 830,000, that Shreveport will be second with approximately 237,000, and Baton Rouge third with 220,000.

Agriculture. Modern Louisiana is still an agricultural state. Nearly 300,000 people live on farms and produce field crops, livestock, poultry, commercial and farm woodlot timber, vegetables, and fruit which in 1974 were valued at almost a billion dollars. Farms are steadily becoming larger and their number is decreasing. In 1950 there were slightly more than 124,000 farms in the state; by the end of 1974 they totaled less than 50,000.

Many different crops are grown, ranging from cotton, sugarcane, and

293

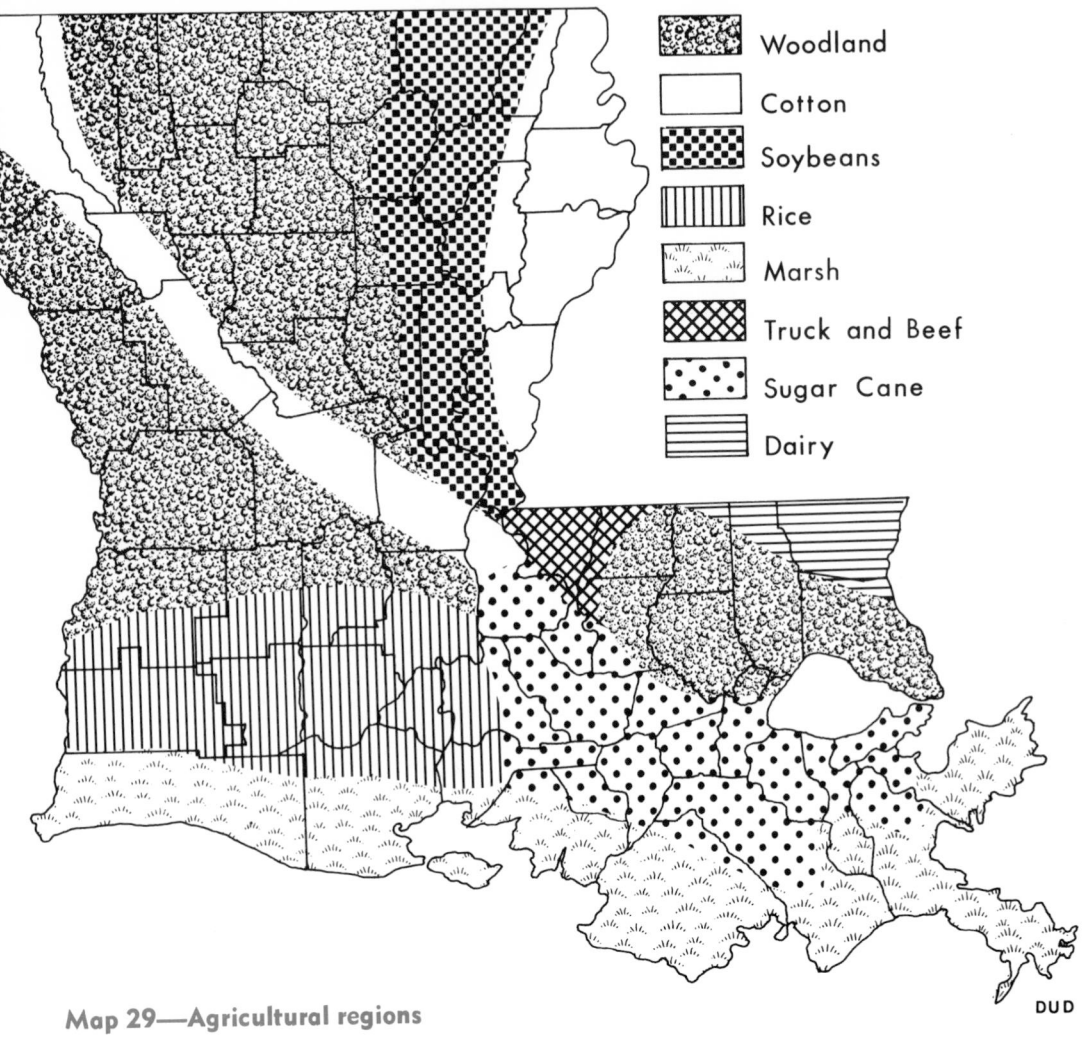

Map 29—Agricultural regions

DUD

tobacco to rice, sweet potatoes, strawberries, pecans, and truck-garden products, and include even lily bulbs and vetiver, a grass whose roots are used in making perfume. Some crops, particularly rice, have to be irrigated, but most depend upon natural rainfall. Louisiana has a particularly long growing season, which in some cases makes possible the growing of two or more crops a year. The state ranks high in

294

the national production of several crops—sugarcane, sweet potatoes, early spring strawberries, rice, cotton, several varieties of beans, and a few truck crops.

For many years rice was the state's most important crop, but during recent years it has given way to soybeans. Although soybeans are rather generally grown in all sections, rice is grown principally in the southwest sec-

A modern cottonpicker in Washington Parish

tion of the state. In 1974 soybean production totaled over $130,000,000, and the total value of rice grown was over $120,000,000. Other leading crops included cotton lint and cottonseed, sugarcane, hay, and sweet potatoes. The most unusual crop is Perique tobacco, which is only grown in St. James Parish, Louisiana. It is used for flavoring tobacco mixtures. Some fruits are grown, and the area surrounding New Orleans is an immense truck-gardening district.

During recent years Louisiana has developed into an important livestock-producing state. About two-thirds of the farmers raise cattle, hogs and sheep. The raising and marketing of beef cattle is a $100,000,000-a-year business. Dairying is also important and in 1971 more than two thousand dairy farmers sold products valued at more than $185,000,000. Hogs are raised in every parish, but generally are sold to packing houses rather than being butchered and processed for the use of the farmer and his family. Sheep, and a few goats, are raised in the highland areas. Many farmers have yards for the production of various types of poultry, most of which are sold to wholesale and retail markets.

Many factors have aided in the improvement of agriculture since 1920. There have been inventions and improvements in agricultural machinery, as for example the cotton-picker and the sugarcane harvester. The Louisiana State Department of Agriculture and Immigration and the United States Department of Agriculture have greatly aided agriculture through various livestock, poultry, plant, and other programs. A relentless attack has been declared against pests and diseases of all varieties. The Louisiana Agricultural Extension Service now operates in all parishes, and farmers are taught how to operate their farms more efficiently. Some years ago Bicniar Prioux of Iberia Parish wrote that "the Extension Service is the best thing that ever happened for the farmer who has to make a living from his farm."

Agricultural fairs and festivals have encouraged farmers to take greater pride in what they raise or grow. Today the Louisiana farmer is a business-

Sugarcane was cut by hand before the invention of mechanical harvesters.

man engaged in the raising of plants and animals which are needed by the people of the state or the nation.

Lumbering and Forest Products. Louisiana has over 16,000,000 acres of forested land, practically all of which is of commercial value. On about two-thirds of this total acreage grow oak, ash, hickory, and other hardwoods, while the remaining third grows several varieties of pine. In 1974 about 40,000 people were engaged in the

various wood-products industries, and their total production was valued at over $600,000,000.

The lumbering and forest industries are greatly assisted by the Louisiana Forestry Commission. This commission helps enforce laws, guards against forest fires and pests, replants cutover areas, and conducts experiments for improving the various types of trees.

Wood products include lumber of all types, shingles, barrels and hogsheads, veneers and plywoods, boxes,

Mechanical devices do the bulk of cane harvesting today in Louisiana.

railroad ties, telephone and telegraph poles, furniture, wooden fixtures, pulp for paperboard and containerboard, and other articles.

Oil, Gas and Minerals. Louisiana has been blessed with large deposits of oil, gas, and nonmetallic minerals. It is impossible even to estimate the total value of these underground resources for new deposits are being found every year. There is little metallic mineral in the state.

There are oil or gas wells in almost all the state's sixty-four parishes. While several fields were already in produc-

Offshore oil drilling platform.

DEPARTMENT OF COMMERCE AND INDUSTRY

tion in 1920, large-scale drilling did not begin until after this date. By 1926 the state had over thirty oil fields, and the number of gallons pumped each year had more than tripled. Today the state ranks second in the nation in crude oil production.

In 1947 drilling was begun in the offshore or in tidelands areas off the southern coast of Louisiana in the Gulf of Mexico. This led to a con-troversy with the Federal government over the ownership of the offshore water and land, which has not yet been settled by the Federal courts.

Salt was discovered in both North and South Louisiana over a hundred years ago but did not become indus-trially important until after 1920. Dry salt and salt-in-solution are now produced in many sections of the state.

South Louisiana salt mine

The Calcasieu sulphur field was exhausted early in this period but was replaced by fields at Jefferson Island and Grand Écaille. By this time the Herman Frasch system of sulphur mining was in general use. Water was heated to a very high temperature and then pumped through pipes into the sulphur beds deep underground, and the molten sulphur was then forced up to the top of the ground by compressed air. This system greatly increased production. Today's annual production is over 5,000,000 tons.

Other important Louisiana minerals include stone, lime, sand, and gravel, shell and clays.

Manufacturing. Louisiana has made gigantic strides in the field of general

299

manufacturing since World War II. At the present time there are over 6,000 industrial plants well spaced throughout the state.

Much of this progress is due to the work of the Department of Commerce and Industry in advertising Louisiana's natural resources and in encouraging manufacturers to build plants in the state. Since 1936 new industries have been permitted to apply for a tax exemption for a period of ten years. This also encourages the building of new manufacturing and processing plants.

Another of the major reasons why Louisiana has progressed so rapidly in the manufacturing and industrial field is the fact that the state has tremendous water supplies. The state has an average daily raw-water flow of over 600 billion gallons. Over 300 billion gallons of this total is in the Mississippi River, which has enough water to supply about 2,000 gallons a day to every man, woman, and child in the United States. The Exxon Chemical Company's refinery at Baton Rouge

Refinery complex at Baton Rouge.

BATON ROUGE CHAMBER OF COMMERCE

uses daily more water than does the city of Cleveland, Ohio.

In 1973 the manufactured products of Louisiana were valued at over five billion dollars. Chemicals and chemical products ranked first; foods and foodstuffs, second; petroleum and coal products, third; and pulp, paper, and wood products, fourth. Other classifications of goods produced included transportation equipment, metal products, stone, clay, and glass products, machinery, furniture, leather goods, and many others. It would take many pages to list all of the individual goods made in Louisiana today: candies, fertilizers, soda, boxes, mattresses, boats, vinegar, perfumes, chocolate, wigs, sails, beer, tombstones, oil tanks, and numerous others.

Owing to the fact that Louisiana has many basic raw materials—oil, gas, salt, sulphur, water, wood, stone, and clay—it seems destined to become a great manufacturing state. It has been predicted that the section along the Mississippi River between Baton Rouge and New Orleans will become one of the greatest industrial centers in the nation.

Economic Importance of Wildlife and Fisheries. The wild game and fish of Louisiana's lands, streams, and Gulf waters are of much economic value; and the Department of Wild Life and Fisheries regulates, aids, and helps preserve these natural resources. Louisiana's wildlife preserves are among the world's largest. Its bird and migratory waterfowl sanctuaries were the first established by any of the states and were the result of a movement led by Edward Avery McIlhenny of Avery Island.

There are over a score of these sanctuaries and preserves, of which the largest are the Sabine Migratory Waterfowl Refuge, the Delta Migratory Waterfowl Refuge, and the Pass à Loutre Game and Fish Preserve. In addition, there are several sanctuaries maintained by foundations, companies, and private citizens. The Louisiana Wild Life Federation, a nonprofit, nonpolitical organization, was organized in 1940 to assist in preserving the wildlife of the state.

Among the fur-bearing animals are coypu (commonly called nutria), which were brought from South America in 1938, raccoon, squirrel, muskrat, mink, opossum, otter, fox, and even wildcat. The annual production of nutria pelts now outnumbers muskrat pelts by about seven to one. Raccoon is in third place, with mink, opossum, and otter following in that order. Although fur production has declined during the last three decades, Louisiana is still the largest fur-producing state in the Union.

The catching and processing of fresh- and salt-water commercial fish is one of the important industries of present-day Louisiana. Commercial fresh-water fish include catfish, buffalo, gaspergou, garfish, and other varieties, while the salt-water fisheries catch shrimp, oyster, turtle, crab, Gulf menhaden, trout, redfish, flounder, red snapper, sheepshead, and mullet.

The first commercial canning of shrimp was done in 1867 by the Dunbar family at Grand Terre Island, but the shrimp packing industry did not really begin until 1918. At that time seines were discarded in favor of huge nets called "trawls," which were handled by motors on board large shrimp boats. The marketing of headless shrimp began in 1934. Today shrimp are packed in many ways, and, although production has declined since the middle 1950's, it is still an important industry with an average annual catch over the past ten years of about 250,000 barrels. Oysters, hard-shelled crabs, soft-shelled crabs, crawfish, frogs, and turtles are found in great supply in Louisiana's waters and add millions of dollars to the state's yearly income.

In addition to direct state income, the wildlife and fishing lands and waters have brought fine sport to thousands of citizens and have provided many a zestful meal for their tables.

Transportation. There are over 50,-000 miles of highways and roads in modern Louisiana. They are divided into three classes: interstate highways, state highways, and parish roads. At the present time there are more than 1,500,000 automobiles and trucks registered in the state.

In 1970 the more than 4,500 miles of railroad track in the state were used by over thirty different railroads. After a continuing downward trend in railroad car loadings in favor of truck loadings, railways are attempting to regain their former position through the use of trailer-on-flatcar, piggyback service, and the delivery of automobiles by tri-level flatcars. Freight-train schedules are being speeded up and new types of refrigerator cars are being designed.

More than a dozen airlines serve the state. The Louisianian can now fly to almost any city within his state, or to other American or foreign cities. He may take off either in a privately owned or commercial plane from one of the numerous private or commercial airports, heliports and seaplane bases. New Orleans International Airport serves as a crossroads for flights to and from Latin America.

The navigable waters of Louisiana, on which pleasure or cargo boats may operate during all or part of the year, total about 9,000 miles. These streams, bayous, rivers and inland waterways carry heavy boat and barge traffic. The completion of the Intracoastal Waterway, the Barataria Waterway, and the Old River Lock are good examples of the constant improvement of Louisiana's inland waterways.

Commerce. Louisiana imports and exports many different types of raw materials and manufactured goods. The business of commerce and trade gives employment to many thousands of persons and plays an important part in the general economic life of the state.

The chief imports include "tanker

imports" such as minerals, fuels, lubricants, animal and vegetable oils and fats, and chemicals; and "dry-cargo imports" including food and live animals, manufactured goods, machinery, crude or natural materials, and miscellaneous manufactured goods. Specific items include sugar, molasses, bananas, coffee, bauxite, rubber, steel, vegetable oil, and hundreds of other goods.

The most important exports are "tanker cargoes" of animal and vegetable oils and fats, foodstuffs, and

One reason for the growth of New Orleans as a shipping center is that it has a Foreign Trade Zone. This zone is a fenced-in area where foreign goods may be stored, processed, and repackaged, free from any American customs, duties, excise, or other taxes. These goods may then be shipped to other countries or imported into the United States.

Recently completed facilities for the display and sale of all types of goods or for the promotion of foreign trade in-

New Orleans International Airport, one of the major airports in the United States.

NEW ORLEANS AVIATION BOARD

chemicals of many types. The leading "dry-cargo" exports include foodstuffs, grain, machinery, sulphur, and chemicals. Specific major items include wheat, corn, flour, feeds, cotton and cotton products, refined oils, and greases.

clude the International Trade Center, which includes the International Trade Mart and the Rivergate, and International House, a private organization of businessmen and professional men interested in the promotion of trade.

303

Night activity at a Lake Charles dock.

New Orleans is Louisiana's largest port, followed by Baton Rouge, Lake Charles, Morgan City, and New Iberia. The port of New Orleans is the second largest port in the United States and is the world's largest exporter of grain. At the present time its freight tonnage averages over 120,000,000 tons a year.

The port of Baton Rouge ranks seventh in the entire nation and is its largest inland port. Its annual tonnage averages over 50,000,000 at the present time. The port of Lake Charles averages about one third the tonnage of Baton Rouge. Morgan City and New Iberia have recently built port facilities. It is expected that a new Gulf of Mexico Superport will be constructed south of Houma to handle oil, petroleum, and other liquid products.

However, not all of Louisiana's commercial business is the handling of manufactured goods. The Louisiana tourist industry is now the second largest industry in the state. The four most important tourist attractions are New Orleans, Baton Rouge (home of the State Capitol and the state university), the Natchitoches country, and the Acadian country. The Louisiana Tourist Development Commission maintains tourist stations to assist all visitors and to furnish them with information on the many interesting attractions in Louisiana.

Labor. Although Louisiana had many labor unions prior to 1920, it was generally considered to be a nonunion state. Labor Day was not officially recognized until 1928.

The modern organization of labor unions had begun during the period from 1910 to 1914 when the Brotherhood of Timber Workers succeeded in securing better wages and a nine-hour day. The State Federation of Labor made its appearance in 1916, and the movement continued until 1929, when the number of labor unions began to decline. Since 1938, however, hundreds of unions representing different labor groups have been organized.

The Legislature has passed numerous laws regulating labor. Women's and children's labor laws regulate the labor of these two groups, while the Workmen's Compensation Law protects those who are injured while on the job. Employers must furnish reasonable medical, surgical, and hospital service and most employers provide these services through workmen's compensation insurance. The State Department of Labor has a Division of Employment Security, which works with the Federal government in taking care of laborers during periods of unemployment. The state maintains employment offices located throughout the state to assist people in finding work. Today working conditions and wages are good in Louisiana.

29. CULTURAL PROGRESS IN THE MODERN ERA

Educational Advancement. The modern educational system of Louisiana is the result of the work of many teachers, city and parish educational leaders, state officials, and other interested people who have worked diligently since 1920. The drive toward education for all has steadily gained momentum.

In 1920 there were slightly more than 550,000 children of school age in the state, only a small percentage of whom were attending school. By 1974 these students numbered more than one million—almost all of whom between the ages of six and eighteen were enrolled in public or private schools.

In 1920 there were fewer than 10,000 school teachers; by 1974 the number of teachers in the public schools had grown to over 40,000. And by 1975 practically 100 percent of these teachers had received four or more years of college training.

The above figures amply illustrate that public education has become one of the most important activities of Louisiana government.

Probably the most significant progress has been made in the movement toward giving complete and equal opportunity to all groups and classes of Louisiana's youth.

In 1954 the United States Supreme Court handed down a unanimous decision to end the doctrine of "separate but equal" public education. This action, after many court battles, eventually resulted in the opening paragraph of Article VIII, the section on Education, in the new Louisiana Constitution of 1974. That paragraph states that the goal of public education in Louisiana is to provide opportunities for learning "in order that every individual may be afforded an equal opportunity to develop to his full potential."

The state's educational door is now open—from the first grade to postgraduate and professional legal and medical courses in the colleges and universities of Louisiana.

The State Department of Education, headed by an elected State Superintendent, is responsible for elementary and secondary education.

In 1972 William J. Dodd, who had headed the department since 1964, met serious opposition. Louis J. Michot, Lafayette businessman, vigorous-

306

Louisiana State University, Baton Rouge

ly attacked Dodd's administration and promised that, if elected, he would reorganize the department along business lines and remove it from politics.

Michot led Dodd in the first primary by over 150,000 votes. Dodd withdrew from the second primary, and Michot won in the general election without difficulty.

Public Elementary and Secondary Schools. The people of Louisiana elect the State Superintendent. He and his department serve in a professional capacity for the administration of policies set forth by the State Board of Elementary and Secondary Education.

The voters in each of the state's sixty-four parishes elect a parish school board. The Constitution of 1974 also provides that the cities of Monroe and Bogalusa "shall be regarded and treated as parishes

307

Southern University, New Orleans, 1882

Southern University Law School and Library, 1975

and shall have the authority granted parishes," thus having separate city-school systems.

The State Department of Education carries out the policies of the State Board of Elementary and Secondary Education in the constant improvement of every aspect of state-wide education.

Courses of study are constantly being improved. Not so many years ago the student frequently studied only arithmetic, reading, and writing. Today he studies a wide range of subjects, all of which help fit him for modern life.

Teachers today are much better qualified than they were even ten years ago. In past years there was no classroom supervision of instruction. Today classroom supervisors, especially trained in teaching methods and in definite fields of subject matter, help teachers to give the most effective possible instruction to their students.

In 1921 there were over 3,400 public schools in Louisiana. Through consolidation and school bus transportation, this number was reduced until in 1948 there were only 2,250 schools. Twenty-three years later the number of public schools had been further reduced to 1,400, augmented by 460 nonpublic schools.

Prior to 1928 textbooks were not supplied to the pupils. It was in that year, however, that the Legislature passed the first Free Textbook Law, and additional laws have been passed since then, so that today the schools are furnished free textbooks, library books, audio-visual aids, and other special equipment. The Louisiana school lunch program was begun in 1932, received its first legislative appropriation in 1939, and by 1974 there were over 2,000 such public, private, and parochial school programs serving an average of over 750,000 pupils daily.

Higher Education. There are thirty-four universities, colleges, and junior colleges in Louisiana, of which eighteen are supported by the state and sixteen by funds from private endowments or religious institutions. In 1974 more than 125,000 students were enrolled in these schools.

All of the state colleges and universities are now (since the Constitution of 1974 went into effect) under a State Board of Regents responsible for planning and coordination. This includes the Louisiana State University system and the Southern University system, though each of these has its own Board of Supervisors. The other state institutions of higher learning are managed by the State Board of Trustees for State Colleges and Universities.

LSU, with a total enrollment of more than 42,000 on all its campuses (about 24,000 on the Baton Rouge campus) is the largest of the universities. The University of New Orleans is a part of the LSU system, and there are campuses at Shreveport, Alexandria, and Eunice. LSU's medical, nursing, and dental schools are located in New Orleans and Shreveport.

The largest of the other state university are Southern University at Scotlandville, the largest predominantly black institution of its kind in the United States, and the University of Southwestern Louisiana at Lafayette. There are also branches of Southern at Shreveport and in New Orleans.

Tulane University and Loyola University of the South, both at New Or-

leans, are the largest private institutions of higher learning. Sophie Newcomb College is the women's division of Tulane. One of the oldest schools in the state is Centenary College, at Shreveport.

The State's Libraries. Louisiana State University's library at its Baton Rouge campus is the largest in Louisiana and in the entire Lower Mississippi Valley. It houses nearly 1,500,000 volumes,

The Louisiana State Library at Baton Rouge.

additional thousands of magazines, newspapers, and pamphlets, and over 1,000,000 historical manuscripts and state and local governmental archival documents.

The Louisiana State Library, with its parish branches, provides information and book services to the people of the state, to state and local officials, and through book loans to other libraries. Its materials for the blind, Louisiana historical materials, films, recordings, and other specialized collections are loaned to other libraries, groups, and individuals. Every year several million circulation loans are made.

The ranking parish libraries are: Jefferson Parish, East Baton Rouge Parish, and Ouachita Parish. The Shreve Memorial Library at Shreveport, with holdings of more than 210,000 books, and the New Orleans Public Library, with holdings of over 500,000 books, are the largest public libraries in the state.

Louisiana's libraries are fortunate in having had some noted librarians who were much interested in collecting material on the history of the state. James A. McMillen was the librarian at Louisiana State University for a number of years and was largely responsible for the building of the university's great collection of books, pamphlets, newspapers, magazines, and government documents pertaining to the history of Louisiana. William Beer was the head of the Howard Memorial Library of New Orleans

(now a part of Howard-Tilton Memorial Library, Tulane University), and he was one of the nation's greatest book collectors.

In 1906 the state established the Louisiana State Museum, appointing Dr. Robert Glenk as the first director. Dr. Glenk served for over thirty years and during that period accumulated for the museum's research library a great collection of published materials on the history of Louisiana. The museum was opened to the public in the old Cabildo building, adjacent to the St. Louis Cathedral in New Orleans, in 1911.

Preservation of Louisiana's History. Despite the fact that Louisiana has one of the most colorful pasts of all the states, it has done less than almost any of the others to preserve its historical records. The French were careless recordkeepers, but the Spanish kept and carefully preserved the records of every division of government. They were especially careful with the records of their American colonies. Early state officials had good intentions but lost many important historical records. A great number of state, parish, and local records were destroyed or lost during the Civil War and the period of military occupation. Even in modern times public officials have upon occasion, when they needed office space, hauled records of great historical value to the city dump, or burned them.

The modern Louisiana movement

311

for records and archival preservation began when the Department of Archives at Louisiana State University was organized in 1935 by Edwin A. Davis, a member of the history faculty. Most of Louisiana's universities now have such departments or library divisions for the collection, preservation, and organization of historical records.

A state agency for the preservation and better organization of Louisiana's historical and present-day archives and other records, officially titled the State Archives and Records Service, was created by the Legislature in 1956. Passage of the act followed a state-wide records survey sponsored by Secretary of State Wade O. Martin, Jr., supervised by Edwin A. Davis, and headed by John C. L. Andreassen, who became the first director of the agency. The service made steady prog-

The Louisiana State Exhibit Building at Shreveport. The building, designed by Frank Lloyd Wright, houses a large museum.

ress under the leadership of A. Otis Hebert, Jr., for several years after 1966, until Hebert became director of the Acadian Folklore Museum at the University of Southwestern Louisiana in 1974. Archives and Records Service also furnishes archival and historical information on Louisiana to all interested persons.

The Louisiana Historical Society, which has had active and inactive periods from the time of its organization in 1836, established the *Louisiana Historical Quarterly* in 1917. The Society is now active only in New Orleans, and the *Quarterly* went out of existence in 1958 despite the efforts of Dr. Joseph G. Tregle, Jr., then of Loyola University, to keep it alive.

The Louisiana Historical Association was organized in New Orleans in 1889 by a group of Civil War veterans for the purpose of preserving the records and relics of that conflict. It established the Confederate Memorial Hall in New Orleans and for a number of years was very active in its work. In 1958 the association was reorganized at Alexandria on a statewide and broader historical basis. Its official journal, *Louisiana History*, sponsored by Louisiana State University, was established by Edwin A. Davis, the founding managing editor, in 1960, with A. Otis Hebert, Jr., associate editor. Glenn R. Conrad, director of the Center for Louisiana Studies, University of Southwestern Louisiana, became managing editor

upon Davis' retirement in 1973, and the University assumed sponsorship of the publication.

The North Louisiana Historical Association was organized in 1952 when Mrs. D. H. Perkins, Dr. A. W. Shaw, and a small group met at Centenary College in Shreveport. A *Bulletin* was edited for a short period by J. A. Manry and from 1959 to 1969 Max Bradbury, who soon earned the title of "Mister North Louisiana Historical Association," edited a *Newsletter*. In 1969 Morgan Peoples, a member of the history department at Louisiana Tech, became the founding editor of the *North Louisiana Historical Association Journal*.

The Attakapas Historical Society was organized in 1966 with Harris Periou as its first president. The *Attakapas Gazette* was established the first year, after an editorial committee had been appointed. The committee edited the *Gazette* until 1968, when Mathé Allain became editor of the historical journal. The Attakapas Historical Society, like the North Louisiana Historical Association, is an active regional historical organization.

Altogether there are more than twenty-five local, parish or regional historical organizations that are now studying and discussing in their meetings the fabulous and romantic history of Louisiana. Similar organizations should be established in every locality and parish to study the history of its own particular area.

Organizations interested in particular phases of the state's history include the Louisiana Genealogical and Historical Society, which is chiefly concerned with family history, and the Louisiana Landmarks Society, which works for the preservation of historic buildings and other landmarks.

The State's Museums. The New Orleans Museum of Art, formerly the Isaac Delgado Museum of Art, houses one of the South's finest collections of paintings and sculpture. The R. W. Norton Art Gallery in Shreveport owns one of the finest collections of Western art in the country, including a large group of paintings by Charles M. Russell. There is also a gallery of art in the Louisiana State Exhibit Museum in Shreveport.

Jay Broussard, under whose direction the Louisiana Art Commission achieved a national reputation, is now director of the State Department of Art, Historical and Cultural Preservation. His department oversees the activities of the Louisiana State Museum complex in New Orleans, the State Art Gallery and the Old Arsenal Museum at Baton Rouge, the Camp Moore Confederate Museum and Cemetery at Amite, and the Orleans Landmarks Commission, which marks historic sites in New Orleans.

The largest historical museums in the state are the Louisiana State Museum and the Louisiana Historical Association's Confederate Memorial Hall, also in New Orleans. The Louisiana State Exhibit Museum in Shreveport also has historical exhibits, as does the Louisiana Arts and Science Center in Baton Rouge. The Arts and Science Center has an outstanding planetarium as well. The Museum of Natural History in Lafayette also houses a planetarium.

The Museum of Natural Science at LSU is one of the outstanding museums of its kind in the country. Its Gallery of Louisiana Birds, which is open to the public, contains mounted specimens of most of the 411 species of birds found in the state and will eventually include all of them.

The Acadian House at Longfellow Evangeline State Park near St. Martinville exhibits Acadian and Creole articles. The Marksville Prehistoric Indian Museum displays Indian relics. The New Orleans Jazz Museum has an extensive collection relating to the history of jazz. Altogether there are more than fifty museums of different types in the state.

Newspapers, Radio, and Television. Louisiana is well equipped to furnish news and other information to its citizens through the media of newspapers, radio, and television. Today there are over twenty daily newspapers in the state and about one hundred weeklies and semiweeklies. There are fifteen commercial television stations and approximately ninety radio stations.

The Louisiana newspaper with the largest circulation is the New Orleans *Times-Picayune.* The *Louisiana Weekly,* also published in New Orleans, is one of the South's most important Negro newspapers. The *State-Times* and the *Morning Advocate* are published in Baton Rouge, and the *Times* and *Journal* in Shreveport. Other important Louisiana dailies include the Lake Charles *American Press,* the Monroe *Daily World* and *News-Star,* the Alexandria *Town Talk,* and the Lafayette *Advertiser.*

Radio appeared in Louisiana in 1922, when WAAB and WWL began broadcasting in New Orleans. This was soon after the first American radio programs were broadcast from KDKA in Pittsburgh, Pennsylvania. KWKH of Shreveport became the first Louisiana radio station to attract national attention when W. K. Henderson, a retired businessman, publicized his fight against chain stores. WDSU in New Orleans was the first American radio station to make direct broadcasts from ships and planes.

Television made its appearance in Louisiana for the first time in 1948 when WDSU-TV began broadcasting in New Orleans. WAFB-TV in Baton Rouge began broadcasting shortly afterward. By 1971 eight out of ten households in Louisiana had color television sets.

Literature. Little was written in or about Louisiana during the years from about 1900 to 1920, but the state joined the "reawakening" in Southern literature during the 1920's.

The new literary movement was centered in New Orleans, which for a time was one of the most important such centers in the entire nation. William Faulkner was among the authors who gathered there. Some of the Mississippi writer's first stories were published in the *Times-Picayune.* James J. McLoughlin wrote his fascinating newspaper yarns in dialect under the name of Jack Lafaience, and Walter Coquille became known for his Bayou Pom Pom stories. Roark Bradford wrote humorous stories and books about Negroes on the plantation, including *This Side of Jordan* and *Ol' Man Adam an' His Chillun.* E. P. O'Donnell wrote about the people of the Lower Mississippi River area south of New Orleans. And Lyle Saxon became the state's most beloved author with his *Father Mississippi, Fabulous New Orleans, Old Louisiana,* and other books. His *Children of Strangers* is one of the most sensitive novels ever written about the Negro.

New Orleans newspaperwoman Gwen Bristow also made a reputation as a novelist during the 1930's, and newspaperman Harnett T. Kane began a prolific career in 1941 with *Louisiana Hayride,* followed by *The Bayous of Louisiana, Deep Delta Country,* and other books. Hewitt L. Ballowe, a retired doctor who lived in the Mississippi River delta country, wrote *The Lawd Sayin' the Same* and *Creole Folk Tales*, which are now a part of American folk literature.

Two of the most important Louisiana writers of recent years are Shirley Ann Grau of New Orleans, who won a Pulitzer Prize for one of her novels, *The Keepers of the House*, and Walker Percy of Covington, who won a National Book Award in 1962 for his novel *The Moviegoer*. Percy has since won high critical acclaim with two other novels.

The Louisiana-born black writer Ernest J. Gaines now lives in California, although he uses Louisiana settings in his stories and novels. His novel *The Autobiography of Miss Jane Pittman* won the 1972 Louisiana Literary Award.

Historical Writing. Louisiana historical writing entered a new era with the death of Grace King in 1932. Since that time, numerous men and women have researched and written in the extremely broad field of Louisiana history. Publication of scholarly historical material was given great encouragement during the 1930's with the establishment of the Louisiana State University Press and with the university's sponsorship of the *Journal of Southern History*, whose founding editor was Wendell H. Stephenson of the history faculty.

In 1937 black historian Charles B. Rousseve published *The Negro in Louisiana*, the first English language account of the role of the Negroes in the history of the state. In 1949 Garnie W. McGinty published *A History of Louisiana*, the first complete history of the state since Henry E. Chambers published his *History of Louisiana* in 1925.

During recent years a great number of specialized and general works have appeared. Edwin A. Davis published his broad-coverage *Louisiana: A Narrative History* in 1961 and *Heroic Years: Louisiana in the War for Southern Independence* in 1965. John D. Winters' scholarly *The Civil War in Louisiana* also appeared in 1965. The two most important books on the Huey Long years by Louisiana authors were published almost thirty years apart and present opposite interpretations of the man and his regime in Louisiana. Harnett T. Kane published *Louisiana Hayride: The American Rehearsal for Dictatorship, 1928–1940* in 1941. T. Harry Williams brought out his detailed, sympathetic *Huey Long: A Biography* in 1969.

Two top-ranking scholarly works published during recent years are *Church and State in French Colonial Louisiana* by Father Charles O'Neill of Loyola University and the two-volume *Rudolph Matas History of Medicine in Louisiana* by John Duffy, formerly of Tulane University.

During recent years New Orleans journalist Charles L. "Pie" Dufour has inherited the mantle of Robert Tallant as the state's most popular

Old State Capitol, 1902

New State Capitol, 1931

author in the field of Louisiana history. Perhaps Dufour's best-known work is his *Ten Flags in the Wind*.

A recent biography of special interest is Frank James Price's *Troy H. Middleton*, the story of the general who made key decisions in the World War II Battle of the Bulge. General Middleton was president of Louisiana State University, 1951–1962.

Art. Since 1920 New Orleans and other sections of the state have attracted and produced numerous painters. Alexander J. Drysdale painted moss-draped misty Louisiana live oaks and swamp scenes. His work is now prized by collectors. Weeks Hall, of "The Shadows" at New Iberia, is remembered for his paintings and artistic photographs. E. H. Suydam sketched throughout the state and illustrated the books of Lyle Saxon. Conrad Albrizio executed murals for many public buildings. William Spratling taught art at Tulane University for several years and became noted for his paintings of Louisiana houses and people.

Juanita Gonzales, a young scupltress of great promise, died in 1935. Her heads of Governor Francis T. Nicholls and General Richard Taylor at the State Capitol are considered excellent work. Richmond Barthe's sculptures gained wide recognition, as illustrated by his *Toussaint l'Ouverture*, *The Crab Man*, and other works. Caroline Durieux gained international recognition with her etchings, "atomic prints," and other works of art. The black sculptor Frank Hayden, of the art department of Southern University, has achieved international attention.

Two distinguished works in the field of photography have appeared during recent years. The photographs of W. Darrell Overdyke of Centenary College at Shreveport in his *Louisiana Plantation Homes, Colonial and Ante Bellum* are unequaled in this historical subject area. *The Face of Louisiana*, which brings together over 150 of Louisiana photographer Elemore Morgan's photographs, was published in 1969, three years after his death. The sensitively written narrative by Charles East is of exceptional quality.

Drama. Professional drama has declined in importance in Louisiana since the appearance of motion pictures, radio, and television. However, the major cities of the state now have civic auditoriums and are visited by traveling companies of players. The amateur theater movement, on the other hand, has made much progress. Little Theaters, Civic Theaters, Town and Gown Players, and Players' Guilds have been established in many towns and communities. And all of the state's colleges and universities have speech departments that sponsor the production of plays.

Louisiana has produced several important American playwrights includ-

317

This was King Oliver's Creole Jazz Band of the early 1920's. Louis Armstrong kneels in the foreground with his slide trumpet.

ing Lillian Hellman, who was born in New Orleans, and Tennessee Williams, who although not a native of the state has lived in New Orleans and did much of his writing there. Also in the world of drama Douglas Turner Ward, a black and a native of Burnside, is a contemporary American playwright as well as an actor and director.

Music. Serious music in Louisiana declined after the Civil War but revived strongly after about 1900. The New Orleans Philharmonic Society was founded in 1906 and by the 1920's

was giving concerts and bringing noted musical artists to New Orleans. A second symphony orchestra was organized in New Orleans some years later, but the two afterward merged under the name New Orleans Philharmonic Symphony.

Today Shreveport, Baton Rouge, and Lake Charles also have symphony orchestras, and Shreveport and New Orleans have civic opera companies.

The music department of Louisiana State University gained a wide reputation during the 1930's with its opera productions. Dwight Greever Davis, former director of bands at North-

Louis Armstrong

western State University achieved a wide reputation as a conductor, band-music arranger, and organizer of a central music organization for the states of Arkansas, Louisiana, and Texas. John Morrissey, Tulane University director of bands, gained a national recognition through his compositions on Louisiana and Latin-American themes.

But Negro and Creole folk music has been the most characteristic of all Louisiana's music, and Louisiana Negroes, in particular, have contributed notably to American folk music. Jazz originated in Louisiana near the end of the last century, spreading from New Orleans over the entire world. Originally, small bands playing on the streets or in the dance halls used no printed music but composed it as they went along. These bands developed what they called "ear" music. Jazz did not become popular until about the time of World War I.

Louisiana has produced many famous jazz musicians, among them the great Louis Armstrong, Kid Ory, Jelly Roll Morton, Sidney Bechet, Louis Prima, King Oliver, Buddy Bolden, Al Hirt, and Pete Fountain.

Modern Louisiana. Everyday life in Louisiana has witnessed many changes since 1920. In the 1920's, and even in the 1930's, many homes in the state had no indoor plumbing. The gas range and the electric refrigerator did not come into general use until the 1930's. Many Louisianians had automobiles from the beginning of the period, but there were no highways as we know them today on which to drive. At the end of 1929, for example, there were only 268 miles of paved road in the whole state of Louisiana. Those who traveled some distance between cities, or to cities in other states, usually traveled by train. Passenger bus travel began with the coming of the highways, in the 1930's.

The depression years of the thirties were bleak ones for many Louisianians. Many lost their savings when banks closed; jobs were hard to find. But most managed to live comfortably. Almost every family in the small towns of the state had its own garden; many kept chickens in their back yards, and some had their own cows.

With the end of the depression and the coming of World War II, life in Louisiana, as in the other states, inevitably changed. The whole country was geared to a wartime economy. More than 325,000 of the state's boys and men volunteered or were drafted to serve in the armed forces. Army and Air Force bases were located in various parts of Louisiana, and these drew thousands of servicemen from other parts of the country. Camps for German and Italian prisoners of war were also located in the state. Louisianians at home mingled with those from far away; Louisiana's fighting men were scattered around the country and the world.

It was a time for patriotism. Louisianians, like other Americans, saved scrap iron to build guns, ships and tanks. They invited visiting servicemen into their homes. When rationing came, they learned to use less sugar, to get by with their quota of tires and gasoline—to manage without such things as nylon stockings and butter.

In the years since 1920, and especially since the end of World War II in 1945, the state has made rapid progress, and many features of the "Old Louisiana" are but memories of the older generation. The new generation of Louisianians live in better houses than their parents and grandparents did. They work shorter hours and their work has been made easier. They have more and better automobiles. On longer trips they travel by jet. The many inconveniences of the old days have all but been forgotten.

Country life has become much more attractive with the installation of rural electrical systems, modern plumbing, and natural or bottled gas. The farmers have built new homes, barns, and farm buildings; many of them now have air conditioning. The day of the walking plow and the old palm-leaf fan has passed.

Today's rural and city dwellers get the day's news over radio or television. They hear and see plays, concerts, baseball and football games, and other athletic events; through radio and television they become acquainted with the people and countries of the entire world; they can be guests at political conventions and at sessions of the Legislature, or the Congress. They are better informed, better educated, and better entertained than any previous generation.

Passing of the Old Creole Civilization.
The old Creole civilization of South Louisiana is rapidly fading. A generation ago there were comparatively few roads in the region, none of them being paved or hard surfaced for easy travel in rainy weather. Many of the larger towns and cities were accessible only by boat. In those days people traveled between farms, plantations, or communities on horseback, or in buggies or *pirogues*. While buggies and *pirogues* are still occasionally seen in South Louisiana, they have disappeared from general use.

Children of French-speaking Louisianians have largely stopped learning the French language and now speak only English. However, many of the old Creole customs and folkways have been preserved and rightly so, for these, with the French language, are all part of a Louisianian's heritage. Many still call a modern clothes closet an *armoire;* they still drink *café noir,* strong and black, or *café au lait,* with hot milk. Occasionally, when you make a large purchase at a store or pay your monthly bill, the proprietor will give you a little gift as *lagniappe.*

During the past few years Louisianians have come to realize that much of their old heritage should be preserved. Today the Louisiana Folklore Society and other organizations are trying to preserve many old customs, buildings, and historic landmarks.

Amusements. Modern Louisiana probably has more different fairs and festivals than any other state in the Union —they total slightly over seventy in number. They are generally staged for three purposes: to educate the people, to advertise a particular natural re-

321

Aerial photograph of Ruston in north Louisiana.

source or product, and to provide recreation. The State Fair of Louisiana is held in October each year at Shreveport and the entire state participates.

Noteworthy fairs and festivals include the Breaux Bridge Crawfish Festival, Holiday in Dixie (Shreveport), the International Rice Festival (Crowley), the Dairy Festival (Abbeville), the Peach Festival (Ruston), the Shrimp Festival (Morgan City), the Strawberry Festival (Hammond), the

Sugar Cane Festival (New Iberia), the Yambilee (Opelousas), the North Louisiana Cotton Festival (Bastrop), and the Ouachita Valley Fair (West Monroe).

In 1956 the state celebrated the two-hundredth anniversary of the coming of the Acadians to Louisiana. A group of citizens from all sections of the state organized a program of activities for the entire year. The celebration closed at St. Martinville, the

Acadian capital of Louisiana, with a great festival which attracted thousands of tourists.

One of the most interesting Louisiana celebrations is the Natchitoches Christmas Festival, which is completely supported by the community. It originated in 1927 when Max Burg-dorf suggested that Natchitoches put on a lighting and fireworks display, and has developed until today at Christmas time the entire city is lighted.

Mardi Gras, of course, is the biggest and best known of the Louisiana celebrations. The center of the carnival

A Rex Parade draws thousands of Mardi Gras celebrants to Canal Street.

The Monroe Civic Center. The complex contains a theater, an arena, and a conference hall.

activities is New Orleans, where there are over a dozen regularly scheduled day or night parades and literally dozens of balls held by the various carnival organizations. The King of the Carnival on Mardi Gras day is Rex, the Lord of Misrule, while Comus is the Lord of Mirth and Laughter. New Orleans is jammed with masked revelers. At six in the evening masks are removed, but the fun-making continues until midnight ushers in Ash Wednesday. The Lenten season has begun, and the revelry must cease.

Some years ago a visitor to Louisiana wrote: "Though New Orleans can strike a serious note, it is a gay-hearted city. New York is too hurried even to smile, London on a sunny day can only look complacent and cheerful, but New Orleans can riotously laugh. During the carnival, Rex, its king, is the merriest, maddest, gayest of all living monarchs."

324

Although New Orleans has the most important carnival in Louisiana, many other towns and cities have their own Mardi Gras carnival parades and balls.

Louisianians are still a fun-loving people, and newcomers to the state rapidly develop an enjoyment of those amusements which the natives of the state have enjoyed for generations.

Sports. One of the state's greatest assets is its wide variety of recreational facilities. Its mild climate, numerous streams, bayous, and lakes, rolling hill country, broad prairies, and great forests offer outdoor sporting opportunities possessed by few states. Hunting and fishing are universally enjoyed. The coastal marshes, streams, and lakes are combed for ducks, geese, and other wild fowl; the upland areas for quail, squirrels, and rabbits; and the interior ridgelands and swamps for deer. The sportsman can fish in the fresh-water bayous and streams for bass, crappie, and perch; in the Gulf of Mexico for shark, king mackerel, flounder, or tarpon; and in the coastal lagoons for trout, sheepshead, and redfish.

The state now maintains seventeen parks, of which Lake Bistineau State Park in Webster Parish, Chicot State Park in Evangeline Parish, Fontainebleau State Park in St. Tammany Parish, and Sam Houston State Park in Calcasieu Parish are a few. These parks have various types of recreational facilities, including vacation cabins, picnic shelters, beaches, small game courts, and group-camp buildings. Outdoor Louisiana offers many opportunities for camping, swimming, boating, and hiking.

Louisianians love competition in their sports, and all types of racing are popular: *pirogue* racing, horse racing, power-boat and sailboat racing. Racing meets and regattas are held annually at various race tracks and on various waters.

Louisianians enjoy intercollegiate sports such as football and basketball, and these contests attract many thousands of spectators annually. Tiger Stadium in Baton Rouge is filled to capacity for most home games during the LSU football season. The Mid-Winter Sports Carnival is held annually at New Orleans in the last week in December and ends with the Sugar Bowl football game on January 1. New Orleans is also the home of professional football and basketball teams. The cities and towns have recreational parks, golf courses, tennis courts, and picnic grounds where the young and old find excellent sports and recreational facilities.

Foods and Fashions in Cookery. An English visitor to New Orleans once wrote that it was the one city in the world "where you can eat and drink the most and suffer the least"; another traveler said that New Orleans was the "only city in America where street quarrels may be heard over the respective merits of certain restaurants and dishes." These comments need

The modern look of many Louisiana towns is well illustrated in this aerial photograph of Shreveport. Interstate I-20, seen in the foreground, has recently been completed through the city.

not have been restricted to the city of New Orleans, for the whole state of Louisiana is renowned for its excellent food.

Louisiana cookery is basically of two types: the cookery of northern, western, and southeastern Louisiana inherited from English-speaking ances-

tors from the eastern states of the South, and Creole or South Louisiana cookery, which combines the French love of delicacies with the Spanish taste for piquant seasonings. However, the members of every national group living in Louisiana have contributed to the great variety of dishes, and today

326

the Louisianian eats everything from French and Spanish bisques, gumbos, and jambalayas to Hungarian kapostas and goulashes.

Many of the old-time dishes are still prepared by Louisiana cooks. *Congri* is a combination of kidney beans and rice and is sometimes still called *moros y cristianos* (Moors and Christians). Gumbo is still a favorite. *Coush-coush* (sometimes spelled *kush-kush*), corn meal soaked with milk or hot water and fried in a little fat, is still eaten for breakfast.

Over the entire state, but particularly in the rural areas, "pot liquor and corn pone" is an old favorite, pot liquor being the water in which any type of greens have been cooked with a piece of salt meat or ham. Huey Long once took time out in the United States Senate to explain how it should be made properly.

Religion. Some years ago a survey made by the National Council of Churches revealed that Louisiana had the highest percentage of church-going people in the United States, with over 80 per cent of the white population attending Protestant or Roman Catholic churches or Jewish synagogues. Slightly over 50 per cent of these people are Protestant, a little more than 40 per cent are Catholic, and the rest are either Jewish or belong to some other faith. About 80 per cent of the Negro population is Protestant.

The Roman Catholic religion is of course the oldest faith in the state. Until recently, South Louisiana had few Protestants, and North Louisiana had few Catholics, but now Catholics and Protestants alike live in all sections of the state. Many old Catholic customs are still observed, though others are passing from common use. In New Orleans, particularly, the custom of offering public thanks to some saint by way of a newspaper advertisement is still practiced. The celebration of All Saints' Day with the gathering of people in the cemeteries, with hundreds of candles lighting the graves, is still to be witnessed in South Louisiana. Fishing boats and fleets are still blessed, the most important of these ceremonies being the annual blessing of the shrimp fleets at Morgan City and Delcambre.

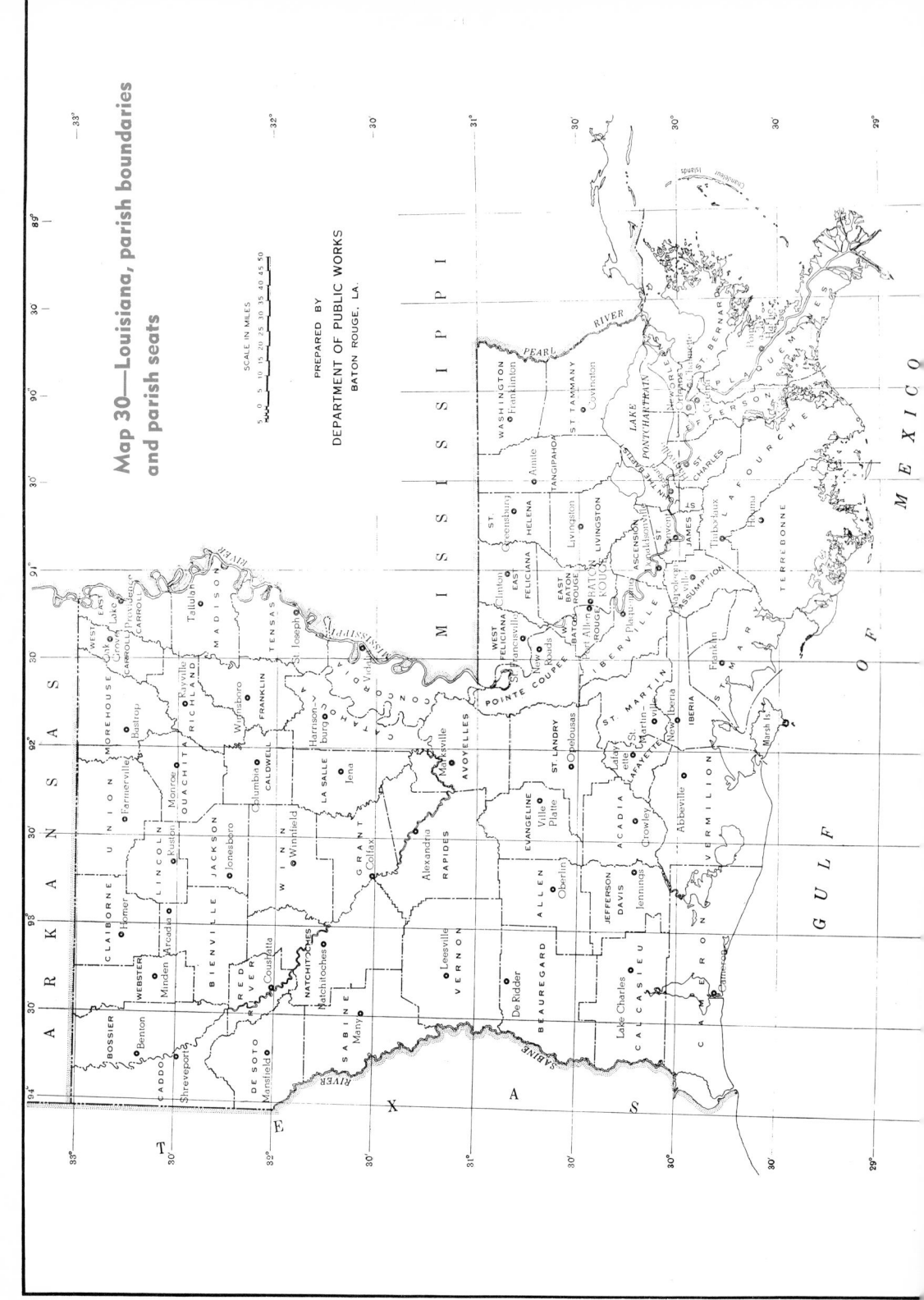

Map 30—Louisiana, parish boundaries
and parish seats

SCALE IN MILES
5 0 5 10 15 20 25 30 35 40 45 50

PREPARED BY
DEPARTMENT OF PUBLIC WORKS
BATON ROUGE. LA.

PARISHES OF LOUISIANA

Parish	Parish Seat	Area	Date Created	1970 Population
Acadia	Crowley	656	1888	52,109
Allen	Oberlin	779	1912	20,794
Ascension	Donaldsonville	312	1807	37,086
Assumption	Napoleonville	369	1807	19,654
Avoyelles	Marksville	883	1807	37,851
Beauregard	DeRidder	1,181	1912	22,888
Bienville	Arcadia	858	1848	16,024
Bossier	Benton	853	1843	64,703
Caddo	Shreveport	933	1838	230,184
Calcasieu	Lake Charles	1,107	1840	145,415
Caldwell	Columbia	553	1838	9,354
Cameron	Cameron	1,674	1870	8,194
Catahoula	Harrisonburg	739	1808	11,769
Claiborne	Homer	776	1828	17,024
Concordia	Vidalia	747	1810	22,578
De Soto	Mansfield	879	1843	22,764
East Baton Rouge	Baton Rouge	473	1810	285,167
East Carroll	Lake Providence	452	1877	12,884
East Feliciana	Clinton	453	1824	17,657
Evangeline	Ville Platte	699	1910	31,932
Franklin	Winnsboro	638	1843	23,946
Grant	Colfax	673	1869	13,671
Iberia	New Iberia	1,055	1868	57,397
Iberville	Plaquemine	635	1807	30,946
Jackson	Jonesboro	584	1845	15,963

Parish	Parish Seat	Area	Date Created	1970 Population
Jefferson	Gretna	771	1825	338,229
Jefferson Davis	Jennings	653	1912	29,554
Lafayette	Lafayette	279	1823	111,745
Lafourche	Thibodaux	2,039	1805	68,941
LaSalle	Jena	669	1908	13,295
Lincoln	Ruston	477	1872	33,800
Livingston	Livingston	689	1832	36,511
Madison	Tallulah	647	1836	15,065
Morehouse	Bastrop	806	1844	32,463
Natchitoches	Natchitoches	1,237	1807	35,219
Orleans	New Orleans	363	1807	593,471
Ouachita	Monroe	639	1807	115,387
Plaquemines	Pointe-a-la-Hache	1,986	1807	25,025
Pointe Coupee	New Roads	591	1807	22,002
Rapides	Alexandria	1,369	1807	118,078
Red River	Coushatta	419	1871	9,226
Richland	Rayville	562	1868	21,774
Sabine	Many	999	1843	18,638
St. Bernard	Chalmette	1,930	1807	51,185
St. Charles	Hahnville	390	1807	29,550
St. Helena	Greenburg	419	1810	9,937
St. James	Convent	260	1807	19,733
St. John the Baptist	Edgard	351	1807	23,813
St. Landry	Opelousas	937	1807	80,364
St. Martin	St. Martinville	831	1811	32,453
St. Mary	Franklin	1,036	1811	60,752
St. Tammany	Covington	1,141	1810	63,585
Tangipahoa	Amite	839	1869	65,875
Tensas	St. Joseph	640	1843	9,732
Terrebonne	Houma	1,893	1822	76,049
Union	Farmerville	912	1839	18,447
Vermilion	Abbeville	1,416	1844	43,071
Vernon	Leesville	1,350	1871	53,794
Washington	Franklinton	667	1819	41,987
Webster	Minden	620	1871	39,939
West Baton Rouge	Port Allen	209	1807	16,864

Parish	Parish Seat	Area	Date Created	1970 Population
West Carroll	Oak Grove	365	1877	13,028
West Feliciana	St. Francisville	426	1824	11,376
Winn	Winnfield	971	1852	16,369
			Total	3,643,180

LOUISIANA POPULATION, 1810–1970

Year	Total	White	Negro	Free Negro	Slave
1810	76,556	34,311[1]	42,245	7,585	34,660
1820	153,407	73,867	79,540	10,476	69,064
1830	215,739	89,441	126,298	16,710	109,588
1840	352,411	158,457	193,954	25,502	168,452
1850	517,762	255,491	262,271	17,462	244,809
1860	708,002 [2]	357,456	350,373	18,647	331,726
1870	726,915	362,065	364,210		
1880	939,946	454,954	483,675		
1890	1,118,588	558,395	559,193		
1900	1,381,625	729,612	650,804		
1910	1,656,388	941,086	713,874		
1920	1,798,509	1,096,611	700,257		
1930	2,101,593	1,322,712	776,326		
1940	2,363,880	1,511,739	849,303		
1950	2,683,516	1,796,683	882,428		
1960	3,257,022	2,211,715	1,039,207		
1970	3,643,180	2,552,572	1,088,734		

[1] Beginning here this column includes all races, excepting black, 1810 to 1860.
[2] Beginning here this column includes all races, excepting black, 1860 to 1970.

LOUISIANA POPULATION BY PARISHES

Parish	1810	1860	1900	1930	1960
Acadia	....	....	23,483	39,326	49,931
Allen	....	....	....	15,261	19,867

Parish	1810	1860	1900	1930	1960
Ascension	2,219	11,484	24,142	18,438	27,927
Assumption	2,472	15,379	21,620	15,990	17,991
Avoyelles	1,209	13,167	29,701	34,926	37,606
Beauregard	....	....	....	14,569	19,191
Bienville	....	11,000	17,588	23,789	16,726
Bossier	....	11,348	24,153	28,388	57,622
Caddo	....	12,140	44,499	124,670	223,859
Calcasieu	....	5,928	30,482	41,964	145,475
Caldwell	....	4,833	6,911	10,430	9,004
Cameron	....	....	3,952	6,054	6,909
Catahoula	1,164	11,651	16,351	12,451	11,421
Claiborne	....	16,848	23,029	32,285	19,407
Concordia	2,895	13,850	13,559	12,778	20,467
De Soto	....	13,298	25,063	31,016	24,248
East Baton Rouge	1,463	16,046	31,153	68,208	230,058
East Carroll	....	....	11,373	15,815	14,433
East Feliciana	....	14,697	20,443	17,449	20,198
Evangeline	....	....	....	25,483	31,639
Franklin	....	3,251	8,890	30,530	26,088
Grant	....	....	12,902	15,709	13,330
Iberia	....	....	29,015	28,192	51,657
Iberville	2,679	14,661	27,006	24,638	29,939
Jackson	....	9,465	9,119	13,808	15,828
Jefferson	....	15,372	15,321	40,032	208,769
Jefferson Davis	....	....	....	19,765	29,825
Lafayette	....	9,003	22,825	38,827	84,656
Lafourche	1,995	14,044	28,882	32,419	55,381
LaSalle	....	....	....	11,668	13,011
Lincoln	....	....	15,898	22,822	28,535
Livingston	....	4,431	8,100	18,206	26,974
Madison	....	14,133	12,322	14,829	16,444
Morehouse	....	10,357	16,634	23,689	33,709
Natchitoches	2,870	16,699	33,216	38,477	35,653
Orleans	24,552	174,491	287,104	458,762	627,525
Ouachita	1,077	4,727	20,947	54,337	101,663
Plaquemines	1,549	8,494	13,039	9,608	22,545
Pointe Coupee	4,539	17,718	25,777	21,007	22,488

Parish	1810	1860	1900	1930	1960
Rapides	2,200	25,360	39,578	65,455	111,351
Red River	....	....	11,348	16,078	9,978
Richland	....	....	11,116	26,374	23,824
Sabine	....	5,828	15,421	24,110	18,564
St. Bernard	1,020	4,076	5,031	6,512	32,186
St. Charles	3,291	5,297	9,072	12,111	21,219
St. Helena	....	7,130	8,479	8,492	9,162
St. James	3,955	11,499	20,197	15,338	18,369
St. John the Baptist	2,990	7,930	12,330	14,078	18,439
St. Landry	5,048	23,104	52,906	60,074	81,493
St. Martin	7,369	12,674	18,940	21,767	29,063
St. Mary	....	16,816	34,145	29,397	48,833
St. Tammany	....	5,406	13,335	20,929	38,643
Tangipahoa	....	....	17,625	46,227	39,434
Tensas	....	16,078	19,070	15,096	11,796
Terrebonne	....	12,091	24,464	29,816	60,771
Union	....	10,389	18,520	20,731	17,624
Vermilion	....	4,324	20,705	33,684	30,855
Vernon	....	....	10,327	20,047	18,301
Washington	....	4,708	9,628	29,904	44,015
Webster	....	....	15,125	29,458	39,701
West Baton Rouge	....	7,312	10,285	9,716	14,796
West Carroll	....	....	3,685	13,895	14,177
West Feliciana	....	11,671	15,994	10,924	12,395
Winn	....	6,876	9,648	14,766	16,034
Total	76,556	708,002	1,381,625	2,101,583	3,257,022

CITIES AND TOWNS OF OVER 5,000 (1970 Census)

Abbeville	10,996	Jeanerette	6,322	Pineville	8,951
Alexandria	41,557	Jefferson Heights*	16,489	Plaquemine	7,739
Baker	8,281	Jennings	11,783	Port Allen	5,728
Bastrop	14,713	Jonesboro	5,072	Rayne	9,510
Baton Rouge	165,963	Kaplan	5,540	Reserve	6,381
Bayou Cane	9,077	Kenner	29,858	Ruston	17,365

Bayou Vista	5,121	Lafayette	68,908	St. Martinville	7,153
Bogalusa	18,412	Lafayette (SW)*	5,498	Scotlandville	22,557
Bossier City	41,595	Lake Charles	77,998	Shreveport	182,064
Bunkie	5,395	Lake Providence	6,183	Slidell	16,101
Cooper Road*	9,034	Laplace	5,953	South Fort Polk*	15,600
Covington	7,170	Leesville	8,928	Springhill	6,496
Crowley	16,104	Little Farms*	15,713	Sulphur	15,247
Denham Springs	6,752	Mansfield	6,432	Tallulah	9,643
DeRidder	8,030	Marrero	29,015	Terry Town*	13,832
Donaldsonville	7,367	Metairie	136,477	Thibodaux	15,028
Eunice	11,390	Minden	13,996	Vidalia	5,538
Ferriday	5,239	Monroe	56,374	Ville Platte	9,692
Franklin	9,325	Morgan City	16,586	West Monroe	14,868
Gretna	24,875	Natchitoches	15,974	Westwego	11,402
Hammond	12,487	New Iberia	30,147	Winnfield	7,142
Harrahan	13,037	New Orleans	593,471	Winnsboro	5,349
Harvey	6,347	Oakdale	7,301		
Houma	13,922	Opelousas	20,387		

*Unincorporated

GOVERNORS OF LOUISIANA

FRENCH PERIOD:

Pierre le Moyne, Sieur d'Iberville	1699
Le Sieur de Sauvole (acting)	1699–1701
Jean Baptiste le Moyne, Sieur de Bienville (acting)	1701–1713
Antoine de la Mothe Cadillac	1713–1716
Jean Baptiste le Moyne, Sieur de Bienville (acting)	1716–1717
Jean Michiele, Seigneur de l'Epinay (Lepinay)	1717–1718
Jean Baptiste le Moyne, Sieur de Bienville (acting)	1718–1724
Pierre du Bugue (Gue), Sieur de Boisbriant (acting)	1724–1725
Étienne de Périer (acting, 1725–1727; Governor, 1727–1733)	1725–1733
Jean Baptiste le Moyne, Sieur de Bienville	1733–1743
Pierre Rigaud, Marquis de Vaudreuil	1743–1753
Louis Billouart, Chevalier de Kerlerec	1753–1763
Jean Jacques Blaise D'Abadie (informed of transfer to Spain September 10, 1764; thereafter acting Governor for Spain)	1763–1765
Charles Phillippe Aubry (acting Governor until arrival of O'Reilly)	1765–1766

SPANISH PERIOD:

Antonio de Ulloa (did not publicly assume governorship)	1766–1768
Charles Phillippe Aubry (acting Governor until arrival of O'Reilly)	1768–1769
Alejandro O'Reilly (Captain General and Governor of the Province of Louisiana)	1769
Luis de Unzaga y Amezaga	1769–1777
Bernardo de Gálvez	1777–1785
Estevan Miro	1785–1791
Francisco Luis Hector, Baron de Carondelet	1791–1797
Manuel Gayoso de Lemos	1797–1799
Sabastian Calvo de la Puerta y O'Faril, Marquis de Casa Calvo (acting)	1799–1801
Juan Manuel de Salcedo	1801–1803

FRENCH INTERIM PERIOD (November 30–December 20, 1803):

Pierre Clement de Laussat	1803

TERRITORIAL PERIOD:

W. C. C. Claiborne (actually "Commissioner" in charge of Civil affairs, December 20, 1803–October 2, 1804)	1803–1812

STATEHOOD (Antebellum Period):

W. C. C. Claiborne	1812–1816
Jacque Philippe Villeré	1816–1820
Thomas Bolling Robertson (resigned to become U.S. Judge)	1820–1824
Henry Schuyler Thibodaux (president of the Senate; served until end of Robertson's term)	1824
Henry Johnson	1824–1828
Pierre Derbigny (died in office)	1828–1829
Armand Beauvais (president of the Senate; resigned early 1830 to become gubernatorial candidate)	1829–1830
Jacque Dupre (succeeded Beauvais as president of the Senate; thus succeeded Beauvais as Governor)	1830–1831
Andre Bienvenu Roman (no opposition in gubernatorial campaign; Dupre resigned before end of Derbigny's term)	1831–1835
Edward Douglass White	1835–1839
Andre Bienvenu Roman	1839–1843
Alexandre Mouton (term shortened by Constitution of 1845 going into effect)	1843–1846

Isaac Johnson	1846–1850
Joseph Walker (term shortened by Constitution of 1852 going into effect)	1850–1853
Paul O. Hebert (as provided by Constitution of 1852)	1853–1856
Robert C. Wickliffe	1856–1860
Thomas Overton Moore	1860–1861

CONFEDERATE GOVERNORS (1861–1865):

Thomas Overton Moore (completed term)	1861–1864
Henry Watkins Allen	1864–1865

UNITED STATES WARTIME MILITARY GOVERNORS (1862–1865):

General George F. Shepley	1862–1864
Michael Hahn (elected in area controlled by United States armies; Resigned)	1864–1865
James Madison Wells (president of the Senate)	1865

PERIOD OF MILITARY OCCUPATION (1865–1877):

James Madison Wells (removed from office by General Philip Sheridan)	1865–1867
Benjamin Flanders (appointed by General Philip Sheridan)	1867–1868
Joshua Baker (appointed by General Winfield S. Hancock, who had succeeded General Sheridan; removed from office by General U. S. Grant)	1868
Henry Clay Warmoth (elected under Constitution of 1868; appointed Governor prior to inauguration by General U. S. Grant after removal of Baker; impeached in December, 1872)	1868–1872
P. B. S. Pinchback (black president of the Senate, who had become acting Lieutenant Governor after the death of Oscar J. Dunn, also a black, thus became acting Governor, December, 1872–January, 1873)	1872–1873
William Pitt Kellogg (declared elected over John D. McEnery, who had received most votes)	1873–1877

STATE OF LOUISIANA, Since 1877:

Francis T. Nicholls (term shortened by Constitution of 1879)	1877–1880
Louis Alfred Wiltz (died in office)	1880–1881
Samuel Douglas McEnery (succeeded as Lieutenant Governor; duly elected in 1884)	1881–1888

Francis T. Nicholls	1888–1892
Murphy James Foster (reelected in 1896)	1892–1900
William Wright Heard	1900–1904
Newton C. Blanchard	1904–1908
Jared Y. Sanders	1908–1912
Luther E. Hall	1912–1916
Ruffin G. Pleasant	1916–1920
John M. Parker	1920–1924
Henry L. Fuqua (died in office)	1924–1926
Oramel H. Simpson (succeeded as Lieutenant Governor)	1924–1928
Huey P. Long (elected U.S. Senator in 1930; took oath as Senator on January 25, 1932)	1928–1932
Alvin O. King (qualified as Governor, January 25, 1932)	1932
Oscar K. Allen (died in office)	1932–1936
James A. Noe (succeeded as Lieutenant Governor)	1936
Richard W. Leche (resigned)	1936–1939
Earl K. Long (succeeded as Lieutenant Governor)	1939–1940
Sam H. Jones	1940–1944
Jimmie H. Davis	1944–1948
Earl K. Long	1948–1952
Robert F. Kennon	1952–1956
Earl K. Long	1956–1960
Jimmie H. Davis	1960–1964
John J. McKeithen	1964–1972
Edwin W. Edwards	1972–

EMBLEMS AND SYMBOLS OF LOUISIANA

State Seal. The Great Seal of Louisiana was adopted in 1902 under the administration of Governor William Wright Heard. Governor Heard directed the Secretary of State to use a seal described as follows:

"A Pelican, with its head turned to the left (the pelican's left—the viewer's right), in a nest with three young; the pelican, following the tradition, in act of tearing its breast to feed its young; around the edge of the seal to be inscribed 'State of Louisiana'; over the head of the Pelican to be inscribed 'Union, Justice'; under the nest of the Pelican to be inscribed 'Confidence'."

The Secretary of State is the official keeper of the State Seal, and with it certifies all official documents, such as laws passed by the Legislature, proclamations of the Governor, and commissions.

State Flag. The state flag was officially adopted by Legislative act in 1912. The act reads as follows:

"The official flag of Louisiana shall be that flag now in general use, consisting of a solid blue field with a coat-of-arms of the state, the pelican feeding its young, in white in the center, with a ribbon beneath, also in white, containing in blue the motto of the state, 'Union, Justice and Confidence,' the whole showing as below."

State Motto. "Union, Justice, Confidence."

State Colors. In 1972 a Legislative act provided that "The official colors of the State of Louisiana shall be blue, white and gold."

State Tree. Act 49 of 1963 provided that "The baldcypress (Taxodium distichum), commonly known as the 'cypress' tree, is hereby designated and hereafter shall be known as the official state tree of the state of Louisiana."

State Flower. In 1900 Act 156 provided that "The magnolia shall be the state flower of the state of Louisiana."

State Bird. In 1958 a Legislative act had specified the pelican as the state bird. Act 457 of 1966 was more specific. It stated that "After July 27, 1966, the official bird for the State of Louisiana shall be the Brown Pelican as it presently appears on the seal of the state of Louisiana, and its use on the seal of the state, other insignia of the state and on all official documents is hereby authorized and directed."

State Song. In 1932 the first official State Song was adopted by the Legislature. The words and music were by Vashti Robertson Stopher, and it was titled "Song of Louisiana."

In 1970 a new State Song was adopted, titled, "Give me Louisiana" and was by Doralice Fontane.

State March Song. A State March Song was adopted by the 1952 Legislature. It was titled "Louisiana, My Home Sweet Home," with lyrics by Sammie McKenzie and Lou Levoy and music by Castro Carazo.

Louisiana Day. In 1954 Legislative Act No. 44 set aside April 30 of each year as Louisiana Day. This was the official date of the Purchase of Louisiana in 1803 and also the official date of the admission of the State of Louisiana into the Union in 1812. The act reads:

"April 30th of each year is hereby designated as 'Louisiana Day', which shall not be a legal holiday.

"All civic and educational organizations and groups, and all service organizations and the governing authorities of all parishes and municipalities are urged to sponsor and arrange programs in celebration of said day, in order better to acquaint the citizenship of our state and particularly its young people, with its wealth, history, romance and legends and to stimulate our pride in its position of importance among its sister states.

"The governor is urged to issue his proclamation each year in advance of said day, calling upon all its citizens to display replicas of its seal, its flag, its flower and all other insignia emblematic of the great state of Louisiana, in order to inspire its youth in the study of the lives of its distinguished citizens, past and contemporary."

Nickname. The nickname of Louisiana most generally used is The Pelican State. Occasionally the term Pelican Land is heard, or, The Bayou State.

QUICK REVIEW OF FACTS ON LOUISIANA

Origin of Name. Louisiana was named for King Louis XIV of France, who reigned from 1643 to 1715.

Area and Shape of Louisiana. Approximately 48,500 square miles (ranks 31st among the states). Actual size is constantly changing—larger one week, smaller the next week. This is due to the rivers and the tides of the Gulf of Mexico that cut away sections of shoreline at one time and fill them in at another time.

Louisiana measures about 375 miles from north to south and about 300 miles from east to west. It appears to be a short, wide boot with a ragged and well-worn sole, heel, and toe.

Water and Water-Covered Marsh Area of Louisiana. Approximately 7,400 square miles of the state's total area is covered by water, as follows:

Rivers	650 square miles
Lakes	3,500 square miles
Water-covered marshland	3,250 square miles

The total square miles of this area are also constantly changing.

Coastline. The length of the coastline of Louisiana ranks sixth in the nation, being exceeded only by the coastlines of Alaska, Florida, Hawaii, California, and Maine.

Louisiana Purchase. The province of Louisiana was purchased from France by the United States, April 30, 1803. The United States took possession of Louisiana at New Orleans, December 20, 1803.

Statehood. After approximately eight years and four months as a United States Territory, Louisiana was admitted to statehood in the United States on April 30, 1812.

The Capitals of Louisiana. Altogether, ten towns or places have been the capitals of a portion of or all of the colony or state of Louisiana, three in present-day Alabama, two in present-day Mississippi, and the others in Louisiana.

French Period

1699–1721   The capital of the colony was located wherever the Governor's (or other chief administrative official's) headquarters were located. The following places, therefore, were the capitals of the colony until New Orleans was officially made the capital in 1721: Old Biloxi, Old Mobile, Dauphin Island, New Mobile, New Biloxi.
1721–1762   New Orleans

Spanish Period

New Orleans was the capital throughout the years from 1762 to 1803 (when the Spanish turned Louisiana over to the French).

Free State of West Florida

The Free State of West Florida (the area of the present-day Florida Parishes of Louisiana) was organized following the revolution of 1810. It was sometimes called the Republic of West Florida. Baton Rouge was the capital of this independent nation during its brief existence, September 22–December 10, 1810. It was officially joined to Louisiana by Congressional act on April 14, 1812.

American Period (1803–1861)

1803–1830   New Orleans
1830–1831   Donaldsonville
1831–1850   New Orleans
1850–1861   Baton Rouge (officially occupied by Governor Joseph Walker, January, 1850).

Period of Dual Government (1862–1877)

Confederate Louisiana (1861–1865):
1861–1862   Baton Rouge
1862–1863   Opelousas
1863–1865   Shreveport

Occupied Louisiana (1862–1877) (government controlled by United States Army):
1862–1877   New Orleans

Louisiana Since 1877

1877–1882 New Orleans
1882–   Baton Rouge

Old State Capitol: The Old State Capitol at Baton Rouge was officially occupied when Governor Joseph Walker was inaugurated there on January 28, 1850.

New State Capitol: The New State Capitol was dedicated on May 16, 1932, and first occupied by Governor Oscar K. Allen. At the time of its construction it was the tallest building in the South. It is the tallest state capitol in the nation. It has approximately 250,000 square feet of floor space.

Isle of Orleans: The Isle of Orleans was that section of French Louisiana lying east of the Mississippi River and south of Bayou Manchac, the Amite River, Lake Maurepas, Manchac Pass, Lake Pontchartrain, the Rigolets, Lake Borgne, and Mississippi Sound. The Isle of Orleans was included in the Louisiana Purchase, 1803. During early French years Frenchmen sometimes referred to Louisiana as the Island of Louisiana.

Florida Parishes: The area east of the Mississippi River and north of the Isle of Orleans was captured from the British by the Spanish under Governor Bernardo de Gálvez in 1779. The inhabitants of this area west of Pearl River fought a successful revolution against Spain in 1810. They established the Free State of West Florida.

INDEX

EDWIN ADAMS DAVIS

BOOKS:

Louisiana, A Narrative History (1961, 2nd ed. 1965, 3rd ed. 1970)

Louisiana, The Pelican State (1959; 2nd ed., revised and updated, 1ꢀ ed., revised and updated, 1969; updated, 1972; 4th ed., revised and ꢀ 1975)

Louisiana, Its Horn of Plenty (1969)

The Rivers and Bayous of Louisiana (1968) (ed.)

Heroic Years: Louisiana in the War for Southern Independence (1964)

Heritage of Valor: The Picture Story of Louisiana in the Confederacy (1

Fallen Guidon: The Forgotten Saga of General Jo Shelby's Confederꢀ mand, the Brigade that Never Surrendered, and Its Expedition to (1962)

A Campaign from Santa Fe to the Mississippi; Being a History of Sibley Brigade, by Theophilus Noel (1961) (ed. with Martin Hardwi

The Story of Louisiana, 4 vols. (1960–1963)

The Barber of Natchez (1954) (with William Ransom Hogan)

William Johnson's Natchez; The Ante-Bellum Diary of a Free Negꢀ (ed. with William Ransom Hogan)

Of the Night Wind's Telling; Legends from the Valley of Mexico (194ꢀ

Plantation Life in the Florida Parishes of Louisiana, 1836–1846; As ꢀ in the Diary of Bennet H. Barrow (1943) (ed.)

REPORTS

Report No. 1, *Survey of Public Records, Louisiana Archives Survꢀ* (with John C. L. Andreassen)

Report No. 2, *Findings & Recommendations, Louisiana Archives Surꢀ* (with John C. L. Andreassen)

EDITORSHIPS:

Louisiana History (official journal of the Louisiana Historical Associꢀ Founding Managing Editor, 1960–1962; Managing Editor, 1970–19ꢀ

Journal of Southern History (official journal of the Southern Histꢀ ciation) Founding Editorial Associate, 1935–1936

WALL MAP HISTORICAL EDITORSHIP:

American Geographic Approved Map of Louisiana (American ꢀ Inc., Fenton, Michigan, 1972). (Historical editor, with A. Otis Hꢀ

EDUCATIONAL PHONOGRAPHIC RECORDS SERIES

Dramatic Moments in Louisiana History (four 12-inch, long-play, ꢀ records; eight narratives with musical background, Panoramiꢀ Aids, Inc., Alexandria, Louisiana, 1969)